T0246390

The Green Hour

Also by Alison Townsend

Persephone in America
The Blue Dress: Poems and Prose Poems

The Green Hour

A Natural History of Home

Alison Townsend

THE UNIVERSITY OF WISCONSIN PRESS

The University of Wisconsin Press
728 State Street, Suite 443
Madison, Wisconsin 53706
uwpress.wisc.edu

Gray's Inn House, 127 Clerkenwell Road
London ECIR 5DB, United Kingdom
eurospanbookstore.com

Copyright © 2021 by Alison Townsend
All rights reserved. Except in the case of brief quotations embedded in
critical articles and reviews, no part of this publication may be reproduced,
stored in a retrieval system, transmitted in any format or by any means—
digital, electronic, mechanical, photocopying, recording, or otherwise—
or conveyed via the Internet or a website without written permission
of the University of Wisconsin Press. Rights inquiries should be
directed to rights@uwpress.wisc.edu.

Printed in the United States of America
This book may be available in a digital edition.

Library of Congress Cataloging-in-Publication Data
Names: Townsend, Alison, author.
Title: The green hour : a natural history of home / Alison Townsend.
Description: Madison, Wisconsin : The University of Wisconsin Press, [2021]
Identifiers: LCCN 2021010994 | ISBN 9780299334604 (hardcover)
Subjects: LCSH: Townsend, Alison. | Natural history—Wisconsin.
Classification: LCC PS3620.0957 G74 2021 | DDC 814/.6 [B]—dc23
LC record available at https://lccn.loc.gov/2021010994

for Tom

Where we love is home.

All water has perfect memory and is forever trying to get back to where it was. Writers are like that: remembering where we were, what valley we ran through, what the banks were like, the light that was there and the route back to our original place. It is emotional memory—what the nerves and skin remember as well as how it appeared. And a rush of imagination is our flooding.

—Toni Morrison, "The Site of Memory,"
What Moves at the Margin: Selected Nonfiction

I have come to believe that all essays walk in rivers. Essays ask the philosophical question that flows through time—How shall I live my life? The answers drift together, through countless converging streams, where they move softly below the reflective surface of the natural world and mix in the deep and quiet places of the mind. This is where the essayist must walk, stirring up the mud.

—Kathleen Dean Moore,
Riverwalking: Reflections on Moving Water

Contents

Black Raspberries

I'm not thinking about my mother as my husband, Tom, and I drive past the overgrown woods partway up the long dirt lane that leads to our house. It's high summer in Wisconsin, and wild bergamot blooms in a lavender haze on the prairie behind us, filling the air with its spicy, Earl Grey tea scent, the essence of this place and season. We're returning from a long hike. It's the end of the weekend, my legs are tired, and I'm thinking of all the things I have to do. Then, as if by magic, a whole family of sandhill cranes appears, the adults in Quaker gray plumage, the youngster, about half the size of the parents, still a warm cinnamon brown, all of them capped in red so bright it looks enameled on. They're in the tangle of black raspberry brambles under the oaks, where we've never seen them before, feasting on pebbled globes of ripe fruit.

We watch, charmed, as their shiny beaks dart out like ebony needles, plucking the berries from the canes in one adept movement. Then the male steps away from the rest and begins to pace slowly up the hill ahead of us. Afraid we'll startle him with the car, I get out and follow behind on foot, careful to keep my distance, Tom creeping along behind me. The crane's legs unfold like lacquered, black bamboo, each step deliberate. The female burbles, not the usual, rattling crane call, but more a worried, *where-are-you-going?* murmur. Past the stately oaks, past the hickory saplings, past the old mulberry tree with a big limb arched low over the driveway. I follow, focused on looking, so quiet I can hear the faint scritch of the crane's feet on the gravel.

That's when it comes to me. *My mother taught me this.* A zoologist by training, an artist by inclination, a 1950s mom, she embodied the art of observation, an act of attention so deep and devoted, akin to prayer, the viewer vanishes into something larger. "Look and see," my first-grade reading book exhorted. "Look and see," I read aloud to my mother, marking the words with my finger, then glancing up from beneath my lashes to see her looking, anchoring me with her attention, the angle of her gaze then lifting and opening across the woods and fields. The words forgotten, but their matching-up to things in the world etched into my brain, I looked too, my gaze following hers.

Pine trees, maples, sumac, and wide green fields filled with hay waiting to be cut. Bobwhites, eastern cottontails, bluebirds, and tadpoles we raised into tiny jade frogs and later released. Sunlight in puddles of silver on the river, the pearl mystery of the moon shining in the heat of day, and stars scattered like sequins across the sky at night. The whole world was there to be contemplated; everything was waiting to be noticed and seen. The proper attitude was wonder.

My gaze still focuses close then sweeps out the way my mother's did, ranging across time from that long-ago moment into the here and now, this shimmering, vibrating world we call the present. My mother has been dead for over fifty years; I spent only my early girlhood walking beside her. But here she is, a part of everything—the oaks, the cranes, the blackberries shining on their prickly branches, my own walking—her spirit woven into the green world she taught me to love. I follow the great, gray bird up the hill, letting him lead the way, Tom driving cautiously behind me, as we move along, each step bringing us closer and closer to home.

Prelude

Genius Loci

Gazing into the Green

Tell me the landscape in which you live, and I will tell you who you are.

—José Ortega y Gasset, "La Pedagogía del paisaje" ["Teaching via the Landscape"], *Obras completas*, vol. 1

The little house that Tom and I would later call Deer Run stands on four acres of restored prairie and oak savanna, tucked into the north side of a drumlin hill in the farm country outside Madison, Wisconsin. The previous owner had thought carefully about how to situate the house on the land. Although only five years old, the steep-roofed brick bungalow looked not only as if it belonged, but as if it had always been there. And yet it took several months for us to understand this place could become our home. We looked at the house six times before we bought it. Each time we visited, I was filled with a tense, jittering anxiety I could not attach to a source. *What's wrong with you?* I asked myself, as I studied the welcoming front porch, bordered with snow-covered flowerbeds I knew I could fill, come spring, or stood in the four-season sunroom that seemed to float among stately oaks, airy yet protected, like a tree house. *It's perfect. So private, and just the right amount of space.* But no matter how much I admonished myself, I felt haunted by worry and fear I hadn't experienced since my mother died when I was a girl.

The truth is, though the red brick dwelling was appealing in many ways, it wasn't my dream house. Imprinted by the drafty, charming, forever-in-need-of-repair colonial houses of my northeastern girlhood, I was looking for the shelter and history old houses provide. I had moved thirteen times, the tacks marking the stations of my journey pressed into every part of the United States map except the Deep South. Although I'd grown to love the places I'd lived—a former summer camp cabin on a pond in Vermont, a knotty pine–paneled apartment above a carriage house in California, a tiny, modern ranch built over the foundations of a pioneer settler's home beside the Marys River in Oregon—I yearned for the sense of comfort and succor old houses offer, embedding me in times and lives older than my own. Could I make a home in a house that was so new?

I wasn't sure. But the housing market was tight in 2001 and we'd been looking for two years. The old farmsteads I'd dreamed of, imagining Tom's and my life together when we embarked on what was the second marriage for both of us, proved few and far between, restored to beauty beyond our price range or in need of so much work they'd consume all our small resources. We returned to the little brick house again and again, accompanied by Nancy, our wise and patient realtor. She understood that purchasing a home—especially for the first time, as this was for me—is an emotional decision, one informed by both memory and hope. We bring the histories of who we are and who we dream of becoming to choices about houses and the land that holds them. I didn't know then that houses and the landscapes they are embedded in sometimes choose us, working on our psyches in ways we don't understand until we learn to inhabit them fully, a process I am still engaged in today.

I walked through the echoing white rooms, each one bright with the stark light of winter that reveals things for what they are, trying to imagine them filled with my maternal grandmother's antiques, their walls lined with the hundreds of books I have acquired as a reader, writer, bookseller, and teacher. Could I make the house *look* old, at least on the inside? I thought so. When it comes to nesting, I have always been able to make the places where I live cozy and inviting—a knack I inherited from the women in my family. But still I hesitated. It felt like such a big decision. What was it that held me back, making me afraid to leap into all that was unknown about this place? I could not say at the time. It is only recently, after living at Deer Run for twenty years, that I realized Tom and I looked at the house in mid-December, during Advent, the same time of year that my mother had died of breast cancer when I was nine years old. No wonder I was anxious.

My mother's death occurred just a few months after my family's first move, from rural, eastern Pennsylvania to New York State, so my father could take a better job. It meant leaving our dirt road with its spine of soft grass, our little white house with its red roof, the echoing green barn, and the tall pines standing sentinel along the driveway—the beautifully named

Wild Run Farm—and the pastoral five acres that had shaped my early girlhood. My parents didn't have much money; they'd bought the place with a loan under the GI Bill, thanks to my father's service in the army during World War II. But in its green peace and pastoral isolation, Wild Run Farm had everything I needed. The move signaled the end of childhood and the belief in safe places. Nearly every move after that, but especially those made in my thirties—a time of unwilling itinerancy as my first husband searched for work—had been fraught, difficult, and painful, each one imbued with loss.

Did buying a house, putting down roots in Wisconsin, mean an end to that? I hadn't wanted to live in Wisconsin. But after a divorce and some difficult years remaking my life in Madison, the state had given me both meaningful work and new love, which changed the way I felt about the place. But I still worried. Was I settling? And what did it mean to settle anyway? One of the original meanings of *settle* is "come to rest." Would buying this house allow me, a woman who had lived more places than she ever wanted or intended, to rest? Was it possible "to establish a permanent residence" (another meaning of *settle*) when one felt as displaced as I did?

Raised in rural Pennsylvania and New York State, I'd gone to college in Vermont, then headed west after college. I lived first in Southern California, where I found my writing voice. Then I moved to western Oregon, where I recovered the soulful relationship with the natural world I'd known as a child, living once again in close relationship with a country place. Although I still felt a strong affinity with the West, by this time I'd lived in Wisconsin for a decade. If I settled here, was I capitulating or giving in, making things permanent? Was I taking my foot out of the door, committing to something, someone, a place that could be taken away as quickly as my mother and Wild Run Farm had been?

Because my first move had coincided with the trauma of childhood bereavement, the feelings of loss, leaving home, and geographic displacement are linked in my psyche. In my child's mind, moving from a beloved place equals death. The association isn't rational, but it's real. For me, place itself is stained with the ink of what has gone away forever. I am haunted by lost places. "And how shall they comfort each other / who have come young to grief?" asks poet Adrienne Rich. "And what would comfort be?" Even in my sixties, I'm not sure I know the answer. But the one constant for me has been the natural world. The power of the land itself—what the ancient world called *genius loci*, the spirit or soul of place—has comforted me. Originally envisioned as a guardian spirit, *genius loci* has come to signify what I think of as the innermost character of a place—how it affects us, how it makes us feel. As I have discovered, the *genius loci* of Deer Run is a special one.

During our first visits to Deer Run, Tom and I concentrated on the house itself, opening closet doors and measuring rooms. But one afternoon we walked around the property, slipping and sliding on snow and ice that had melted and refrozen. Standing under the bare oaks, which range from one hundred and fifty to over two hundred years old, I looked down the back hill at Island Lake, shimmering like a frosted jewel box across the fields. I envisioned the trees leafed out, a whispering green canopy that would shelter me in the summer. Still new to the Upper Midwest, I didn't yet know that this kind of landscape is an elemental part of our psyche, which some theorize dates from our origins in the African savanna. Tucked into the waving grass beneath the trees, we can look out from where we are and feel sheltered. Dappled with light, oak savanna is a mother-grove, a refuge offering comfort and protection.

Even in the middle of winter I could feel that Deer Run offered exactly that. When I had been focused on the house, I hadn't reckoned with the power of the land, its particular *genius loci*. It was the pull of the place, its arboreal sanctuary and its prospect overlooking the surrounding farmland and Island Lake that convinced us to purchase the house. Standing there under the oaks I felt a soothing calm that I hadn't experienced in a long time, even in Madison, one of the most pleasant cities I'd ever lived in. I felt something flicker and turn over inside me—a green page I had not yet read, one I would come to know as well as the land here, all of it anchored by the largest, oldest oak at the bottom of the hill, the one we would later call Grandmother in honor of her age and wisdom. I knew, standing there in the chill, the December wind cutting under the oaks, that we would buy the property.

One month later, heading down the long dirt driveway in the blue February dusk after we visited the house for the first time since we'd closed on it, after turning the shiny brass key in *our* lock, I noticed the silhouette of a deer. She was looking at us over the barbed-wire fence from what I'd learn was a deer trail that ran beside it, one of several braided into this place long before we settled here.

"Look," I said, pointing her out to Tom. "She's blessing us."

Nodding his head, he said, "Yes. Let's call our house Deer Run."

How many times since then have we seen deer or been watched by them? This summer a slender, tawny whitetail has feasted on so many of my favorite green and white hostas that I've had to fence the plants in a chicken-wire enclosure. Just last week, I watched a doe and her fawn, spots splattered across its back like eastern dogwood petals, run across the lawn in pouring rain, then down the back trail, clearly on a familiar thoroughfare. But twenty years of life here blur my memory of the time when everything was new, a landscape where we discovered something amazing every day—sandhill cranes, great horned owls, with two downy owlets, peering down from an old hawk's nest, a family of red foxes (one year with eleven kits), the silky feel of Indian grass as it slides between your fingers in late summer, the many variations of blue in Island Lake, how most storms move from west to east across the land, and how it feels to be snowed in for several days, something I hadn't experienced since I was a child and my father and a neighbor snowshoed out with a sled to get milk at Wild Run Farm.

Not long after we moved in, Tom cut the winding trails we still use, looping through the front woods and the savanna on the back hill. He built four raised vegetable beds and began growing Yukon Gold potatoes, leeks, and tomatoes, from which he makes batch after batch of marinara sauce that he freezes, pulling it out all winter, the taste of summer in each mouthful. I filled the flower beds with perennials and native plants—bleeding hearts, Virginia bluebells, giant lobelia, cardinal flower—the cottage-style borders I dream of forever out of control, but filled with bees.

We learned about the land too. Although it scared me after so many years in the West, where dangerous wildfires grow worse every year, we burned the prairie, renewing what the original owner had planted. It still astonishes me that one can hold a match to the dead plants and grasses every spring so the prairie returns, restored within weeks to what it was meant to be, the small tongues of new growth rising through the blackened earth like green flame. I delighted in the wild bergamot, purple coneflowers, and false sunflowers swaying among the grasses, and learned that prairies are dynamic, never quite the same every year. Once, when I lay down alone in the middle of it all, I felt like I could disappear in the sea of grass I had only read about in novels. Deer sometimes bedded down here. Was I in one of their resting places?

Tom and I became familiar with the oak savanna, also a disappearing ecosystem. We loved the great trees for their gravitas and presence, and created a sitting place beneath them from which to view Island Lake on summer evenings. Our tiny portion of savanna is a work in progress. We have opted to restore without herbicides, beating back invasive honeysuckle, multiflora rose, and reed canary grass as best we can with clearing, digging, and fire. Just last summer though, when our Grandmother tree, a vulnerable red oak, was threatened by oak wilt, which can kill a tree in weeks, we consented to have her treated. She survived, to our relief. But it felt like having an elderly relative on chemotherapy, using poison to fight a toxic disease. Before we did so, we stood under her rich dark green canopy, our hands on her rough bark, explaining what we were doing and why.

It takes time to grow into a place, letting it work on you as you work with it. Sheltered by the oaks and with the house nestled gently into the hill, we attuned ourselves to the seasons and natural cycles at Deer Run. We learned the land's personality and its many moods. Each one has its special qualities. My favorite occurs in late spring—I call it the green hour. In early evening the light slants low across Island Lake, the neighboring farm fields, and the wilder Department of Natural Resources land beyond them, illuminating everything so brilliantly it seems to glow with the verdant radiance the twelfth-century mystic, healer, and philosopher Hildegard of Bingen called *viriditas*, or "greening power." Each blade of grass, each leaf, each aspect of the geography in the scene is lit so brightly it almost doesn't seem real, but an imagined place, a mythic world from a childhood book, or a tiny scene in an illuminated manuscript. I could look out across the land forever, savoring the slant of sun inside the green. But of course it is ephemeral, beauty made more special because of its brevity.

I had experienced this kind of green in other beloved places, especially in Pennsylvania, New York State, Vermont, and Oregon. Each one took me in, cradling my life, healing me, connecting me to times deeper than my own hours on earth. But Deer Run did it differently, revealing its mysteries gradually, the daily growing memorable before I understood its significance. I paid attention to the land before me and entered into relation with it, participating in what I later learned my Scottish ancestors might have defined as *dùthchas*, the ancient Gaelic spirit of connection to the land and kindness to it in return for its gifts. Robin Wall Kimmerer's "grammar of animacy," a concept in the Potawatomi language expressing the idea that everything in nature—rocks, wind, trees—is alive and has spirit, helped clarify this experience. I'd known these things from the time

I was a child, but I understand them differently now, having resided among them more deeply.

The land set me dreaming, summoning memories of my other soul-scapes and psychogeographies, layering them over one another in a palimpsest, many times and places present within me at once. When I stood on the back hill, I found myself wondering if an immigrant woman settler from Norway had stood here in the nineteenth century, perhaps hanging her laundry between the same oaks from which mine is strung. And before her, had Ho-Chunk women gathered acorns or made a camp here, their blue-black hair shining? And before that?

The deepening awareness about where I lived seeped into my creative life, like the springs that feed Island Lake. During our early years here, gazing into the green from the bedroom or my study window, no other houses in sight, I finished a book of poems, my heartsong for my mother, something I hadn't been able to write until I was in my forties. Then I wrote another book about mothers and daughters, exploring that relationship through a contemporary retelling of the Demeter and Persephone myth. My mother's death was the defining event of my life, her absence a constant presence that affected everything I experienced. Poetry helped me articulate that, redeeming the psyche of the girl I had been. And all the while the land called out to me in a language I was learning, one that seemed so all-embracing it required something more expansive. Although trained as a poet, I have also always written essays, a form I love for the way it mirrors the movement of the mind on the page. Writing about my observations in my journal, I segued, without thinking about it, to the essay as a way to understand the land and my relationship to it. It felt completely organic.

The word *essay* means a "a trial" or "an attempt," a definition I've always liked because it doesn't try to resolve things. Looping, musing, and meandering, essays were my way of moving toward an understanding of my connection with Deer Run and the landscapes with which my body and soul have been intertwined, as well as the way they have healed me, offering solace and sustenance as I navigated a world, at times rudderless, without a mother. They represented my effort to map home ground, both within myself and in Wisconsin, where the circumstances of life had kept me, half a continent away from where I might have chosen to live if left to my own devices. Essaying my way through time and place, trying to figure out what my own story meant in the context of this big country, I felt like an explorer on the page, never sure what might come up next. Even when it wasn't going well, the writing, like the land, was a refuge, a place where I could hear myself think.

In the way that experiences in our lives sometimes align, I found myself teaching creative nonfiction, nature writing, and a women's studies class on gender, ethnicity, and the environment in my job at the nearby state university. I'd come of age as a writer outside the academy, returning only later for an advanced degree, and so was always a bit uneasy in that environment, knowing there is another world outside it where most people live. I could "pass" in the academic world and do well there, moving up the ranks of the tenure track, although it made me feel squirmy and rebellious. Despite my misgivings, my university proved to be a good place, filled with hard-working, caring colleagues and students I adored. The workload was crushing, but the classes I taught allowed me to immerse myself in thinking about both essays and the natural world. And always, when I came home from work, Deer Run was waiting. As I drove up our long dirt driveway, windows open to the spicy-sweet scent of the autumn prairie, alive with asters, goldenrod, and swaying bronze grasses, the work world fell away.

Life, like essays, is messy, and what I'm describing here all sounds neater and easier than it really was. I loved Deer Run, but I was still bedeviled by questions about place that seemed unanswerable. I knew that place, at least for me, is inextricably bound with a sense of home and identity, remembrance and loss. There was—and remains—something I couldn't put my finger on about it all. Place-based studies were in vogue, and books about home and bioregions and landscape piled up in my study, many of them wonderful, but none giving me the answers I sought as I underlined furiously.

In class, I pestered my patient students—who, like Tom, were native Wisconsinites, with deep and sturdy roots I envied—with questions from our text. If we are shaped by the places that make us, what are we and how do we define ourselves? If we move around a lot, as I had, does that mean we keep changing and being remade? What gives us a sense of place anyway? How does the land act on us, and how do we make homes in new places, the inner geography of the self changing when we change our outer geography? As I asked questions, images of places I had lived swirled inside me, in a 360-degree geographic panorama. Living at Deer Run had grounded me enough to study and write about these other locales, seeing what they added up to and who I was a result.

All our lives begin with a specific landscape. "Where do we find ourselves?" Ralph Waldo Emerson asks at the beginning of his essay "Experience." Where, indeed. His words suggest a literal place (where have we
arrived after our travels?) and a looking back in order to figure out where
we have come from. Place defines identity. It's where we map our inner
geography, what writer and psychologist Sharon Blackie calls "the songlines and placelines of our lives," the greatest of which is home. Even settled, I was still looking for home, missing places I have loved and left,
reexperiencing my childhood expulsion from the personal Eden of Wild
Run Farm. The water there ran bright and cold and clear from the old red
hand pump. I am forever nostalgic for its taste, even as I know I will never
experience it in the same way again.

The word *nostalgia* entered our lexicon in the nineteenth century as a
way to describe immigrants' failure to adapt or take root in a new place.
Considered a medical condition, nostalgia was the clinical description for
homesickness, that aching, yearning, pining malady eased only by a particular place. The origins of the word describe it clearly. *Nostos* means "return
home" and *alogos* means "pain" in their Greek roots. But one wonders how
doctors treated this malady. Was there a prescription for homesickness, a
tonic or tincture that would ease its pangs?

The reality, of course, is that even if we have the ability to return to
places we miss, they aren't the same. Like illness, homesickness can become
chronic, the sufferer yearning for a lost place it is impossible to return to,
what my Welsh forbears would have called *hiraeth*. It is as simple and as
complex as that. My search has been about finding a place on earth that
I can call my own, my emotional home, one with which I can be in such
an intimate relationship that I know it as well as the landscape of my body,
this house of blood and bone within which I walk through the world and
that is, in the end, the one home I can rely on. For the last twenty years,
longer than I've ever lived anywhere else, home has been Deer Run, shelter
of my body and soul. It has informed my inner landscape, allowing me
to be, as writer-naturalist Nan Shepherd says, "the instrument of my own
discovering." When I grow impatient with my restless questing, walking
the trails up and down the hill calms me, and I am reminded that discovery
is an ongoing process.

It took a while to understand that, while every inch of our four acres is
imbued with *genius loci*, the Grandmother oak at the bottom of the back

hill is the center of that soulfulness. As I approach the tree, the grassy trail down the hill turns to emerald moss, its velvety softness muffling my footsteps. Before I ever looked up at the tree, I found myself looking down, drawn by the moss, which reminded me of clumps I'd loved in childhood, when I used to build fairy houses between the roots of the big maple in the backyard at Wild Run Farm. The moss, which covers some of the oak's great, slate-gray roots, directs the eye to the tree. Like a set of shallow, curved stairs, the roots grip the ground with purpose and a beauty sculpted by weather and time, an invitation to climb among them and find a sitting spot.

The place I like best is a flat, sandy cove nestled between a V of large roots on the protected, uphill side of the oak. Leaning my back against the thickly ridged, blackish-gray bark, much of it inscribed by hieroglyphs of bluish lichen, I close my eyes and try to adjust my rhythms to the oak's slower ones. We know trees breathe, giving us the oxygen we need, and that they communicate through their roots. More recently, it's also been determined that they have heartbeats and move their branches slowly up and down at night, water pulsing up through their tissues. If I slept beneath the oak, would I feel or hear the beat, resounding within the wood like the drum of time? The very idea of it calms me, as being held by my mother or playing beneath the roots of the maple tree did when I was a child. For a moment, all these forms of solace are present at once and I am content, part of something wiser and older than I am.

I lean back and look up through the Grandmother's outspread branches, which tell me she is a true savanna tree and grew with plenty of space around her. There are some dead black limbs and several raised, breast-like scars where branches dropped off years ago. But above them the oak's thick foliage rustles in the breeze beneath the blue roof of sky. Just this year I learned that there is a word for the sound of wind in leaves—*psithurism*. How many different melodies have been played on the leaves of this old oak over the decades, ranging from the gentle, surf-like rise and fall I hear now, to the rougher, rain-driven blasts of thunderstorms that make the leaves stick together in a sodden mass, to the winter gales that snatch the few rattling leaves from the branches, crumpling them together like wet tissue.

In the autumn, the Grandmother's leaves change color late, extending the season as they turn a dark reddish brown that lightens to amber, so it looks like you're gazing up through honey. In midsummer, her sharp-pointed, shallow-lobed leaves are a deep Lincoln green. But the light filtering through them is dappled, nearly the same as the light of the green hour that I love so much. I hadn't realized it was present at other times and am reminded to look more closely. Perhaps other things and places I miss are also with me in ways I don't fully understand. For some reason, lines from an old Kate Wolf song come into my head: "It's a journey with my soul that I am taking, / one that only goes from the cradle to the grave." What impact has this landscape had on my identity, and where are we going together? Perhaps the soul is really a green-crowned oak, guardian spirit of this place, wind shushing through her leaves as she lets me rest against her, the two of us held together in what Kathleen Dean Moore calls "a *refugia*, a place of safety where life endures." I press my cheek to the Grandmother's rough bark. I sense her presence, but she keeps her counsel. All I can hear is wind.

I'm a slow study when it comes to understanding landscapes. While I always have an immediate emotional response to a place, intuiting its essential nature, it takes me a long time to really know it, to learn its flora and fauna, to feel I have the right to write about it. The bedrock of my soul was shaped by Pennsylvania, where, guided by my parents, I learned the names for other beings, matching up killdeer, mourning cloak butterflies, and bobwhites to pictures in my Golden Guides. But I am an amateur naturalist when it comes to other locales. I haven't lived anywhere long enough to understand the land's language like a native. Still, I have paid close attention, which has led to devotion, as I allowed myself to be led by this land where, against all expectations, I find myself not only settled but sheltered—south-central Wisconsin, a place I have only gradually learned to call home. During our years at Deer Run, I've studied what this small piece of property has to teach me as I've headed up and over our back hill each morning, Togo and Annabelle, our pair of tricolored collies, running ahead as I've trod the grassy path, the deer trail a secret thread braided through it.

Here, in the middle of the country, on the north side of this hill that was once farm and grazing land, and before that unspoiled oak savanna, the home and hunting grounds of the Ho-Chunk people, I am well-situated to reflect on the passage of time and place. If there were ever an appropriate landform for one afflicted with a lifelong case of homesickness, it's a drumlin. The glacier stopped just south of here. The hill, shaped like an inverted spoon or a half-buried egg, is composed of material from many places the ice dragged with it as it chewed its way south. Retreating, it left parts of those places behind, making it a perfect habitation for someone like me, a woman composed of many places. Sometimes, perched on the large, wave-patterned glacial erratic at the crest of the back hill, I can almost feel the memory of movement that lies embedded in the rock.

I muse on the secret, sacred, and mysterious life of this land, with its oaks and prairie grasses, its deer and coyotes, and the sandhill cranes who gather spring through fall at Island Lake, their primeval voices ringing out across the water. I think about the hickories and the bluebirds, the ice that shaped this hill, and the winter nights when we've watched the aurora shaking its green silk sheets across the northern sky. I absorb the energy of the earth. As I do, I remember and mark the places I've lost or left behind, Deer Run somehow the accumulation of all the homes I carry inside me and yet utterly itself. I am amazed and grateful at how the past, present, and future sometimes occur simultaneously, woven into that continuum Native Americans call "ceremonial time." This is the way memory works, too—our lives like drops of rain fallen into the long history contained in a lake left by a glacier. Sometimes, when dipping my hands into Island Lake as we canoe there on a hot day, things blur and I am outside time completely, a girl again at Wild Run Farm, baptized into being by the wild, cold sweetness.

I

Her Intricate Weave

A Strand in
Her Intricate Weave

Sometimes it seems the world began with my mother brushing my hair. It is not my first memory, but the one most vivid in my recall because it happened every day and is what my body remembers. It is an early morning in the late winter or spring of 1962. My mother and I stand in front of my mirrored Victorian dresser—which she found for a song at an auction and repainted pink at my request—as she brushes and braids my waist-length hair the way she does each morning before I leave for school. She undoes my braids from the day before, slipping their rubber bands over her wrist and unbinding the sleek, tea-colored plaits, which have frayed a little overnight as they rubbed against my pillow. Then she runs her fingers through my hair, loosening it so that it falls around me in a cascade of Pre-Raphaelite ripples. A busy mom with three kids, my mother keeps my hair bound tight most of the time, no doubt with an eye to making her own life easier. But I adore this moment of undoing, when she sets my hair free to fall around me in a shimmering veil. When my mother unbinds my braids—which I love for the way they make me stand out in a sea of pixie cuts—she releases something in me, an energy that tells me who I am even as she prepares to re-create me.

Set free for a moment, I run my fingers through my hair and toss my head the way that Chestnut Hill—the gentle, bay gelding on whom I am taking long-dreamed-of riding lessons—does when we trot down the trail. With my hair down I look and feel like a different person. If my mother is distracted for a moment by my little brother and sister, I pile my hair on the top of my head in the way I imagine Jo March in *Little Women* must have done before she cut hers. Then I let it spill around me again for the pleasure of feeling it fall, softer than my own skin, the weight of it warm as a silk shawl. Sometimes I twirl in front of the mirror, my hair flying out around me like a spin-art painting at a country fair, in one of those spontaneous dervishes of childhood, so much of which is spent in a trance of imagination, the body moving in time to its own metronome.

Just as quickly, though, my mother returns, holding the half-round, boar bristle hairbrush exactly like the ones at her own mother's house in Philadelphia. Like the artist she is when sketching with bright pastels that dust her fingers with grains of color like pollen, she holds the brush in the air over my head for an instant. She contemplates me, her first child and eldest daughter, as if I am *prima materia*, a blank page in her drawing pad, waiting to be filled. Then she lowers the brush and begins to drag it through my hair, raking it with such vigorous strokes that she pulls my head back with every one, my knobby shoulders pressing into her body. If I utter the slightest protest, she sings out, "It's painful to be beautiful," in a joking voice, then continues with her ministrations, gentle but firm as a mother cat, holding her kitten down with one paw as she washes it. She's an advocate of one hundred strokes a day, and the brushing and braiding is her undisputed territory—so completely that I don't know how to braid my own hair yet, but must depend on her to weave me together again each morning.

The brush rustles through my hair, its rhythm regular as the beat of the poem I have memorized for Miss Obie's second grade class from a book called *Silver Pennies: A Collection of Modern Poems for Boys and Girls*. "I am the dryad of the wood," I recite, as my mother's brush flies, pulling me against her with each stroke. "I shimmer in my solitude. / Men call me the birch tree, yet I know / in other days it was not so." Although my mother sometimes yanks my hair as she brushes, I never cry out. Unlike my little sister, Jenny, who ran around the house screaming, "Don't touch me! You're murdering me!" until my mother gave up and had her short blonde braids clipped into a pixie, I am a stoic. As invested in my hair as my mother is— indeed, because she is—I stand, patient and biddable, beneath her touch, wondering what she means by equating beauty with pain. At eight I haven't much of a long view, and while I can tell by the tone of her voice that my mother is kidding, there's some authority underneath it that makes me a little uneasy.

Although my mother often tells me how pretty both my sister and I are, exclaiming, "I have the two most beautiful girls in the world," I puzzle over the notion that pain is a prerequisite of beauty. What does this mean?

I know it hurts when I fall down and scrape my knee. And I remember the dull ache that took up permanent residence in my chest when she was in the hospital for two weeks the previous summer. But what is the connection between pain and being beautiful? Although simple on the surface, her words seem to hide a world of meaning as mysterious and inaccessible as the New Math I cannot master. Unable to get any farther, I turn her words over in my mind as she brushes until they begin to sound like a poem. *It's pain-ful to be beau-ti-ful* echoes through my head with each rustle and swish of the brush, until it seems hooked together with "I am the dryad of the wood."

When she has dressed my hair to her liking, my mother draws it all back from my face, so tight I can feel it yank at the root. Then quick as can be— her speed and dexterity part of what fascinates me about the process—she draws the end of a tortoise-shell, rat-tail comb from the top of my forehead to the nape of my neck, redoing the center part (which is almost etched there) and dividing my hair into two equal portions, as if marking territories on a map. She divides each of these sections into three strands and begins to weave them into braids. Under and over, under and over, her long pianist's fingers fly through my hair, as fast as if she is playing a reel. She draws the strands tight, so tight I feel my eyes slant as the skin in my temples goes taut. Under and over, under and over, she interweaves the strands, tugging on the length of the braid as she does. I lean away from her, increasing the tension, as I know it helps her make tightly woven, glossy braids. But even as I stretch away from her, I am connected. My braids are like the reins I am learning to handle on Chestnut Hill, or the ropes of hair the witch climbs in Rapunzel, my favorite fairy tale after Cinderella, though I won't understand the significance of the braids in that story for many years, yet alone equate them with anything in my own experience.

Rustle and swish, rustle and swish. My mother is finished with one braid and working on the second. Section by crisscrossing section, she weaves her way to the bottom, doubling the rubber band over and around the fluffy switch at the end that reminds me of Chestnut Hill's tail, and which I like to draw back and forth over my upper lip like a paint brush when I am reading. "I am the dryad of the wood," I murmur. "I sway, I bend, retreat, advance." She's almost finished, but I would stand there all day if she asked, floating in a half-dream state, connected to the waking world through her flying fingers as she plaits me into being, corralling my wild tresses, ordering me, preparing an image with which I can navigate the world, my face a pale oval within the frame the braids make, their weight a part of my body.

"There," my mother says, coming to the end of the second braid. "How's that?"

I stand before her, looking at the heavy plaits that hang down my chest. They are always perfect, evenly matched and without any lumps or messy places, and I always tell her so.

"Well then," she says. "I guess we're ready, aren't we?"

With one last, quick motion, she licks her index finger, and light as a butterfly landing, smooths my eyebrows out. Then she stands with hands on my shoulders for a moment. We look at each other in the glass, a tall blonde woman in a homemade calico shirtwaist and a girl in plaits, wearing a hand-me-down green sweater and a Black Watch kilt. We stare into one another, my blue glance falling into her hazel-gray in an invisible figure eight of motion. If I were to look close, I'd see the whole scene reflected in our eyes. But it is an ordinary morning and neither my mother nor I know how sick she is, let alone that she is dying. I do not even really understand that she is sick at all, despite her hospital stay the summer before, because she acts so normal, just like always. If I knew otherwise, would I stop and attend to each detail as I do to the words of the silly poem I still remember? Would the whole picture mean something different and would I hold it closer? In memory, the meaning of the scene unfolds as I slow it way down into still shots, parsing each frame for its emotional significance.

In life it is just another day, starting as it always does. A painfully shy child, anxious about presenting my poem, I am focused on that, not on some dimly understood, half-conscious exchange with my mother. "I am the dryad, slim and white," I repeat, feeling, if not quite like a dryad, then at least a little beautiful, for no one I know has hair like mine. I flip my braids back over my shoulders, pick up my battered plaid school bag, and clatter down the red stairs to the kitchen, where my brother and sister are already eating their oatmeal. Tethered and then released by one who made me, my whole being a strand in her intricate weave, I couldn't do it any differently. My braids bounce against my back as I go, my mother following close behind, as it seems she always will. It does not occur to me that we are rushing together toward the beginning of the end of a world.

Beyond Wild Run Farm

A Travel Guide to an
Eastern Pennsylvania Childhood

If we opened people up, we'd find landscapes.

—AGNÈS VARDA, *The Beaches of Agnès*

Begin here, with Pennsburg, the township where Wild Run Farm, the verdant world at the center of my childhood, lies. Start with its five acres of gentle woods and fields, faded green barn, and little white colonial house with wide window sills and an elaborate brass floor register. Here is the maple tree, between whose roots I create miniature houses. Here are the tall pines bordering the driveway, prickly and hard to climb, but with smooth, cylindrical cones I love to collect. Here is the arbor of rosy grapes, from which my father makes pink wine. Here is the laundry, linens smelling of Ivory Snow and fluttering white on the line, while my little brother and sister and I run, laughing, between the tents of sheets. Here is the sandbox our father built, with triangular seats in each corner where we sit, sifting sand between our fingers, inventing small worlds. Here is the old-fashioned red hand pump. A few strokes and the coldest, sweetest water I will ever drink gushes from it like a silver river, telling me exactly where and who I am.

Here is the garden, where we each get a patch to plant whatever we want—popping corn, watermelons, and green beans for their leaves, which our guinea pigs squeal for when they see us coming. Here is the red mailbox with our family's name—Townsend, which makes me imagine the end of town, a place where paved roads turn to dirt like ours—painted on it in my father's precise scientist's hand. It is the mid-1950s and the nation is optimistic, everyone beginning again after the war. This is the only world I know. I believe Pennsburg was settled by William Penn, though in fact it wasn't; it was just "purchased" by him from the Lenape people for "two watch coats, four pairs of stockings, and four bottles of cider," then named in his honor, like so much else. In my child's mind, Penn is a benevolent great-grandfather, floating over the entire state like a cumulus cloud, not an intruder.

We kids drive with my mother into town, crossing a causeway over one branch of the deep blue reservoir, the land around it wild, pheasant chicks chittering away from the car into the tall grass behind their mothers in balls of tawny fluff. Here is the Five and Ten, with its black and white swinging doors, where my siblings and I purchase a nested set of pastel mixing bowls for our mother's birthday. Here is the Farmers National Bank, where I learn to save money in a little green passbook. Here is the feed mill, where my mother picks up grain for her chickens and ducks in flowered muslin bags she later makes into pillowcases. Here is the orchard, where she buys baskets of Elberta peaches that she slices into a blue bowl and sprinkles with mint. I yearn for a small pine doll's cradle with scalloped edges, but know not to ask for it. On the way home there is a tavern at the top of the hill that (oddly) sells icy cylinders of orange sherbet, shot through with a vanilla star in the middle, a combination of flavors I will love the rest of my life.

Visit the two closest towns, Red Hill and Green Lane, with their matching names that sound like Christmas. Stretched along Route 29 with Pennsburg, they are sometimes called Upper Perk, after the Perkiomen Creek, which winds through my childhood, its waters a silver voice I still sometimes hear in my dreams. In Red Hill I look in vain for a brick-colored summit and wait while my father gets gas at the station. A scarlet horse with wings like the one in *Fantasia* carries me away on her back into the sky while the numbers flip past, their sound clicking like Chiclets above the steady *kachunk* of the pump. Sometimes I am permitted a bottle of Coke from the red bin. The bottle sweats, the color of sea glass in my hand, as I sip the fizzing sweetness.

In Green Lane I imagine grassy boulevards instead of roads, never the Green Lane Reservoir that flooded our previous home, the Old House, by right of eminent domain. Nothing's left there but foundations, rising ghost-like one summer in a drought, though the reservoir area became a county park where we go swimming. Each afternoon my brother, sister, and I watch our mother stroke out into deep water for some time alone. I feel the tug to follow as we stand there, forbidden to go in past our waists, her going-away even for a short while unbearable—what I will remember when she dies two years later—the mineral scent of the water rising around me in invisible clouds.

Pennsburg, Red Hill, Green Lane. Say their names out loud, the holy trinity of my childhood. String them through my mind like prayer beads that smell of pine and spring water, dirt roads and creeping Charlie in the grass, beginnings and ends.

Go further afield to Quakertown, where I believe Quaker Oats are made (though they are not), the smiling man on the box with his broad-brimmed black hat another William Penn look-alike, but with a catchy adage: "Nothing is better for thee than me." Attend the auction in Kutztown, where my mother bids—shy, but raising her hand again and again through the clotted, incomprehensible gabble of the Pennsylvania-Dutch auctioneer—for an antique dough tray on legs that she later strips and refinishes. It stands behind my sofa today, its wood satiny and worn. Drive to Phoenixville, where my Uncle Chic and Aunt Sally live with their three kids and I once went swimming in an old quarry where I feared I would drown, no bottom anywhere, the water dark green and still as the air in midsummer.

Follow the Conestoga Turnpike, which both Daniel Boone and the settlers in covered wagons took west, to Chester Springs, where my maternal grandmother's country house, a fieldstone colonial near Anselma, waits, an abrupt hill rising behind the barn. Fields full of black-faced sheep stretch out around the yard like it's Scotland or Wales. I believe these sheep supply wool for the legendary family mill in Philadelphia, but they don't and I am wrong again, as I am about many things. My parents married here, walking up through the formal rose garden. There are photos of me taking my first steps, tottering through the sunlight toward my mother's outstretched hands, her love so palpable I almost remember how it felt. In summer I lie on the cool marble slab of the spring house for hours, watching clear silver bubbles float up and holding wriggling black commas of tadpoles in my hands for a moment before letting them go.

I learn to put my face in the water of the small pond nearby, love the sweetness inside the skin of Concord grapes that grow along the driveway, and see my Aunt Betty kiss her Hungarian émigré lover, Eugen (pronounced *Oy-gen*), in the brick-walled patio we kids call The Secret Place. Neighbors across the road, the minister Gilbert and his wife, Sylvia, let us pick out puppies, wiggling black and white Welsh corgi-beagle mutts we name Megan and Tina. At night I sleep in a two-hundred-year-old spool bed, in a room with a tall armoire that should scare me but doesn't, the window screened by a curtain of ivy that tints everything green as if breathed on by a spirit. I have never felt so safe.

Say Conshohocken, King of Prussia, Bird-in-Hand, Brandywine, the names of places alive in my mouth, a spell that weaves around me, an incantation that lifts who I was and where I began into who and what I am now.

Drive to Pottstown with my mother, twelve miles from Pennsburg, in the old Plymouth wagon we kids call Gray Car, past the Ringing Rocks to Wyndcroft, the small independent school we attend because our Quaker-educated mom doesn't think the local schools are good enough. God knows how our parents pay for it; everything I have for the first day is either homemade—from my red calico-print dress to the purple bloomers my mother stitched up on her Singer Featherweight—or second hand. My plaid, messenger-style school bag with the brass clasps from Goodwill is perfect until I see how worn it looks beside the other kids' new ones. Wyndcroft, with its peculiar spelling, where I am too shy to speak but win ribbons on Field Day for running and hoop racing, plus a patch for my jacket, the embroidered school insignia like a genie's lamp. Wyndcroft, where my second-grade teacher gives me a pass to the fifth-grade library when I run out of books to read in her room, words from *Little Women* a paisley shawl I wrap warm and tight around me. In the winter, my mother kneels on the cold white to put clanking chains on the car.

There is more in Pottstown, where my mother grocery shops at the A&P after picking us up from school. She purchases *The Golden Book Encyclopedia* there, volume by volume, which I read from A to Z, the set divided between my siblings and me one Christmas. She buys records too, one a week, placing them in the red, leatherette-bound *Standard Treasury of the*

World's Great Music. I listen to it all, one disc at a time, on my father's Victrola, dancing up and down the braided rug in his study to Chopin, Ravel, Mozart, Beethoven, and Stravinsky, and more, the collection my first introduction to classical music, the notes burned into my brain. I do not realize my parents struggle to make ends meet. Every night my mother plays the piano, an old upright Cunningham, the notes in the refrain from a song about a cat, called "I Love Little Pussy," alive in memory, so clear I sometimes think I still hear them as I fall asleep at night.

On the way home from Pottstown, stop in Birdsboro, site of Daniel Boone's farm, and also where my first crush, Rick Gosh, lives. Rick has liquid brown eyes and a buzz cut, his plushy hair sleek and dark as an otter's. Shy and left-handed like me, he has a slight stutter and stands, hands jammed in his chino pockets, in a way that seems—how do I know this?—manly. We recognize something in one another while our mothers chatter, laughing over what they remember about Smith College, surprising me. Did they know one another before Rick and I were born? On the wall is a calendar with the days crossed out, one by one, with a giant X, just like ours at home. Is this how time passes everywhere?

Say Paradise, Intercourse, Blue Bell, Ambler, Sellersville, New Hope—all of them uttered in the nasal, eastern Pennsylvania accent, with its softened consonants and rounded vowels—"woder" for water, "sewda" for soda, "hay-ouse" for house. No matter where I am when I hear it, I can pick it out in an instant, the voice of home, as if the earth itself could speak.

Find Media, where my father was born, on the map. Imagine the paradise of Montcalm, the farm where his father worked, and their little white house by Pickering Creek—sweet refuge after life in a tent for two years during the Depression—everything vanished when my father tries to find it decades later, paved over into a parking lot. Late in his life, he writes an essay about it that makes me weep.

In nearby Newtown Square my paternal grandfather is the gardener at the Ellis School for Fatherless Girls. Every summer, when my grandparents host our family, too many for their tiny bungalow, they put us up in a screen-walled camp cabin across a creek from the house. It's a wonderful adventure, with even our parents tucked into bunks. But late one night the sky explodes with rain. I wake wrapped in a blanket, carried in my grandfather's strong arms across the raging stream. He brushes my hair back gently with his big, work-roughened hand, and I remember watching him help plant the vegetable garden at Wild Run Farm—how he raked the coffee-colored loam fine, then scooped some up in his hand, crumbling grains of dirt between his fingers in a gesture I understood was love. I am told I have his eyes, bright blue as sky reflected in water.

Say Radnor, Berwyn, Malvern, and Devon, where I am given riding lessons one summer on the friendly bay gelding, Chestnut Hill, who I pretend is mine and never forget. The warmth of his body and scent of leather and sweat is a comfort, though I do not know my mother is sick or that this her last birthday gift to me ever.

Allentown, with the closest hospital, is where my siblings and I are all born—me a difficult labor that ends in a high forceps delivery, my brother much easier, my sister a slick fish, almost loosed in a taxi. Allentown, where the Liberty Bell was hidden from the Redcoats during the Revolutionary War. Allentown, which Billy Joel later immortalizes in a song. Allentown, where my mother shares a maternity room with another woman, Jean, whose daughter Ellen, born a few hours before me, is my almost-twin. The two families gather every year on our birthdays at Wild Run Farm or in Gettysburg, where Ellen's father teaches at the college. Gettysburg, with its hallowed, bloody ground, turning point in the Civil War, but which at first I associate with joy—Ellen, with her deep brown eyes and brown pixie haircut. Ellen, my first friend, my lost twin. Where is she now?

Say New Jerusalem, Bally, Lehigh, Skippack, and Doe Run. Say Bala Cynwyd, which feels beautiful in my mouth, the map of childhood frayed soft around the edges from folding and refolding.

There are other places too, big because seen and remembered through the small lens of *then*. Hershey, where the candy is made and the air smells like warm cocoa, where even the streetlamps are shaped like chocolate kisses, every other one opened, the rest still wrapped. Once a week my mother tapes a nickel in my lunch box and I buy a whole Hershey's bar at the school store, doling its squares out in slow delight, letting each one melt in my mouth.

There are also darker places where I never go, like Bethlehem, with its famous steel, where I-beams were invented and are made, or Scranton, up in coal country, each a different hell—one filled with blast furnaces, the other's anthracite clawed from the ground, black "diamonds" and roaring blue flames that it seems will never go out, until they do. Wilkes-Barre, with its funny name, home of Vulcan Iron Works, the town where there's also a terrible mine disaster, the Susquehanna River flooding the pits, King Coal going down. Boring Harrisburg, memorized because it is the state capital and I need to know it for tests, is as far west as I have ever been. Pittsburgh is a foreign land, distant and unknown, hard to even imagine.

Slide my finger east on the map, then loop west from Philly out along the snooty Main Line, where rich people talk like they have pebbles in their mouth. Say Overbrook, Merion, Narberth, Wynnewood, Ardmore, Haverford, Bryn Mawr, and Paoli—the phrase "Old Maids Never Wed and Never Have Children, Period" a mnemonic my parents tell me was made up to remember the names of the train station stops.

Go to Lansdowne, where my grandmother and her sister grew up, the name of the town like a long blue hallway back to their almost-Edwardian past, when they were Bessie and Floss, not Elizabeth and Aunt Florence, the elderly maiden hovering around the edges of parties, a lace-trimmed hankie tucked up the sleeve of her pink cashmere cardigan. She gives my family a subscription to *National Geographic* each year, tucks a five-dollar bill in a paper wallet at Christmas. When she dies, I inherit her sterling silver hair pick, a tea strainer shaped like a miniature kettle and engraved with her initials, and a lapis-inlaid marble mantle clock that plays Westminster chimes on the hour, just like one my grandmother has in her house. The chimes seem like the music of time itself, the back-and-forth call between their notes so lovely it catches in my throat.

Say Honey Brook, Coatesville, Yellow House, Spinnerstown. Say Reading, the Pretzel City, with its many bakeries and Japanese pagoda, the heavy industry that once fueled the place silent and impoverished now, a railroad named after it in Monopoly the only memory of better times. Say gone.

Visit Lancaster, where the Amish live, their black, horse-drawn buggies moving in slow time along the roads beside lush green fields where men walk behind the plow and oxen as if it were another century. They make beautiful furniture, wear black collarless coats and long dresses, use oil lamps at night, and seem like serious people. They are not to be confused with either the Mennonites in their lawn caps or the Pennsylvania Dutch (who are not Dutch but German) with their strange food—scrapple, chow chow, apple schnitzel, shoofly pie—all of which seems normal, even delicious, because I live here. Hex signs float on the side of their well-kept barns to ensure good luck and a bountiful harvest—stars in circles, pairs of birds, trees of life. They seem a beautiful voodoo, mysterious as the guttural Pennsylvania Dutch language.

Say Sugartown, Avondale, Downington, Kimberton. Say West Chester and Newtown Square again, where my father came home to his parents after the War, a miracle, alive. He sent special-delivery letters to my mother every day after they met, following Arthur Murray's famous magic footsteps in a dance class at the Statler Hotel in downtown Philly.

Go to Valley Forge with its woods and fields, its reproduction log huts and cannons. We have picnics with our cousins where George Washington's Continental Army camped in the winter of 1777–1778. The soldiers froze and ate firecake. Only one in three had shoes. They left bloody footprints where we play hide-and-seek, statues, red rover, and sardines.

Say Kennett Square, Red Lion, Longwood Gardens, and Chadds Ford, where Andrew Wyeth paints his precise and moody pastorals. Some look so familiar when I study them in college I want to lie down inside them.

An hour away from Wild Run Farm, Philadelphia waits, City of Brotherly Love. "What about sisters?" I ask. "Why isn't it Sisterly Love, too?" But no one can give me a satisfactory answer. Here are Philadelphia's many neighborhoods, history alive on every block. Mount Airy with its big houses. Chestnut Hill, where I go to Doctor Lee for checkups and vaccinations, once climbing a lab ladder to escape the hypodermic. He saves my life when I am hospitalized with a mysterious fever, and writes my father every Christmas until I am eighteen to ask how I am. Last of all, Germantown, star in the heart of the mandala of the known world, where my mother grew up. A Quaker neighborhood with mossy brick sidewalks and cobblestone streets, it is leafy, quiet, and comfortable. Here my grandmother raised her ten children, so many they seem mythic, like a clan of giants. The great, stone-faced house at 134 West Coulter Street floats like a lit ship that shelters all, a refuge for everyone until she dies at ninety-six. "Well, hello, hello, hello!" she cries as she rushes down the steps to greet us, elegant in her nipped-waist floral dress and choker of chunky, fake pearls, waving a handkerchief. When she hugs me, I feel like the only grandchild in the world, her favorite, although I have thirty first cousins.

Philadelphia, home of the Museum of Art, where I like best the scary armor within which I swear I can see eyes move, and the costumed ladies in the basement, almost breathing in their long silk dresses. At the Academy of Natural Sciences the tyrannosaurus rex skeleton rears up and life-size dioramas of bioregions and their animals loom, like rooms I could step into and vanish. At the Philadelphia Zoo I pity the giraffe, reaching high for a hank of hay, and must be led away, crying. We drive into the city along the Schuylkill River, where rowers skim like swallows over the water in their sculls, each one a scene from a Thomas Eakins painting.

My parents take us many times to Independence Hall, where the Liberty Bell is displayed in those years. I place my hand on its crack and feel the weight of time and history, cool and heavy beneath my fingers. My father lifts me up to trace its inscription: "Proclaim Liberty Throughout All the Land Unto All the Inhabitants Thereof." I picture Ben Franklin, Betsy Ross stitching her mythical flag, the noble Continental Army and the dangerous Redcoats, the clever Quaker girls who were secret spies (their messages hidden beneath cloth-covered buttons), who blur into runaway slaves and the Underground Railroad, then the Lenape people, of whom there is almost no trace. It all makes me feel tiny, a fleck of tea steeped in time. My grandmother buys us reproductions of the Declaration of Independence on fake parchment, and a miniature replica of the bell that I'll move from place to place, sentimental, until I misplace it years later in California.

Philadelphia is also the home to the Free Library, where my father stops after work to check out books he brings back to the country and reads aloud at night—*Little House in the Big Woods*, *The Children of the New Forest*, *The Incredible Journey*, *Ring of Bright Water*, *The Golden Eagle*, *Kidnapped*. Philadelphia, where my grandmother takes me to Gilbert and Sullivan operettas and to see *Babes in Toyland*, bolstered by chocolate milkshakes at Schrafft's. At Christmas we go to see the holiday light show at

John Wanamaker's, sit terrified in Santa's lap, watch the famous monorail zip around the top of the store, sip milky Earl Grey and eat sugary petit fours in the Crystal Tea Room. On New Year's Day, the Mummers Parade dances up Broad Street, all sequins and feathers, glitter and strut.

Philadelphia, where my father works as a biochemist for Merck on Spring Garden Street, at least until someone reads the elegant narrative of his lab notes and he moves from bench science to copy writing to advertising and accounts, leaving behind his white mice, except the two he brings home as pets. He works on S.T. 37, an antiseptic hexylresorcinol solution our family swears by, which comes in a cobalt blue bottle, and Sucrets sore throat lozenges, mint green, tasting like candy but not, in a cunning metal tin we play with when it's empty. He works on first-generation antidepressants, one of which will play a role in my life many years later. Before they marry, my mother works in a lab, then for the Red Cross, and later for the American Friends Service Committee, the Quakers so ever-present I'm surprised to learn her family is really Presbyterian and Episcopalian.

Philadelphia is where my mother went to Germantown Friends School and both parents graduated from Penn, he on the GI Bill, which saved him from pipe fitting in the shipyards, she because the funds for Smith ran out (although she claims the girls were too snobby). We are given a special library card at Germantown Friends the summer she is in the hospital for so long that our whole family moves in with my grandmother, the world as I know it swaying and precarious, delicately balanced as the teeter-totters my siblings and I play on at Penn Charter School, wondering if our uncles did so when they went there as boys. Philadelphia holds the wonder, solace, and mystery of my grandmother's house—Thanksgiving dinners with the candlelight and silver, family faces shining around the long white table; the nursery on the third floor with its Victorian dollhouse and toys; the book-lined library where I find all my mother's Louisa May Alcott books lined up, as if waiting for me. I am given her copy of Frances Hodgson Burnett's *A Little Princess* to keep, and I marvel at what seems its ancient inscription: "To Mary, Christmas, 1928."

Philadelphia, where the city lights wink out behind our family as we drive home to Wild Run Farm in the alfalfa-scented dark. I drowse, lying half asleep on the front seat beside my father. My mother sits in back, with my brother and sister on either side, their heads pillowed on her lap. I listen to my parents' voices weaving back and forth in the dark, my eyes blinking shut, the air through the window green and fresh. Perkiomen Creek glimmers and shines, a silver necklace spangling the dark beneath the echoing WPA-era bridge with its mossy cement railing. The whispery, shushing sound of the dirt roads—first Bowers Mill, then Wild Run—with their grassy centers that brush the bottom of the car, is soft and familiar, as is the slight rise when the vehicle turns and lumbers into the driveway, and the porch light that has been left on, guiding me up the golden pathway into the house of everything that matters, where all it seems I'll ever need to know awaits me.

In the distance, Blue Mountain, that misty ridge that forms the eastern Appalachians, floats, invisible now on the indigo horizon, like something sensed in a dream. Myriad creeks and rivers twist and twine through the land, their names often Native American, words that summon the sound of running water—Perkiomen, Wissahickon, Schuylkill, Susquehanna, and the massive Delaware, which flows to the sea. The collective memory of the land sighs and stirs, scarred and legendary, alive with ghosts of all who ever walked here, from coonskin-capped explorers to Continental soldiers to Quaker women in their plain bonnets to German farmers, and most of all the spirits of Lenape or "true people," who were forced to give it up for almost nothing. Beneath everything, under the rolling hills of the Piedmont, lie the Precambrian and Paleozoic bones of the earth, broken many times by glaciers into granite, quartzite, and schist, rocks that hold this world together, though they can be collected and labeled for our nature museum in the spring house, their eons cupped, warm in the palm of my hand.

Over everything lies the rich brown dirt, surprisingly sweet when I taste it once while making pine needle upside-down cake for my dolls. It is cool and soothing when I strip on a hot summer afternoon and paint my body with a paste of mud, a girl dressing herself in the skin of her world, dancing herself ecstatic. Until I am the land and it is mine, and I am one with everything that made me, the sound of the little quail I love calling from the fields around the farm—*Bob-WHITE, Bob-WHITE, Bob-WHITE*—their clear whistle back and forth an anthem that etches the scroll of time, though I am, of course, too young to know that.

Say Red Hill, say Green Lane, say Pennsburg. Say Wild Run Farm and begin and remember. Say earth, say heart, say hearth, say home.

Planting Pansies

We think back through our mothers if we are women.

—Virginia Woolf, *A Room of One's Own*

It was the latest spring that I had ever experienced and too early to plant pansies. But when I saw them lifting their sweet, splotched faces at the Bruce Company nursery, brave in the thirty-eight-degree Wisconsin weather, I couldn't resist buying a few to tuck in a rustic basket near the front door, as I do every April. It is my annual ritual and the first act of the gardening season, though it's almost always some weeks before I can do much else. This was reinforced by the fact that the pansies at the Bruce Company were displayed under a protective awning. One garden assistant I consulted, asking if it wasn't too early for pansies, confessed that they were wheeling the carts into the greenhouse by late afternoon. Their pansies weren't even hardened off. I knew I'd be carrying the basket in and out of the garage every night. But who can resist pansies, their bright faces, their velvety petals and the sense of possibility they bring after winter?

The next day was sunny, and as I transferred the root-bound pansies from their flimsy plastic containers to a large pot that fit inside the basket, I couldn't help feeling hopeful. I had selected purple-on-purple "black" pansies with inky centers, and the bright yellow ones with black faces that look like little lions. They are my two favorites, although I also like the white ones with purple faces and the solid orange ones with the strange name (at least for the season), Halloween.

I've loved pansies since I was child at Wild Run Farm, where my relationship with gardens and the larger natural world began. Each spring my mother bought me an entire flat of pansies to plant in a flowerbed alongside the house. Turk's cap lilies—the kind with spotted cheeks—grew at the back of this bed. Although they cannot have been in bloom at the same time (lilies are midsummer flowers), in my mind's eye they always are, memory's magic lantern superimposing one frame over another in a composite that fascinates me, even as I know it to be inaccurate.

Although I never felt poor as child—in large part because of my mother's ingenuity and powers of imagination—finances were tight. My mother made our clothes, tended a huge vegetable garden and put up most of its produce, raised chickens for both eggs and meat, built me a dollhouse using her jigsaw, and scavenged auctions for antique furniture she painstakingly refinished. Purchasing an entire flat of pansies must have been an extravagance. Still, she did it every year because pansies were my favorite flower. I loved them for their silky petals and faint sweet scent. I pressed my nose to each one before I planted it, inhaling its blossom, each sniff a sensual delight, the parasol-like petals pressed against my nostrils as if part of me. Which they were, on some level, for one of the pansy's many supposed medicinal attributes is its power to strengthen our memory.

Kneeling on the damp grass before the newly spaded bed, the flat of flowers beside me, I'd dig a hole for each plant, sprinkling in a bit of compost as my mother had instructed, then press the earth—*be gentle but firm*—into place around each one. As I did this, my mother taught me other names for pansies, beginning with the most obvious and well-known, *pensée* (French for "thought"), for what dwells, hidden inside. "There's pansies, that's for thoughts," my mother said, quoting Ophelia in *Hamlet*, though it would be years before I read the play myself, pricked by the vulnerability in the line when I did. But there are other names for pansies too, ranging from heartsease to love-in-idleness to flame flower to stepmother to herb trinity (its three colorful petals symbols of the Trinity).

Of all these names, I think I like heartsease—which is Elizabethan in origin, signifying innocence and unspoiled love—best for the tenderness and sense of rest it suggests. Maybe this is why my mother, so soon to die of breast cancer, bought them for me. I cannot know what she thought, watching me as she worked in another part of the yard, perhaps already ill. I know only that I was aware of her presence, as I am sometimes aware of her spirit today. After my mother's death there were many years when I did not have a garden. But I will never forget the feeling of being turned loose and entrusted with my own piece of ground and a flat of pansies. It was my first garden, coming even before the plots she lined off for us in her vegetable patch, and it marked me for life as one who is happiest with her hands in the earth. Even in my sixties, a rubber pad cushioning my knees, planting pansies each spring grounds me, reminding me that, though I did not have her very long, my mother gave me vital gifts that still sustain me.

These personal legacies are part of a larger tradition, for pansies are one of the oldest flowers in cultivation, and the varieties we get at nurseries today are ancestors of the wild pansy. Elizabethan writers and herbalists celebrated the pansy for both its beauty and its usefulness. Dried and purified, it was mixed into a cordial believed to be helpful in heart disease, another reason, perhaps, why it was called heartsease. But it was also used to heal wounds, treat blood disorders, build up weak nerves, combat exhaustion, ease nervous complaints, and counteract jaundice. As a poet who is at times prey to debilitating depression and anxiety, I wonder if brewing a tincture of pansies would strengthen my nerves. Instead, I content myself with sprinkling their little cousins, Johnny-jump-ups, into my salad. Their bright faces are blue, gold, and deep violet, and I take delight in being a blossomovore, like a bee or a rabbit, or the doe and fawn that ate my pansies when I lived in Oregon, each nibble so delicate I couldn't bear to stop them.

Without saying a word about it, my mother taught me with that first flowerbed that gardening is a form of love, an emotion with which pansies have a long and profound association. My Celtic ancestors brewed a tea made from pansy leaves, which they used as a love potion. The heart-shaped leaves were also used to cure broken hearts, though I can't imagine how, except perhaps in the form of a poultice. When I encountered *A Midsummer Night's Dream* in college, I reveled in the fact that the play is shot through with pansy lore, where even a bit of the juice "on sleeping eyelids laid, / Will make a man or woman madly dote / Upon the next live creature that it sees." I wonder, did I fall in love with gardening because the first thing I saw after sniffing my flat of pansies was a plot of earth waiting to be planted? I cannot say for certain. I can only say that every garden since has been an echo of that original one at Wild Run Farm, our first love always our greatest.

As is obvious from their appearance, pansies are related to—and developed from—violets. The domestic tricolored violets or Johnny-jump-ups that I like in my salads, and which grew, self-seeded, at my parent's farm, their bright faces springing up even between cracks in the concrete pad before the barn, were developed from violets and are the ancestor of the modern pansy. According to garden writer Diana Wells, in her fascinating book *100 Flowers and How They Got Their Names*, Johnny-jump-ups were first bred by a gardener named Thompson, who worked for a British naval commander in the early nineteenth century. In 1810 Thompson bred from a stray bed the first "blotched" pansy, which he poetically described as "a miniature impression of a cat's face steadfastly gazing at me." Perhaps it is this quality of looking back at us, as if there were some mysterious exchange going on, that we find so appealing about pansies. After Thompson's discovery, pansies became fancier and fancier, bred in pastel colors, some with double blossoms. But I prefer the simplest ones and comb garden centers for antique varieties. Close relations of their wild purple cousins, they feel pure and real to me, and most like those I planted as a child.

In the spring, at about the same time we planted pansies, violets bloomed in the Pennsylvania woodlands. My mother and I loaded buckets and spades in the back of her old gray Plymouth station wagon and set forth on what she called wildflower expeditions, looking for plants to dig up and transplant into our garden. She took special delight in violets, which she loved for their scent and color. Violets come with their own load of lore, stretching back to the Greeks, for whom they were a symbol of fertility. Both the Greeks and the Romans drank a wine made from violets and made violet conserves and cosmetics. Violets have always been associated with love and were the original heartsease.

Pansies' connection with love was made tangible for me when we visited my grandmother in Philadelphia. We went to visit the Liberty Bell, as we always did, as if it were a relative or family friend, dipping our small hands through the cool fissure of its famous crack into things that came before us. It was spring, and I think there were pansies growing outside Independence Hall, though I am not certain. But as I stare into the deep violet wells of my own pansies, I can almost see the pansies of the past. Like rows of sentries in a neat bed between the cobblestone walk and brick building, I glimpse them out of the corner of my eye as my brother and sister and I race toward the main attraction. My grandmother says something to my mother. Passionate gardeners and observers both, they pause before the flowers, stooping low to see them better, my mother's blond head almost touching my grandmother's elegant white one. My mother has a rebellious spirit, and I sense there is sometimes tension with her mother. But in that moment, something passes between them, their hearts eased toward one another by the presence of flowers they both love. Running past, I take it in and hold it inside me, delicate as a pansy pressed between the pages of a book.

Eight years after my mother's death ended our wildflower forays, the taste of violets took me back to the Pennsylvania woods and my first full garden. In high school, immersed in an accelerated program in French, I often shared Anis de Flavigny violet pastilles with my friend Kathy as we studied together. The sweet, almost ineffable taste of the candies was an instant trigger, recalling sugared violets my mother once put on a cake. Produced since the ninth century, Flavigny candies are made from a single anise seed, spun round with layers of a violet-flavored sugar coating. The company brags that each batch of pastilles takes over fifteen days to make, and I imagine the individual candies turning and turning, sweet and nacreous layers building up around them, each one like a tiny pearl. Best of all, the pastilles come packed in a charming keepsake tin, decorated with Victorian-era paintings of violets, good for storing tiny treasures when the candy is gone. Several of the tins rattled around my desk for years, so pretty I could never bear to throw them out.

I was introduced to Flavigny violet pastilles by Madame DeBaerstrand, my high school French teacher, who shared them with Kathy and me once after class. We adored the idea that we were eating flowers, and Flavigny became a habit. Lost in the sea of our senior year, unabashed romantics (me in patchouli-scented, Indian print dresses, she in wide-wale corduroy miniskirts or jumpers), Kathy and I offered pastilles to one another before bending our heads over the lime-green journals from France that Madame had given us to practice our French in. Here, she announced, we were to keep a personal journal, writing in what she called "a more natural and spontaneous manner" than the drills in our textbook permitted. When I taped into my journal a photo of my sister and brother and me playing on the beach at Cape Ann the summer after my mother's death, describing it in my halting French, as "très triste, très calme, et très solitaire," Madame wrote, "C'est comme un rêve," in the margin. "It's like a dream." Alongside another entry, made after Kathy took me to visit the herb farm near our town, I pasted in sprigs of rosemary and thyme, along with a handful of violets, which prompted me to write about Flavigny pastilles. I described them as tasting "une teinte plus fonceé que le bleu du crepuscle"—"One shade deeper than the blue of twilight"—a line I would be happy to write now.

Several weeks after we began keeping our journals, Madame asked to speak with me privately after class. She sat me down, observing that my entries were completely different from those of my classmates, and then asked a question that moved me forward into my life: "You do realize don't you, Simone" (her pet name for me, since mine did not, according to her, translate well into French) "that you are the real thing? A writer. Un écrivaine?" I didn't, of course, but Madame's words, coming at a lost and painful time in my life, when I was being bullied and abused by my stepmother, inspired in me the same sense of possibility planting pansies with my mother had so many years earlier. Scribbling words down until I "got" something gave me the same feeling of quiet satisfaction and wholeness that I'd felt when I patted earth firm around the pansies in that long-ago garden, their happy faces looking up at me, as I sat back on my heels, contemplating what I had created. Madame's perceptive observation planted something too, taking me back to a world I thought I had lost and suggesting I could go forward, taking it with me in words.

It saddens me now that I didn't keep up with French (which I loved). I let go of it in college because I felt intimidated by my male French professor, an aging hippie-intellectual type who was nothing like Madame. My little green journal disappeared in one of my many moves, and I almost never purchase Flavigny violet pastilles in my adult life. But I cannot taste them without thinking of Madame and what she gave me. In the spring, when violets erupt in a sea of purple on my back hill in Wisconsin, I pick them and make tiny bouquets, recalling the hesitancy, vulnerability, and possibility of my adolescence, and before that the hours spent roaming the woods with my mother, searching for wild things to add to that first garden already brimming with pansies.

The violets in my backyard here connect me to the pansies I have planted in the front of the house, which in turn link me back through every year I've ever planted them. They remind me that we love flowers not just for their physical beauty, but for the way they anchor us in our lives, accompanying us through time that stretches beyond our personal history into a past that unfolded long before us, even as we bend to plant this year's flat, the purple and yellow faces splotched with black looking up at us as if they know all this and more. *Begin again*, the pansies tell us, their petals shining with the gift of the oldest possible story. And so I do, each spring as I kneel before them, my mother's gardening hands alive in mine.

My Mother's Dress

"You've got something from the veterinary clinic," the UPS courier shouted, as he dumped a large box on my front porch in Madison late one May afternoon, a few months before my second marriage was to take place. "The *veterinary* clinic?" I opened the screen door and stood there for a long moment, gazing down at the mailing label. Blue and white, it had an official look that connoted business and importance, reminiscent of those from the late 1950s and early 1960s, the kind that came on the boxes of beautiful hand-me-downs my Aunt Kitty shipped to my mother whenever her own girls outgrew them. I stared down at the box, lost for a moment in a wave of remembering that swept me up as it rushed in.

We never knew when such boxes might appear, and their arrival at Wild Run Farm, where the mail carrier was often the only one who passed down our dirt road all day, was an exciting event. Although the parcels came several times a year, I can still recall the quality of the filtered green light under our big maple tree the day one particular package arrived. Perhaps it was even the last one we received before my mother died, and like so many other things in our lives, the packages stopped coming. I cannot say for sure. But the day lingers, somehow representative of all the days, suspended in memory's amber. My mother, brother, sister, and I are preserved within it, caught in a moment before we knew sorrow, as we crowd around the box in a circle beneath the tree, eager to see what it contains.

Maybe the reason I remember this box so well is that one item within it symbolized a moment of transition, a passage that my older cousins, Kate and Sally, had already passed through, and one I hadn't, at age nine, even begun to consider. Along with the velvet-collared coachman's coat, the dark raspberry wool suit with an embroidered Tyrolean design on the jacket, and the green Black Watch kilt, the box contained a training bra, size 28AAA. I remember looking at it, then down at my own still-flat chest, wondering about the mysteries ahead, experiences I had yet to grow into. I might have even glanced at my mother's chest for confirmation, unaware that she wore a prosthesis to hide her double mastectomy, as she set the bra aside, murmuring something about how I wouldn't need it for a few years.

All this came back to me as I stared down at the box on my doorstep in Wisconsin. The spring light, filtered through a tall pine in my front yard, dappled the label so it shimmered up at me as if from beneath water. Penned in a strong, spiky hand, the words blurred for a moment, their source murky, then cleared as the silt of time floated and settled, a thousand sunlit particles suspended and dispersing. I could feel the minute and labyrinthine circuitry of memory catch and hold, struggling for a direct connection.

Then, in a split second—or was this *all* a split second, the speed of memory, with its sudden leaps and connections, fast as the speed of light?— I had it. Of course. The box was from one of my cousins, Cookie, who had phoned me a few weeks before to say it was coming. She and her husband have a veterinary clinic, and she'd shipped the package from the office. She'd been sending packages for over a year now, ever since her mother, my maternal aunt, Bea, died. Bea had shared a room with my mother when they were girls. She kept an eye on us after my mother's death, remembering birthdays and holidays from where she lived in Missouri, half a continent away from her Philadelphia origins. Over the years she sent mementoes to me—my grandmother's Royal Copenhagen tea pot, or a hand-painted dish, splattered with roses the size of babies' fists and rimmed in gold, from my great-grandmother's luncheon service. In the absence of my mother, she was a kind and concerned presence, maintaining the strong female legacy in our family as best she could from afar—passing things down, preserving memory, connecting us with our past.

Since Bea's death, Cookie and her sister Karen had stepped into that tradition, sending on things they discovered as they went through their mother's belongings. "I'm sending you some more *stuff*!" Cookie had said in her call. "I just wanted to be sure you'll be home to receive it." Her vivacious Missouri twang echoed out of the phone as if she were in the room. I listened, touched, wondering what "stuff" entailed. Cookie said, "There's a formal portrait of your mother, and some other pictures. There are several clippings of her hair that Grandmother saved—can you believe they saved *hair?*—one from when she was two and another from when she was thirteen. And oh yes, there's also a dress of your mother's."

A dress? I was more disconcerted by this than by the idea of clippings of her girlhood hair. All I could imagine was one of my mother's many homemade creations. Perhaps it was the blue daisy print, with white rickrack around the collar and a pale pink, grosgrain ribbon belt, that she'd made to wear at what, I realized, looking at old photographs, must have been her fortieth birthday party at my grandmother's farm. Or maybe the dressy blue and purple striped silk, used for special occasions? Or was it the pink and white shirtwaist, dotted with carnation-like flowers, each marked with a small black squiggle in the center that always reminded me of tadpoles? Her dresses tumbled through my mind in a swirl.

Did other women remember their mothers' clothes in this way? With this clarity and precision? Certain garments of my mother's stood out like icons or holy relics, permeated with the shimmer and significance inanimate objects assume after their owner dies. I remembered too, the visceral effect of death. After the funeral my father stood in the upstairs hallway, his arms full of my mother's dresses, asking Bea and her oldest sister, Betty, if they wanted any of them. My aunts flinched, taking a half step back, as if the idea of wearing my mother's clothes was physically painful. My mother's death must have been too close, too immediate and unbearable for them to even imagine taking her clothes. It couldn't be any of those dresses in the box on my porch. They were packed off to Goodwill the week after the funeral, along with a pair of silver party shoes my mother had worn once or twice, and her large gray mother-sized purse, which my father had brought back to her from a business trip to Montreal, a pack of Black Cat cigarettes tucked in its small zippered pocket.

Cookie confirmed this. "I think," she said, hesitating for fraction of a second, "that it's the dress your mother wore in my mother's wedding." I knew right away what dress she meant. I have a photograph of Bea after her wedding, my mother and another bridesmaid posed around her, admiring the bridal bouquet. Bea is the centerpiece of the photo, dark-haired and willowy in white satin and lace. But it is my mother's image that draws me, as if, examined up close, it will tell me something about myself, solve some riddle of female identity her death left forever unanswered. Caught from the side, half-turned toward the camera, she wears a floor-length garden-party dress and an organza hat, tied on one side with wide satin ribbons that must match the dress. She looks like a shepherdess minus her crook, and not unlike a small porcelain figurine, one of the "Four Seasons," my grandmother kept on her living room mantle, which I used to stare at with longing. Just twenty-nine, married less than a year herself, she looks dewy, her face radiant above the Peter Pan collar and long line of small fabric-covered buttons.

What the black and white photograph does not reveal is that the dress is a peachy-pink taffeta that when touched rustles with a crisp, whispering sound I had not heard since I played dress-up. Nor does the photograph convey the scent, a mysterious combination of camphor and sandalwood that rose from the tissue paper, even though the dress had been in the box labeled "Mary's Pink Dress" since 1948, and transported me to my grandmother's house in Philadelphia. And it could not anticipate me slipping out of my own clothes on impulse almost fifty years later, lifting the dress over my head, and trying it on.

The gesture was so instinctive I didn't even know what I was thinking as the dress slid down over my body. Inside the bell of pink and peach-colored light the fabric made around me, I was concerned with making sure nothing got caught and that I didn't, in my usual rush and lack of patience, damage it in some way. I never expected it to fit. I'd always thought of my mother as not bigger exactly, but somehow more womanly than me. Frozen in my nine-year-old gaze, my mother was just that, Mother, with a capital M. The first landscape of my life, the female presence I took for granted and in whom I sought refuge, her physical person grew more blurred and indistinct around the edges as time passed, her presence more immense than anything that could be contained in mere measurements. Over the years, relatives had told me I was the image of my mother, but with death's weird erasure, I had no idea what she weighed, how tall she was, or even what size clothes she wore. Like so much else about her, the topography of my mother's body was a mystery, something I'd had to dream up, reconstructing it from fragments, looking for models as I discovered my own. In many ways, my quest to remember her was mirrored by my feelings of displacement and search for a home. It was as if putting the pieces together would in some way create a place where I could settle and rest.

Some of the fragments were tangible. I knew that her wedding slippers, white ballet flats, which my grandmother passed on to me, were size seven, a surprising two sizes smaller than my own feet. Other bits were given to me by family. In an unpublished vignette about my mother, written during

World War II, my grandmother describes her. "Sweet Mary," she writes, regarding my mother across the room:

> How lovely she looks—not the least bit tired after working all day at the draft board. She is still rosy, and her hair is soft and wavy, and she has that really angelic smile. It is hard to believe she can, at times, say such hurting things. She is luscious to look at, quite different from anyone else in the family. Perhaps it is the Irish in her father's family that gives her that wholesome beauty? She is rather large and not thin, but so very graceful and with such a very beautiful complexion.

I liked my grandmother's description. Always worried I was fat, especially compared to my lean, angular sister, afraid my body was too round, I felt reassured by the woman my grandmother describes. Neither perfect nor small, she is nonetheless beautiful and loved, despite her ability to say hurtful things—an unfortunate trait passed down to both her daughters. But that did not tell me what it would have felt like to stand beside her as an adult woman, to borrow her clothes (as I did, in fact, borrow my stepmother's when I was a teen), to measure myself against the body that bore me. And because of this there was some knowledge about my own body that I lacked, something that remained a mystery, untapped even in my mid-forties, as I prepared to marry for a second time. All my life, watching women interact with their daughters, I had been struck by a curious sensation. I didn't know something they did. I didn't have the connection they took for granted. My body felt hollow, insubstantial. No matter what I did, there was a break, a gap, an interruption in my corporeal story of how I became who I was.

I adjusted the shoulder pads of the dress, pulled the very retro side zipper shut, and fluffed out the smocked, yoke waist skirt. I stood before the mirrored bureau, framed with carved oak flowers, which I'd inherited from my grandmother, looking at myself. Knowing my family, I'm sure the dress was custom made for my mother, but it fit me perfectly, "as if it was made for you," a friend would say later. I smoothed it over my hips, feeling the faint ridges of taffeta against my fingertips, a Braille I had forgotten I knew how to read.

I want to say that for a moment I wasn't sure who I was looking at. Family resemblances aside, though, that isn't quite true. It was more as if two transparent slides had been lined up, one in front of the other so, viewed together, they made one picture. Something, a bodily knowledge for which I had no name, came into focus for a moment before disappearing. It reminded me of the way I'd once seen my grandmother's ghost not long after her death, white and insubstantial as a plume of smoke, yet undeniably present as it flitted through this very mirror. But this feeling had to do with my mother, who, through the vehicle of the dress, was mysteriously present as I prepared for my marriage. The fact that Cookie, not yet knowing when I was getting married, had sent the dress to me then, was one of those moments of synchronicity or meaningful coincidence that remind us we are part of a larger order, one we do not control, however much we may wish to do so. That the pink dress fit me seemed a blessing or a gift from a time both before and beyond the grave, an affirmation from my mother of my own approaching wedding. Putting on my mother's dress, I not only established myself in physical relationship to her but participated in something far more soulful, intimate, and primal. I enfolded myself in who she once was, who I had become, and the sense of potential engendered by the dress.

Searching further in the box, I discovered that the dress was accompanied by two yellowed newspaper clippings announcing my parents' wedding at my grandmother's country house, known in the family as the Farm, on September 7, 1947. As I read the clippings, smiling at the dated descriptions—"A garden at Anselma will be the setting for the marriage of Miss Mary Hey Doak of Germantown to Mr. Henry Townsend Jr. of Newtown Square"—something from the past aligned with and affirmed something in the present, my parents' marriage blessing mine. It was as if she, dead for forty years, and he, dead less than a year, were with me in some way, encouraging and approving, reassuring me that this was meant to be.

I'd looked at their wedding photos often in recent weeks, putting them out about the house, joking to my friends that I was trying to give myself courage about matrimony the second time around. But what I was really searching for, besides the mysteries of origin and who my parents were before me, was reassurance. That love lasts. That it is real. That the people I came from loved one another with a depth and intensity so singular that, after his death, my father's third wife told me, "You know, of course, that your mother was the love of his life." I had always known this, but it was good to hear nonetheless.

In the photographs, all is potential. The War is over. My father has not only survived Normandy and Germany but helped liberate a concentration camp. In the stories he'll tell us kids, he was carried on the shoulders of weeping French people at the Liberation of Paris. Like many women during the War, my mother has entered the work force and enjoyed her independence at the Red Cross and the American Friends Field Service. They have met, in a story that seems too romantic to be true no matter how many times I hear it, at the Arthur Murray Dance Studio, and fallen in love.

Looking at the photographs, studying my parents' as yet unlined faces, I was pained by their innocence and vulnerability. They did not know that she would get cancer and die young, that they would lose each other before they were ready, that our family would be destroyed by the event, that he would remarry twice (both unions disasters), that he would die alone in a studio apartment in Albuquerque. As they lifted their glasses toward one another or stood, smiling, to cut the cake, against the dreamy backdrop of my grandmother's garden, everything lay ahead, the future as bright and fresh and full of hope as the carnations and daisies in my mother's bouquet.

Perhaps hope is the point, the mysterious quality that enveloped me when I pulled my mother's pink dress over my head. Wearing her dress, I felt supported by her presence, by that of my aunt who had saved the dress all those years, and by my cousins who sent it to me. Smoothing it down my body, amazed that in my mid-forties I could wear a dress she wore when she was twenty years younger, at a wedding over fifty years ago, I clad myself in something far more meaningful than mere rustling taffeta. I was wrapped in my mother's hope, protection, encouragement, and love.

I would need to find a crinoline petticoat and the right shoes. I would need to find a wide-brimmed, late 1940s-style hat. But the decision to wear the dress had caused something important to fall into place. Call it trust or belief or imagination. Call it hope. My mother would be present at this wedding—in the pink dress she once wore, in the body that was so like hers, in a life that, while it had taken place far away from hers and on its own, was made more meaningful and complete by this connection to her. Wearing my mother's dress, the hollow places inside me would vanish, at least for a while. I would feel more substantial, more womanly and real, as if the bridesmaid she was in the photograph had stepped outside the frame and hugged me, blessing me as only a mother can, the flesh and bones of the one who made me my home country, almost as familiar as my own body inside her rustling dress.

II

The Landscapes inside Us

My Thoreau Summer

If, on an afternoon in midsummer, I happen to find myself near a small lake or pond, opening like earth's blue eye before me, and then catch a whiff of the water's clean mineral scent, overlaid with algae and mixed with the head-clearing resin of white pine, all of it intensified, cooked by sunlight, I am transported to South Pond, in Marlboro, Vermont. There I spent my twentieth summer, living in a cabin without heat, electricity, or running water. No matter where I am when I recall the pond, it is 1973 when I do, and I see myself as I was back then, long-legged and slender, my sun-streaked auburn hair tumbling wild around my back and shoulders. I walk down the soft pine needle–covered path through the woods, past Kenmore, the defunct summer camp, with its abandoned buildings, toward the water. The pond gleams, just ahead through the fringe of trees, radiant with sunlight. No matter how far I travel from that New England summer, I carry the pond balanced inside me, a bowl of bright water. Now trembling, now still, it shows me who I was, who I am, and who I might become if I dive again beneath its shimmering surface.

I wish I could say that, like Thoreau, "I went to the woods to live deliberately." But the truth is, at least in the beginning, I went to the woods because I didn't know what else to do. Halfway through Marlboro College, my heart smashed by a breakup with my boyfriend, horrified that I might have to go home for the summer (where my father and stepmother's marriage was collapsing), I was lost, miserable in the way one can be only when one is twenty. Pale and wan as the heroines of the nineteenth-century novels I favored, I wandered the hills. It was May and the apple trees were blooming on campus. The air glittered, gold with the dust of pollen blown off the pines. But my heartbreak underlay everything, like granite under the Green

47

Mountains. Everywhere I went, I seemed to stub my toe or bash my knee against the unrelenting truth of my loss. Neither old enough to realize that this moment would pass nor psychologically astute enough to understand that my response had to do with earlier losses in my life, I was miserable and obnoxious in my misery. Even my friends were sick of me.

Except for Grace. It was about this time that she asked if I wanted to live at South Pond with her for the summer. The pond, a pure, spring-fed body of water, with an outlet that ran into the Green River, lay a mile away from campus. Shining softly as a polished pewter platter, it was nestled deep in a forest of mixed hardwoods—maple, oak, paper birch—and surrounded by Vermont's signature pine. The word *pond* is elastic in New England, and ours was a small lake, accessible on one side by a long dirt road and on the other by a footpath that led in from South Road, which ran from Marlboro town to the campus. Grace had lifeguarded the previous summer at a small beach called the Ames Hill Association on the north side of the pond. As part of her pay she was given a cabin at the defunct Camp Kenmore, where she acted as caretaker, chasing out any intruders. She'd found it lonely there on her own, however, and this year she was eager for a companion, even a woebegone one. "It will be great," she said in her breathless, excited way. "You're a nature girl. You love the woods. We can be caretakers together."

I liked Grace, and the idea appealed to me because it gave me somewhere to go for the summer that wasn't home. The pond and the woods seemed an oasis too, a private place where I could lick my wounds and brood. All I had to do was secure a job, crucial because I was paying for school on my own. I already worked in the college library, so this was easy to accomplish. There were no formal summer classes at our campus, which was taken over by a classical music festival, so it was an ideal time for housekeeping projects at the library. I was hired to help conduct a manual inventory of the complete collection, going book by book through our holdings, shelf-reading, checking each volume against its card in the catalogue. It was tedious and exacting work, bearable only because I stopped to browse each new discovery as I went along. But it was a job; I told Grace we were on.

I had been to South Pond before, the previous winter, during my ill-fated romance. My boyfriend had given me a pair of bear paw snowshoes, and the path out to the pond afforded the perfect opportunity to try them out. Snowshoeing is easy, even for a novice. I clomped along behind him, enjoying the splendor of the forest. Vermont is a brilliant place in the winter. Everything sparkled and shone, the pines bent beneath the weight of snow, the chalky birches ghost-gray against the blinding whiteness. We don't get to choose our soul landscapes until we leave home for the first time. Vermont, with its fragrant pines and mountains rolling one into another, was mine. I felt I could become who I was meant to be there.

We lumbered on, and there was the frozen pond, a hushed white field, smooth and untrammeled as tundra before us. My boyfriend strode out over the surface, tromping out "I love you" in three-foot-high letters. I thought it romantic, even as part of me wished he'd left that white space alone, pure and unsullied as it was when we came upon it. As he trudged away from the message, the wind began to blow, filling in the letters, leaving them to lie there until spring, when they would melt and become part of the pond itself. It felt like a wonderful secret, and I clapped my hands together in my brown and white Ice Wool mittens.

I didn't see the pond again until the afternoon in late May when Grace and I moved into our cabin. Three miles down a dirt road, Ames Hill, then two miles along Camp Kenmore Road—a narrow, infrequently traveled track, with a tufted green ribbon of grass running through its center—then downhill through the camp, and we were there, at our own private Walden. On the way to the cabin, Grace's old blue Volvo sputtered to a stop, which would turn out to be permanent, forcing us to rely on foot power and hitchhiking for much of the rest of the summer. The car was laden with everything from bedrolls to a Coleman lantern and camp stove to my large collection of houseplants to an absurd Victorian wicker desk, where I imagined I'd write poems. A battered silver Grumman canoe, which I'd borrowed from the college's outdoor program and planned to use to commute across the pond to work, saving several miles of walking, was strapped to the top of the car. We had everything we needed.

As we got out of the car, the pond called to us. Before unloading a thing, we careened down the path of pine needles, an avenue I'd travel so often I'd learn its every twist and turn and root, even in the dark. Adjacent to the camp's overgrown playing field, the pond opened before us, with a natural cove that seemed made for swimming (where skinny dippers sometimes came, and where we ourselves would take baths in the evening). As I stood under the pine trees, drinking in the way the May light flashed over the water, illuminating each ripple and wavelet, something creaked open in my chest. For a sunlit, pine-scented moment, I forgot my sadness. Looking at the water from the sloping bank, I was taken inside its quiet reflection. There was nothing visible but sky and water, everything encircled by a ruff of green.

I stood there, looking at the pond, and it looked back at me. Something floated between us, and I fell still for a moment, held in the water's clear and pitiless gaze, my troubled thoughts dispelled by its quiet beauty. A presence was there with us, though I could not have said what it was. I sensed that my emotional drama had no place here. The pond asked me to be bigger than that and to turn my gaze outward, regarding the realm of ordinary things—pollen drifting in a gold veil on the pond's surface, the plateaus of jade green lily pads scattered across it, and the scent and sound of water as it lapped in small waves against the shore. I wanted to stay forever.

When I tell people about the cabin beside the pond, they envision a rustic log structure, cozy despite its lack of modern amenities. In fact, the cabin that Grace and I moved into that day was a rickety, rundown former campers' cabin. It was built of slatted brown pine and lacked insulation, so chinks of light glowed between the wallboards. Set up on concrete pilings and reached by a short flight of stairs leading to a tiny landing, the cabin was one big room. Entering through the squeaky screen door, one went blind for a minute in the shadowy space, assailed by the woodsy scent, a mixture of sun-warmed pine, dust, and generations of girl campers' sweat. There was a raised, stage-like platform at one end, with a huge table that we made our cooking area. Built-in bunks were at the other end.

The bunks were missing mattresses, so Grace and I stowed our suitcases on their rusty springs and opted for two metal cots on either side of the cabin, their mattresses covered with faded blue and white ticking. We placed our books on narrow shelves that ran along the wall beside our cots. Grace was studying psychology and working on the thesis required by our small, tutorial-based college. I was reading the Transcendentalists and working my way through the American Impressionist painters, trying to find a focus in American Studies, though all I really wanted to do was write. Photographs of Freud and Jung decorated the walls on Grace's side of the cabin, and cheap prints of landscapes by painters such as Childe Hassam, John Twachtman, and William Merritt Chase glowed beside my bed like dream places.

Although there were six large windows, the cabin was dark inside, even during the day. Beyond our rusting, 1950s screens, wooden shutters were propped open ninety degrees, held in place by splintery supports. The shutters looked more like awnings and sometimes gave way unexpectedly, often at night, with a loud bang that sent us bolt upright in our beds. But at midday, with the front door propped wide open, a rectangle of yellow light fell through the length of the cabin. Looking out the door, we had a perfect view of the pines that crowded the opposite shore, and always the pond reaching toward them, its blue surface undulating like watered silk. This reflection bounced off the walls inside the cabin, painting it in wavering gold, as if it were the background for a religious icon.

At night the cabin was illuminated by the ferocious glare of a large, dangerous, and unpredictable Coleman lantern. It required that one person pump it to the correct pressurization, while the other one darted in at just the right moment with an Ohio Blue Tip, lighting the mantle of fragile ash, which, if disturbed too much, fell apart and had to be replaced with a new one. Starting up the companion Coleman stove was exhausting, requiring two hundred pumps to get it going. But the lantern was plain scary, forever on the verge of flaring up out of control and exploding. Hung from a hook in the middle of the cabin, it lit the rough boards inscribed with former campers' names with the harsh intensity of a rural security light. Grace and I read beneath its eerie glow every evening, but we always turned the flame down with a sigh of relief, our faces disappearing as the incandescent mantle faded to black. We kept flashlights beside our beds, but the velvety dark of the cabin was part of its charm. I loved lying there at night, snuggled in the cheap blue and gold sleeping bag from Caldor's my father had given me when I left home, listening to the wind sigh though the pines, the scent of water washing in over me like a benediction as I slipped into sleep.

Like Thoreau, we weren't cut off from civilization. Some way up the hill stood two crumbling Victorian houses that had once housed camp administrators and were now rented out to music festival participants, a couple we never saw, though the music of their flute and cello sometimes floated through the woods. There was electricity in one of the houses. Grace and I were granted access to a refrigerator there, where we kept a wheel of blond Vermont cheddar and our stash of Colombo yogurt. Whole wheat bread, peanut butter and jelly, and Campbell's Chunky Clam Chowder rounded out our simple meals. For a privy we had the woods, where we kept a good distance away from the water and, like animals, buried our scat in the thick pine needle duff.

From first light, when I'd rise and kneel beside the water, cupping it in my hands and washing my face with Dr. Bronner's biodegradable peppermint soap, to the end of the day, when we shed our clothes and slipped into the indigo-colored depths to bathe, the pond was our compass and reference point. Everything we did—from gathering drinking water, to washing dishes, to bathing and washing our hair, to musing about our lives—revolved around the pond. Still water invites contemplation, and South Pond was a length of silver held out each day before us. The cabin was our ark, but the pond set us sailing.

A blue rowboat came with Grace's lifeguard job, and she used it to shuttle over to work. But my canoe gave us swifter, easier access to the water. I paddled it across the pond every morning, stashed it near another rustic cabin, then hiked out through the woods and up South Road to campus. The rest of the time we used the canoe to explore our watery domain, from Camp Kenmore at one end to a beaver dam at the other, where the plush, industrious creatures were engaged in keeping the pond a pond, damming it at its outlet. Grace and I floated, silent in the long New England evenings, watching the water turn violet then almost black, hoping for a sign of one of the beavers, only to be startled by the emphatic slap of a tail as one surfaced then dove, catching us out before we'd even glimpsed it. Other times we followed the resident loons across the pond, marveling at how far their sleek, speckled tuxedo bodies could travel under water before coming up for air. Sometimes we sat, still as statues, hardly daring to breathe, watching as the doe with twin fawns dipped her black velvet nose to drink in the shallows. Her babies balanced on stilt-like legs beside her, their backs patterned with spots like storms of small white blossoms. The entire family was mirrored in the pond; it seemed the deer drank their own reflections.

At night the pond was another world, its dark blue reflecting the sky above so precisely that, whether we were in the boat or swimming, we lost view of where earth left off and sky began, the firmament liquid too, streaked gold with meteor showers in August. Keats's line, "Bright star, would I were stedfast as thou art" ran through my thoughts, though I felt too embarrassed to say it aloud. A few years later, reading Anne Sexton's poem about "a bowl, / with all its cracked stars shining," I thought again of the nights at South Pond. Getting out of the canoe, Grace and I lounged on the sloping hill where the skinny dippers came by day (former campers, fellow college students, or local hippies, none of whom we ever chased out), staring into the sky as if our futures hung suspended there. More pragmatic than me, Grace—engaged to be married to her high school sweetheart at the end of the summer and destined to become a pediatrician—grounded me in important ways. But something in my romantic sensibility must have appealed to her, too. We complemented one other, as friends who are very different sometimes do, the pond a wide blue net that held us gently balanced. We lay there in the fragrant grass, talking and trading secrets, our faces lit faintly by that circle of bright water drizzled with starlight and reflecting the moon.

By day the water, while not transparent, was sparkling and clear, darkening to the color of deep tea as one went deeper and deeper, and I loved the way my body seemed to merge with it, fluid as the element I moved through. I never swam as much as I did that summer, sliding into the water's cool arms every day after work. A few strokes out from the skinny dippers' cove, past the ghost of a drowned piano, which someone had dragged into the pond many years before, and I was over my head and alone. Turning on my back, I floated, lifting my face to the sun like one of the yellow water lilies that dotted the pond, my hair streaming around me.

I was neither a strong nor a confident swimmer, especially compared to Grace, who cut through the water like a dolphin in her blue-striped Speedo and that summer saved two people from drowning. Swimming lessons, like so many other things, had ended with my mother's death when I was a girl. But as I swam out farther each day, working my way up to crossing the pond, my fear dissolved, and I grew more adept and sure of myself. By July, stroking my way through South Pond every day, I retrieved something of the girl I had been, discovering I possessed a capability I had not realized. In those moments I belonged to the place, as much a part of it as the deer, beavers, loons, or cedar waxwings that passed through, thrilling me with their red-tipped feathers. I floated, alone in that small, shining circle of silence, my body weightless, while the pond worked its magic, its silver hands holding me up as my mother's once had.

Although I loved the long evenings when the light lingered until nine, my favorite time of day at the pond was early morning. If it had been a cool night, the pond steamed, filled with mist, reflecting back a muted, blurry picture, as if the water itself was dreaming. On warmer days it lay perfectly still, polished to a sheen that showed everything so vibrantly the reflected trees seemed more real than the trees themselves. As I knelt at my morning ablutions, dipping my hands into the water to wash, I was sometimes startled by my own face staring up at me, as if my soul dwelled there, just beneath the surface. We had only an old mirror in the cabin, its silver badly foxed, so we combed our hair by feel. I got out of the habit of looking at myself and found it curiously refreshing. Not worrying about my appearance, I moved more naturally and freely, with greater self-possession. I was filled with ongoing delight at how much there was to notice at the pond— the song of the hermit thrush, a glimpse of white turtlehead or cardinal flower, the pattern of the constellation Cygnus in the sky at night. My sadness seemed to fade.

Early morning at the pond felt like the beginning of the world. Although there were two other simple cabins at the far end, there was no sign of human life as I paddled my way across the water to work. The water was so still it held the image of the pond with its wreath of green trees and their reflection as if they were two halves of the same world, a summer snow globe of sky and water. Dipping my paddle as silently as I could, so as not to disturb the stillness, I felt as if I had been granted access to a secret world. I breathed with the pond, part of its tranquil surface, without thinking consciously about the value of solitude and silence it provided. I was too young and confused about life to be able to muse on those qualities with anything resembling larger understanding. I knew only that I loved those mornings alone, the silver pod of the canoe skimming over the sparkling water. When I thought to look down, I saw a young woman who resembled me, dipping the paddle, sailing through her own image, which broke into wavelets behind her.

Most of my memories of that summer are tranquil, still shots in which the pond seems to float, a sterling silver medallion shining at the center of our world. But we had an extended rainy patch in August, when the pond seemed to merge with the sky, and Grace and I were cooped up, miserable in the damp and mildew-saturated cabin, where nothing dried out and even our sleeping bags were damp and clammy. During that time I had one of my few scary experiences of the summer. After going straight from work to a party one night, I found myself hiking in after midnight to retrieve my canoe and head home. It was raining so hard I had to tip water from the canoe, which should have given me pause. Focused only on getting back to the cabin, soaked to the skin from my hike through the woods, I slithered in and pushed off through what felt like a curtain of falling black water, torn open now and then by streaks of lightning.

As I maneuvered away from shore, the sky split open above me. Did aluminum attract lightning? I wasn't sure. But I knew it wasn't a good idea to be out in the middle of the pond, my body the tallest visible target. While I dithered for a moment, deciding what to do, bolts of fire slashed the sky several more times. Each yellow blast filled the air with the scent of ozone, illuminating the familiar landscape of the pond in sharp relief, making it into a ghost picture, everything brilliant white for an instant before being plunged again into the sheets of rain that fell, like darkness falling into darkness. The rain pelted down, thrumming against my skin, so insistent my entire body felt like a drum. With my hair and clothes plastered against me, it was difficult to tell where I left off and the world around me began. Everything was water.

I decided it was safest to hug the shore, even though it would take longer to get home. Blinded by the deluge, guessing at my direction, the canoe rocking, my path illuminated by lightning, I somehow clung to the land and began navigating my way around the perimeter of the pond. Keeping my head low to avoid tree branches, I was aware of shivering and being cold, even as I was exhilarated. Flash after flash lit up the pond and then vanished, leaving afterimages printed on my eyelids. Once or twice I could swear lighting struck the water, fizzing out like enormous, burning brands plunged into darkness. But I couldn't be sure because I could see things only in brief, hallucinatory glimpses.

When I at last reached the marshy shallows at the far side of our lobe of the pond, I had to make a decision. I could shoot straight across and be home. Or I could continue to feel my way around the shoreline, clinging to its edge, fitting myself up against it like a piece from a jigsaw puzzle. In hindsight, it seems clear what I should have done. But I was young and impatient and reckless. Although I had watched my mother die of cancer when I was nine, my own life had never been tested. I chose the easiest route—straight across. Paddling as hard as I could, I shot through the darkness. The rain streamed over me as I pushed right, left, right. My arms ached, my shoulders burned. My breath sawed back and forth in my chest. I felt as if the canoe were an extension of my body as we plunged together through the water.

A few minutes passed and I felt a soft bump as the prow of the canoe hit land. The first lightning since I'd darted across revealed the huge fallen birch where I always hid the canoe. Staggering out of the boat, I hauled it from the water and stowed it behind the tree's thick trunk. I flopped down on the tree for a moment, panting. The rain continued to pound my skin. I was freezing, and could feel my pulse throbbing where my thighs pressed against the tree's sodden bark. I ought to have offered a prayer of thanks for my deliverance and dashed to the cabin. But I didn't. I lifted my face to the rain, exultant and smiling, and sat there for a long moment, drenched with the plentitude of summer.

Grace's fiancé, Bill, traveled from Maine to visit a few times. But for the most part our time at South Pond centered on the rhythms she and I created together. We rose early, cooked simply, and read or wrote letters at night, the incandescent glow of the Coleman lantern casting everything into sharp relief. Grace's maiden name was Miele, which means "honey" in Italian. Sometimes, glancing up at her, I'd be struck by her beauty and earnestness as she bent over her book, her long, brown, sun-streaked hair falling around her in veil. *Remember this*, a voice inside me whispered. *This time won't come again.*

Summer deepened, and I felt myself on more equal footing with Grace. Simple things, like mastering the art of the canoe, having to walk everywhere, and losing my fear of the dark as I stood at the edge of the pond in my nightgown, gazing across the water through the pines, had connected me to myself in ways I hadn't experienced before. Brown and muscular, I thought nothing of walking five miles if I had to. I wasn't aware that I moved with more ease and fluidity until one of my friends pointed it out. Living close to elemental rhythms, I felt able to do things, and I trusted myself in ways I hadn't before. Without even realizing it, I became more self-sufficient, and my heartbreak vanished like something from another life.

As the end of summer approached, the days growing shorter and mist rising from the pond more mornings than not, I found myself wishing our time beside it would never end, though all such interludes do. But Grace's marriage lay ahead of us, the final note in a small piece of music written for two voices, the implicit end of our South Pond idyll, and I started a relationship as well.

Stopping with friends one late August afternoon at Gibbsie's store, the sole place to shop or get gas if one didn't want to go twelve winding, mountain miles down Route 9 to Brattleboro, I'd flirted with my friend PK, who was working as a roofer that summer. We'd been buddies our first semester in college, before we drifted into romances with other people. Like me, he'd had his heart broken, and then he'd transferred to another school, where he could pursue engineering. As he stood on the roof at Gibbsie's that day, bare to the waist and shining with sweat, his skin glazed a warm nut-brown, his dark curls glossy, I saw him in a different way. Impulsively I handed him some grapes I had just bought. "Where are you living?" he called. "At South Pond," I called back. "Come out and see me some time."

He came, bringing with him a little Sunfish sailboat, on which we skimmed around the water. I showed him the pond's mysteries, from the beaver dam to the place where the deer drank to the yellow water lilies that were still blooming here and there, impossible to pick. At some point, as we balanced on the boat's narrow hull in our shorts and T-shirts, both of us spangled with water, our thighs brushed together. It was a Saturday and Grace was lifeguarding across the pond. I took PK back to the cabin. "Pretty underpants," he said as he removed the scrap of silky red fabric printed with flowers, and we moved toward one another, both of us shy and hesitant, afraid of being hurt again.

Afterward, filled with the satisfaction of a twenty-year-old male who has just had sex, PK wanted to go swimming. "C'mon, Abby," he said, the one boy in college to ever call me by my childhood nickname. "Let's go." He grabbed me by the hand and we ran, nude, toward the water. Dropping my hand, he charged ahead and dove in—only to stagger back out, grimacing, clutching his shoulder. Having overestimated the depth of the pond, he had hit bottom, dislocating his shoulder.

I prevailed upon one of the skinny dippers to dress and drive us to the Brattleboro Memorial Hospital emergency room in PK's car. A gruff doctor wrenched PK's shoulder back into place and bound it against his body. I took him back to the pond, where he spent a week recuperating. He and I took up temporary residence in another cabin, where we slept on the floor in a nest of sleeping bags. It was a sweet time, but like the summer, we both knew it wouldn't last.

When PK departed, I moved back into the cabin I'd shared with Grace. But something in the rhythm of our days had shifted. She was focused on the big event, and Bill was due to arrive. Our time at the pond drew to a close, the days dwindling as quickly as the water striders danced over their flower-like shadows. Grace and Bill married in the Marlboro Meeting House at the end of August, after a party at the pond the night before.

After their one-night honeymoon she stayed with me a little while longer, while her new husband went back to Maine to finish his summer job. She was moving to Maine, with plans to send installments of her thesis to her advisor in by mail.

I was living at the pond unofficially and had to leave when Grace did. Before we departed, while Grace was packing, I swam alone for the last time, savoring the blue darkness as it washed around my body. Floating on my back, I studied the heavens, watching as an occasional meteor shimmered through the sky in a silver-gold streak. Knowing I was leaving, it was as if something in my continuous communion with the pond had been interrupted, though not quite cut off. I felt lonely there in a way I hadn't before. I'd begun the process of removing myself from the experience. But I couldn't bear the fact that I was going, departing from that scent of pine and water Grace and I wished we could bottle and keep.

I don't remember the day we left South Pond, locking the flimsy door on our cabin, walking up the pine needle path toward the loaded car, which had finally been repaired. But I do remember how difficult the transition was. I boarded with the college nurse for several weeks before school started, caring for her daughter in exchange. I couldn't get used to being inside all the time. There was never any privacy, and everything seemed too bright, too loud, and too easy. I caught myself thinking I had to boil water before drinking it or pump the recalcitrant Coleman stove to do so. Like a time traveler from another era, I was shocked by how easy it was to flick a switch or turn on a tap. At Camp Kenmore I'd felt close to the natural world even when I was inside the cabin, wind blowing through chinks in the wall, moonlight reflected on the pond's bright surface, and always the water itself, just feet away. Some essential simplicity and goodness seemed missing in the world I now inhabited.

I was homesick for the pond for months after leaving it. I missed the silence and the stillness, nothing but the sound of owls calling at night and wind in the pines. I missed my meditative forays, alone in the canoe. I missed the sight of Grace, reading across the room. But more than anything else, I missed who I was there. Or rather, I missed the way I forgot myself in the pond's presence. Returning to the normal world and resuming my studies was a letdown after living as elementally as I had. As time passed, I'd understand that we had lived much more deliberately at the pond than I realized.

I could not articulate it that way then. All I knew was that I went to the woods unhappy and returned with a larger sense of myself, my spirit opened by the invisible presence of wildness and solitude that I'd sensed the day we arrived. It wasn't until many years later that I understood how transformative that summer had been, a defining moment in my history. Perhaps one is permitted experiences like that only once or twice in a lifetime, when one is least prepared for their impact and thus most in need—as I was then—of a pond's green and silver instruction. The cabin I lived in that summer is long gone, torn down as a fire hazard. But I still have the key to its door in a carved sandalwood box where I keep special things. What I experienced there is alive within me yet, its click familiar in memory's lock, the pond spread before me in a blaze of light as I stand at the open cabin door.

❧

I went west after college and did not see South Pond for decades. But one summer, while visiting family in New England with Tom, I took him to Marlboro. As our green Subaru Outback bumped down Ames Hill Road, then Camp Kenmore Road, the ridge of grass in the middle scraped softly against the car's bottom, as it always had. We stopped at the top of the hill, where the crumbling Victorian house still stood, along with some of the camp buildings. We stepped down the pine needle path and there was the pond, blue and still as ever, a wafer of light fringed with pine. I stood there for a long time, looking out across the water, recalling the sunny afternoon when it first revealed its secrets. Then we walked around the point, to what had been the campers' beach. There we encountered a young woman with a long blond braid, who politely asked what we were doing on the premises. I explained that I'd once spent the summer there, serving as one of the caretakers.

"That's what I'm doing this summer," she exclaimed. "Isn't living here amazing? It's so quiet and private."

"Yes, it's wonderful," I said, my voice soft, knowing what she meant. "It's the best experience in the world. Living here was one of the most wonderful things that ever happened to me."

We chatted a bit, just long enough for me to find out that she, too, was a Marlboro College student. I considered asking her if the beaver dam was still there, but didn't, knowing I wouldn't be able to bear it if the sleek, brown creatures that had given me so much pleasure were gone. Granted permission to wander about, I snapped a few photographs to send to Grace. I knew they would never capture the pond's mystery as we had known it, but wanted to mark that it was all still there, unchanged from how it had been that summer. I stood, looking out over the water, half-expecting to see Grace, lifeguarding on the far shore, or my younger self, skimming home across the pond in my battered silver canoe. We were not there, of course, though on some level we always would be. Kneeling, I cupped my hands in the clear water, as I so often had done that summer. I lifted them and spilled the water over my face and neck, anointing myself, as one should at true and sacred places. And then I walked away, back up the pine needle path to where Tom waited, and back into my present life, the pond glimmering behind me.

California Girl

Beautiful country burn again.

—Robinson Jeffers, "Apology for Bad Dreams," *The Wild God*

In a photo that exists nowhere but in my mind, I am caught, suspended mid-leap between two boulders in a talus field at the base of the mountains that rise above Squaw Valley. It's the early 1990s and I'm in my forties, just clear of a divorce that's burned through my life like a wildfire, and I'm visiting California for the first time since leaving almost a decade before. There to attend Art of the Wild, a conference devoted to nature and the environment, I am trying to write about my experience living in California, how the landscape acted upon me, changing the way I saw myself and the world. But the truth is I've come to see if California—where my ex-husband, David, was born and raised and where we met in graduate school and lived during our twenties and thirties—is still mine. The conference is a foil, offering me structure and purpose I might not have felt traveling to California on my own. While I'm enjoying the workshops and readings more than I expected, it's the landscape that draws me. Rising around Squaw like rough, carved pieces in a board game tossed down by giants, the granite blocks of the Sierra uplift exert a magnetic pull on my body and psyche. Happy to be sprung for an afternoon ramble, I leap, the mountains' distinctive scent of dust-baked granite and pine rising around me in invisible welcome.

My friend Robin, who has traveled with me to the conference from Madison, hikes beside me. Although I haven't been on this particular trail before, having spent more time hiking and cross-country skiing in Yosemite or exploring the mountains in Southern California, each step takes me deeper into something familiar in myself, something that I've forgotten or which has lain dormant, while I have struggled, so homesick for verticality in the Upper Midwest that I sometimes mistake cloud banks for the mountains. As we tramp along, moving into the rhythm of walking, a fizz of happiness rises from deep inside me, like the springs that feed into Squaw Creek, a bubbling tangle of silver rushing downhill beside us. I lift my face to the sun. I feel etched, limned by light, scraped clean as the boulder I stand on, as if I too have been hewn out of the ground, tumbled into a place different from where I started. Sunlight glitters off the granite's rough surface like tiny jewels. Enlivened by the brilliance, I hop from boulder to boulder, darting and flashing like the Steller's jay I tossed peanuts to earlier in the day.

"You look as if you belong in this landscape!" Robin calls out. "I do," I call back. "Oh, I do." And it is here, in the moment when I hang, suspended in the air between pushing off from one boulder and landing on another, that I understand something the land itself seems to be trying to tell me: I am home. Unlike so much else that disappeared in the wake of my divorce, I have not lost California, this place that shaped me, making me someone different from who I was when I first arrived. There are moments like this in a life, most often unbidden, when the invisible energy of a place seems to rise up through our boot soles and communicate itself. It welcomes us, as I am welcomed, there on the side of the mountain, the rocks calling out to me as if they know my name, reminding me that the person I was when I lived there is still alive inside.

It was fire season when I arrived in Southern California in September 1975. When I stepped off the plane at the confusingly named Ontario Airport in the eastern San Gabriel Valley, hot, dry Santa Ana winds were blowing in from the desert. The air was charged, shimmering with heat that made me lift my hand to shade my eyes as I deplaned, overdressed in my blue Shetland sweater and matching skirt, looking for my on-again-off-again college boyfriend, with whom I'd gotten together after the summer romance with PK. Supposedly in California to begin a doctoral program in English at Claremont Graduate School, I was really following my boyfriend. Against my better judgment—for we'd broken up many times before—I hoped things would work out between us.

Full of the illusion that I was moving forward in my life, rather than making choices by default, I'd screeched through my last days of college in Vermont, finishing my thesis at the eleventh hour, my course set stubbornly westward. As waist-high drifts of snow at last melted and the apple trees bloomed, I dreamed about California, unaware that, like so many before me, I was orienting by a mirage, by what I imagined the state to be rather than what it is. When the girl next door in my dorm described watching the sun set over the Pacific from tall bluffs that tumbled down to the beach from her family cottage at Big Sur, I imagined myself there, gazing west, notebook in my hand, describing it as no one else ever had.

Filled with an ignorance that now seems blessed, I went, heedless of the fact that Claremont is in Southern California, nowhere near Big Sur. I didn't know anything about West Coast geography or distance, about water feuds, ethnicity, smog, overpopulation, or freeways. I had grown up with turnpikes and tollways; even the word "freeways" was new to me. I didn't know about Los Angeles, city of angels lost and found. I didn't know about what I would come to see as the Bay Area's patronizing attitude toward the supposedly hedonistic southern part of the state, which I would grow to love. In short, I knew nothing—the best possible condition, perhaps, for setting out on a three-thousand-mile journey.

I traveled with a $2,000 cashier's check in my pocket (everything I'd earned working evening shifts that summer as a pediatric nursing assistant at the Brattleboro hospital), one small suitcase, and my red college footlocker. With the exception of bus and train trips back and forth between college in Vermont and my parents' house in New York State, I had never traveled alone. I had never flown in a plane. I had never been west of Pittsburgh. More concerned with what to wear than where I was going, I didn't even look at a map. I just went, flinging myself westward, as if diving into the cold, green Pacific.

∽

When I came to California, Ontario Airport felt small, almost rural. I never got used to the name of the city, now home to an international airport servicing places far beyond the Inland Empire. Back then, flights landing from the east swooped in over the vineyards of Cucamonga and Etiwanda, which are long since gone. To the north, above Foothill Boulevard, orange groves still backed up against the front ridge, not yet razed for housing developments. Travelers stepped down the stairs from their plane and onto the tarmac, then walked to a terminal that seemed strange, like so many buildings in Southern California, too flat and open, as if the intense sunlight of the place exerted pressure that made everything hunker down on the ground.

The light struck me most. When I think about what is golden in California, I think of the rolling hills, burnished by that light. There's a reason why it's called fabled. Nothing prepared me for the merciless intensity or bounty of the light. Now gin-clear, now filtered by low clouds and fog that roll in from the ocean, now veiled in smog, the color of red ochre in a second-stage alert, now a scorching ball of white, the Southland sun is omnipresent. That first day, it beat down, entering me like a laser. I sensed even then that it was going to penetrate my being, changing me in ways I couldn't imagine. Looking for my boyfriend in the crowd of people in shorts and Hawaiian shirts waiting inside the gate, I had an impulse to step back into the air-conditioned dark of the plane and sit down. Overwhelmed, I wished I could bury my face in the arms of the way-too-warm sweater I'd donned that morning in New York, pinning a pink rose to my collar. What did I think I was doing?

September is the worst month of year in the San Gabriel and Walnut-Pomona valleys. It's the smoggiest time in Southern California and the height of fire season—a conjunction of human-caused pollution and climate that has only intensified since the years when I lived there. Santa Ana winds blowing in from the Great Basin and the Mojave Desert can huff a stray spark into a wildfire in minutes. Although they cleanse the air, blowing the smog toward the ocean, scrubbing the mountains sharp and clear as the 3D pictures in a 1950s View-Master, they are said to induce anxiety in some, a supposed result of their positive ions. In my experience, Santa Anas can energize you or make you feel as if you're filled with swarming bees—sometimes all at once. My skin blasted by desert heat, I didn't know how to react. All I knew was that the wind seemed to blow through me, filling my body for a moment, and then turning me inside out.

Things were over with the college boyfriend in weeks. And there I was in California, alone except for two wonderful female housemates, in the ugly cinder block apartment of graduate student housing where my black-and-white postcard collection featuring portraits of women writers kept falling off the walls. Everything was strange to me, from palm trees to orange groves to the sprinklers that went on in the middle of the night and were, I realized, the inspiration for Joni Mitchell's song "The Hissing of Summer Lawns." I was an American Studies major in a PhD program in English that I sensed from the start was a mistake. My own writing tugged at me. I had no idea how to go about that terrifying endeavor though, so I forged on. Was there anyone ever so young and unworldly, so clueless and innocently hopeful?

The Mount Baldy fire began a few weeks after my arrival. It lit the night sky above the foothills north of Claremont orange, like an earth-bound aurora or a vision out of Blake, a Promethean disaster caused by arson or human carelessness. As I struggled to find my way in an academic program that, in addition to being wrong for me, was run by aging white men who seemed to delight in putting down their female students, the fire raged in foothill communities, damaging Padua Hills, Palmer Canyon, and Potato Mountain. Covered with a layer of gray-and-white-flecked ash, smoke everywhere, Claremont seemed perched on the edge of a con-flagration that made me think of Vesuvius. But rather than being para-lyzed by the choking air, everyone went about life as normal—a bit shaken, but at the same time accepting in that peculiar, life-on-the-edge way only Californians can.

It was about this time I met David at a campus art opening. We sat on a blue leatherette-covered piano bench, drank too much wine, and talked about the fires, a bright red, wall-sized abstract painting blazing behind us. Lean and rangy as a mountain coyote, David had been out running before the show and was clad in hiking shorts and a Mission Bay Marathon T-shirt. An economics student who had just passed his qualifying exams, he was researching his dissertation on exhaustible resources, focusing on water in the West, an irony even I caught, though it also seemed noble.

A little unsure of himself, engaging and boyish, with floppy blond hair, a cleft chin, and an indirect, teasing manner, David was a native Califor-nian who loved the mountains and had hiked everywhere. Different from guys I'd known in college, gentler and kinder, a preacher's kid, he seemed authentic, a boy-next-door type, fresh and new as the landscape in which I found myself. He would become my guide to this place where I struggled to adapt, but gradually came to see as my adopted home.

He would take me hiking in Yosemite (where I saw my first bear), Sequoia, Point Reyes, and the Redwood Parks. We'd camp up and down the coast, from just north of Santa Barbara to Eureka. We'd run in races on the beach at Morro Bay, ride bikes in Cambria-by-the-Sea, and sit for hours on the bluffs at Montaña de Oro, watching sea otters anchored in kelp as they ate abalones, the *tappity-tap-tapping* of the rocks they used to break the shells audible above the waves. We'd house-sit for two summers up a narrow canyon in Mount Baldy Village, cradled in the San Gabriels' rough embrace, Bear Creek pattering beneath our bedroom window, black-tailed deer on the path ahead when we ran on Glendora Ridge Road. Once, while we were hiking the back side of Baldy, seven bighorn sheep crossed our trail, having come straight up an abrupt scree slope. Looking into their eyes, I felt for a few moments beholden, caught in a spell of limitless wildness. For a girl from the Northeast, it was overwhelming. I felt as if the bones in my head were expanding, straining to contain it all. Bigger and more gorgeous than any geography I'd ever known, California stretched my senses, opening me to possibilities I hadn't imagined, enlargement of self being the magic the Golden State does best.

David was distressed by the Baldy fire. Towering ten thousand feet, the highest peak in the San Gabriels, Mount Baldy (officially known as Mount San Antonio) rises behind Claremont like an enormous Buddha, the natural focal point of the area. Several times the evening we met David said, "They're burning my mountains," as if he had a personal stake in the matter. Raised in rural places, I liked his attachment to earth. Even in our first conversation his care for the place filtered into me. David was, from the beginning, so bound up in my mind with the sheer physicality of California that for many years I associated him with the landscape itself, as if he were one of the desert bighorns he loved, here then gone, nothing in their wake but the scent of sage on the wind and the faint skitter of scree. Running or hiking or biking behind him, it didn't occur to me that I was building my own relationship with the place, absorbing its claims on my spirit.

Neither as severe nor as extensive as recent California wildfires, the flames in the foothills below Baldy were quickly contained. The winter rains came—as locals say, "L.A. has two seasons: summer and January"— and David and I became a couple. The following spring I moved into his apartment above an old carriage house behind a Victorian house in Pomona. Paneled in warm, knotty pine, with steeply slanting eaves, it was like a cabin in the middle of town. It overlooked a yard filled with orange, lemon, grapefruit, kumquat, and apricot trees that felt like a paradise. Boiling in the summer, chilly in winter, 355 East Kingsley Avenue in Pomona was a perfect first home. I loved its long, old-fashioned kitchen sink, the black and white Western-Holly stove, and the view to the north, where Mount Baldy stood framed every morning, like something on a Chinese scroll.

Many things happened to me while I lived in that apartment. I finished my MA, got my first real job, began writing, became a vegetarian, started running, went into therapy, lost a child, and survived a depressive episode triggered by that loss. I sewed quilted ornaments for a Christmas tree we cut in the San Gabriel foothills, cooked Lentils Monastery Style from *Diet for a Small Planet*, and made dozens of jars of apricot jam. I listened to Jackson Browne, Linda Ronstadt, Fleetwood Mac, and George Winston, and adopted three cats, who lolled each afternoon in the bank of sunny, south-facing windows in the living room—my family. Most important, I learned how to make a home with another person. But I'd always associate David's and my beginnings with fire, and with how I felt as if I were rising from the ashes of one life into another before they were even cool. Earthquake-shaken California, where the seismograph judders then resumes its path, etched like a trail of blood inscribed with a needle. Rattlesnake California, slipping out of its translucent, silvery skin into a new beginning.

∽

Before I ever went to California I had a long history of dreaming about it. Even as a girl at Wild Run Farm, I'd bent with rapt attention over *To California by Covered Wagon*, a retelling of the Schallenberger party's trip to California in 1845. I couldn't formulate a clear image of the Golden State, but I could visualize the journey across the plains from Council Bluffs. I imagined myself as part of the wagon train that split off from the Oregon Trail near Fort Hall and went south on a route where only one party had gone before them, heading through valleys and rolling hills covered with sagebrush toward the Humboldt Sink and then the Sierra Nevadas. I wrote several pioneer stories in grade school, one describing a band of settlers who struggled over the mountains to a body of water set like a chip of sapphire among the peaks—Lake Tahoe.

The problem was the journey across the country seemed like what mattered. Once I got my pioneers to California, I couldn't figure out what they *did* there. My solution, pushing my stubby pencil over the page like a girl divinity, was to make them keep on having children. My story failed to satisfy me in the end, concluding in a litany of names, like some reverse reading of Genesis. It didn't convey anything about the details of the landscape my imagination had carried me into. How could it? Like everyone who has ever migrated there from another place, I had to live in the state to discover what it meant. Getting there was the catalyst, the spark, the trigger. I tricked myself into thinking I was doing one thing—following a boy, going to graduate school—and believed in it long enough to discover it was about something else entirely.

∽

When I was growing up, California was like the Grail, elusive, mysterious, out of reach, a reward for something I felt I hadn't yet accomplished. From the late 1960s to the mid-1970s, when the five kids in my family were graduating from high school and leaving home at the rate of one per year, my three brothers each read *On the Road*, and then made a ritual trip, hitchhiking across the country. Departing from our two-hundred-year-old house on a dirt road in North Salem, New York, they'd snag a ride to Interstate 684, heading south then west. Their destination was always California, a place so far away it seemed a distant land, given that I was a girl, forbidden to hitchhike (though I often did, locally, my little sister in tow), and didn't know how to drive.

But besides having no way to get there, I couldn't open my sights that wide. Accustomed to an intimate, circumscribed landscape, I couldn't get my mind around anything as big as California, let alone imagine myself there, a part of the landscape, indigenous as sage or scrub oak, bay laurel, or manzanita, names I sometimes repeat aloud to myself now, lying in bed at night, their beauty a language I once knew intimately.

I watched as my brothers loaded their backpacks and constructed elaborate sets of signs, grommeted together with a special gun so that they could flip from one page to the next. I helped them letter the names of cities up and down the California coast—Los Angeles, Santa Barbara, Monterey, San Francisco, Berkeley (of course), and Eureka—coloring in the block letters until my wrist ached and the Magic Marker began to run dry. I too yearned to escape, but I sensed I'd have to do it a different way, one more gradual and less dramatic. Leaving home, for me, was a more extended affair. My brothers traveled to California and then came back, and only one returned to live there. It took me longer to go west, but when I did, I stayed, through the formative years of my young adulthood, metamorphosing into someone I never imagined I might be. But most important is the fact that I made a home there. California took me in, sheltering me in ways I could not have imagined as a girl dreaming of covered wagons.

❧

The summer I was sixteen I was a little too young and (I hoped) a little too cool to have been much influenced by the Beach Boys' innocent version of California, a place filled with dune buggies and long-legged girls clad in skimpy bikinis, which I felt shy in when I started wearing them myself. A fan of the Stones, Jefferson Airplane, and the Grateful Dead, I fancied myself deeper and more complex than the songs on the *Surfin' Safari* album my father embarrassed me with on my birthday, though I secretly loved "California Girls." Despite the dark footage of the Stones' Altamont concert on the evening news, something of the golden California mystique filtered its way into my psyche. I believed everything was beautiful there.

Lying in our backyard, slicked with Bain de Soleil—with a glass of water to pour over myself when I got too hot—I baked myself a color I liked to think of as burnt sienna. I bleached gold streaks into my long reddish-brown hair with Sun In, an evil-smelling spray-on application consisting primarily of peroxide. "What is this, the California look?" my oldest step-brother jeered. I'd felt attractive, even alluring, until he'd said that, drawing some strength I'd never felt from a mythical landscape where the sun always shone and the beaches ran, like sifted gold, down to an azure-green Pacific.

On some level, and with no idea as to what it entailed, I wanted to be a California girl, cool and hip in my beads, flowers, and gauzy Indian-print dresses smelling of jasmine and sandalwood. California, where everything was happening, represented freedom I couldn't find in the Northeast. I wanted to toss my hair, wear hiking boots with dresses, and get so tan I'd never need to shave my legs again, the hair on them blond as sunlight. I wanted to become, as Roseanne Cash would later write, "a California girl, in aesthetics and attitude." I wanted, like every seeker, to make the Golden State's treasure mine.

Like many of the most important relationships in my life, California at first lay a little to the side of my direct gaze, peripheral but present, containing more possibility and potential than I knew. I came to think of it as something a little like the low clouds and fog so often present on Southern California mornings—the result of the Catalina eddy, David explained—but burned off by noon to reveal an enormous landscape. If anyone had told me that I was going to spend most of my twenties and thirties in Los Angeles County, swim at San Onofre Beach on summer weekends, climb the back side of Half Dome on my first hiking trip, learn to drive on the San Bernardino Freeway, attend poetry readings at Beyond Baroque (thinking nothing of driving an hour to get there), live with a ten-thousand-foot mountain visible from my kitchen window, or wear a dumb T-shirt that said "I love L.A.," I wouldn't have believed it.

And if anyone had told me that, in California, I would begin to pursue with intent the writing I yearned for but feared, I might have wept, so shaky was my self-esteem and sense of my own voice—which I recorded in secret, on small slips of paper jumbled in my top desk drawer. Apart from my reading about the pioneers and putting on my mother's old cowboy boots in our dress-up box, California was my first encounter with what felt to me like the American West. The Golden State has been described as existing "west of the West," a place that is its own realm, different from the interior West. In many ways it is. But I think something of the pioneer spirit also lingers there, making the state a psychological frontier. Moving to California, I got to be the woman in the covered wagon I had once imagined, arriving in a new world. As far as I was concerned, this was the West.

Whenever I fly into California, usually landing at Ontario International, I look for the mountains that guide me home. As the plane descends over the dun-colored back of the Mojave, I sit up, alert, waiting to see the jagged spine of the San Gabriel range arch up beneath us like the back of a stegosaurus. I name the peaks I recognize: Timber, Thunder, Telegraph, Ontario, and last, Baldy. They always come up faster than I expect, their scruffy shawls of trees and chaparral zooming into close focus, and every time it feels like we're flying too low, headed for a crash in the rugged terrain. Scared but exhilarated, skimming through the air like the hawks I used to watch soaring above the mountains, I feel I have entered a different realm, my psyche open in ways it isn't elsewhere. I am in California again, the place where anything can happen. I watch the plane's shadow traverse the peaks and marvel at the fact that I have hiked, camped, and lived among them. It seems improbable to me now, something from another lifetime.

Suspended over the mountains that, despite the constant encroachment of humanity, remain familiar as years go by, I can feel time tick through me. "How did that all become the past?" I once asked David, after we had moved to Wisconsin and divorced. He shook his head sadly, as if it was beyond his comprehension as well. We had arrived in the middle of our lives without realizing exactly how we'd gotten there, or why things weren't working, or why loving each other wasn't enough. California, and whoever we had been there, seemed like it was gone, except in isolated snapshots: the two of us posed, grinning atop Mount Baldy or lounging with the *L.A. Times* at San Onofre Beach or cross-country skiing in the Sierras at Yosemite, everything light-dazzled, the sun shining down.

Even after decades in the Midwest, I still catch myself looking for mountains. I have learned (and love) another landscape, but am anxious without them and find their presence comforting. Rough-hewn, enormous, and foreboding, protected by thickets of instantly combustible chaparral, the mountains of California are completely themselves. I studied them each day when I lived in Pomona. I rested my eye on the front ridge as I ran at Puddingstone, a nearby and then-primitive recreation area, named for the conglomerate that defined its rough terrain, in which a small, dammed reservoir lay embedded, a blue gem in the desert. Viewed from the valley, the peaks, crisscrossed within by fault lines, stand out like dragons' teeth on the horizon, so sharp it seems they slice the sky. Heaved up in block faults, their billion-year-old metamorphic rock among the oldest in the state, these mountains are a tangible reminder of what emerges and what remains in a place where geological change occurs all the time, shifting and straining in response to pressures from within. Maybe that's why it's impossible to stay still or remain the same in California. The mountains and the earth around them move, changing you in the process. No wonder I look for mountains, even if, as was the case with the Sierras the Schallenberger party encountered, they seem at first to block the way—a high, snow-covered wall, a last obstacle between the journey and arrival in the Promised Land.

We all have our own version of California. As my late friend and teacher Holly Prado Northup was fond of saying, "Los Angeles is the most imaginative city in the world." She wasn't talking about Hollywood, but something more elemental, something about California that enables us to create (or re-create) ourselves. Writing from the perspective of time, distance, and exile, it's easy to lapse into nostalgia, to see California as somehow better and more magical than it really is. But that, too, is part of the story. Identity changes in increments, as does our relationship with place. I resisted California at first. Then one day, running errands in Claremont, I caught a glimpse of myself in a store window and was surprised. Someone I didn't recognize looked back, a young woman with nut-brown skin and long, sun-bleached hair, wearing a flower-embroidered turquoise dress from Mexico. I understood then that I'd crossed over an invisible border within, one that was as clear and demarcated as if I were entering the Southland through Cajon or San Gorgonio Pass. I'd become the California girl I wanted to be, and a southern one at that, which I've read is the most Californian of all.

~

Moving to California was disorienting, the greatest geographic change in my life, a true exercise in dislocation. But it was also such a big move that there was little I could do but accept it—or rather, live with it, feeling my way into what it meant to live there while sustaining the illusion that I could go back to Vermont any time I wanted. Keeping a copy of Thoreau's *Walden* and Van Wyck Brooks's *The Flowering of New England* displayed on the shelf above my desk, I mythologized the Northeast for several years, not realizing I had already left it behind. Do I mythologize California in the same way now?

Living there, it was impossible to romanticize California. It was too new, as if it had all just been built, too crowded, too bright, too noisy. It would take me years to develop a sense of its history. At the same time, everything that flourished there was a discovery, from camellias in winter to avocados to pomegranates to the scent of eucalyptus trees along College Avenue and Foothill Boulevard. I'd pick up their lance-shaped leaves and fragrant pods, sniffing them as I walked. I'd never lived in a place where geraniums and jade plants grew big as bushes, where rosemary hedges with flowers like blue stars bloomed in front of the low-slung, bungalow-style houses I grew to love, their dark, wood-framed interiors as cool and welcoming as water on a hot day. But I felt bothered by the fact that much of the water came from somewhere far north, the California Aqueduct unimaginable to a girl who had grown up drinking water from her own well.

The palm trees, with their dusty, clattering fronds, were so alien I didn't even know how to look at them. "I hate palm trees," I shouted at David the first summer we lived together, when the thermometer hit 100 degrees and our apartment became unbearable. It took me a long time to appreciate their beauty, to love the way they thrash and shine in the wind, to forgive them for taking root there, only the California fan palm (*Washingtonia filifer*) native, the rest transplants, just like me.

The palm trees were one indication of all the ways I had to keep remind-ing myself that this was the desert—or, as David was always quick to remind me, semi-desert, Mediterranean, really—a fact difficult to keep in mind, given Claremont's oasis-like feeling. Raised to turn the faucet off when brushing my teeth to conserve the ever-abundant water supply of our well back East, I was shocked at the sight of people hosing down their sidewalks instead of using a broom. It seemed profligate, wasteful, unthinking.

Even the Rancho Santa Ana Botanic Gardens, a gorgeous, leafy pre-serve devoted to native Californian plants, relied on tremendous amounts of water to sustain its woodland, rock, dune, and desert areas. Claremont was supposedly built over artesian wells, which sometimes overflowed in the rainy season. But early on in my sojourn there, I was struck by the ten-sion between what was natural in the landscape and what was nurtured through artificial means. When so many transplants flourished, it was hard to tell what was native.

～

Since leaving California, I've often found myself defending it to naysay-ers and attackers, people who have never even visited the state. "I just don't see how you could live there," a bookstore coworker in Madison once said to me as we shelved new titles.

"Well, it's easy," I retorted, on the defensive. "It's just a place like every-where else. It's not like living in a movie. There are neighborhoods and houses and normal people going about their everyday lives."

"Well, I still don't see how you could *live* there," she insisted. "I mean, you're such an outdoors person and all."

I gave up. How do you explain a mountain that was a presence in your life for ten years to someone from Ann Arbor, for whom the horizon was their main point of reference? Or how it felt to hike dusty switchback trails, sweat drying in the sun as fast as it emanated from your body? Cali-fornia is all about living outside, feeling the place on your skin, the air and light of it entering you as it does nowhere else.

But my coworker's question made me think. It reminded me that for those who haven't lived there, California *is* strange, a glitzy, foreign-seeming place perched on our country's farthest western edge, where who knows what might happen. I bridle when people reduce California to clichés. What defines California for me has more to do with the landscape of the imagina-tion and how it is informed by the physical place, my twinned obsessions as I've searched for home. Something about the largeness and the largesse of the West Coast in general, and California in particular, inspires a similar inner state. As Los Angeles artist Tony Duquette said, "The space is vast. The things it holds are colossal and dreamlike. But they will not make you feel small. Your consciousness will be expanded." He was describing his environmental art project "Our Lady Queen of the Angels," designed to celebrate L.A.'s two hundredth birthday, but he could have been talking about the state itself. As my Tom, native Wisconsinite that he is, once observed, "America offers possibility to the world; California is America's possibility." He was right.

Overarching all of this is how we each form our own idea of place and what it activates within us when we inhabit it. Place works on us, shaping who we are, and California, with its sheer range and diversity—of people and terrain—works on us differently than anywhere else in America. At least it did for me. In that first grown-up job, as a publications writer in a federally funded program in the Pomona public schools, I was one of the few Anglos in my office. Hiking and camping my way around the state, I was amazed by its multiplicity of landscapes—mountains, ocean beaches, deserts, farmland, redwood forests, and more, all there for me to explore. I'm not a cultural geographer, but it seems to me that these factors combine almost alchemically to create California's biggest draw and its greatest myth—the dream of self-reinvention in a gorgeous place where there is room (at least in theory) for everyone. Or is it a dream? And if so, isn't it the quintessential American one, taken all the way west? All I know is this: California altered me, on physical, emotional, and spiritual levels. I am not the same person I was before I spent a decade watching that desert mountain framed in my kitchen window every morning. All those mornings live inside me still, shifting, kaleidoscopic, changing, their terrain mine. California's richness and variety, its sense of possibility and permission merged within me and became an internal architecture, its beams supporting the house of who I am.

I carry California with me the way I carry abalone shells from Montaña de Oro, a piece of stone from the trail up the back side of Mount Baldy, and a foot-long cone from a sugar pine I once found on a picnic table in the Sierras. At night sometimes, half a continent away, uneasily exiled, I sometimes think I can hear the ocean, mistaking the rhythm of my own pulse for saltwater, the crash and sibilant hiss of the retreating waves like the sound of rice thrown at a wedding, something mysterious and lovely hidden within. *Shush-shush*, the ocean says, and I listen.

Even now, out driving through a Wisconsin landscape that it's taken me years to see isn't flat but rolling, I scan the horizon for something vertical to get my back up against, a mountain by which to orient myself, something that will tell me that north is nowhere else but north by virtue of its invincible presence. I look for the Sierras floating, like the dreams of some nineteenth century luminist painter, along the edge of the Central Valley, for the Coast Range edging the sea with a fringe of coniferous green. I look for the San Gabriels hunched—in one of the starkest juxtapositions of wilderness and civilization ever—in a jagged shield between the Los Angeles basin, the San Gabriel and Pomona valleys, and the high desert. And I look for "my" mountain, Mount Baldy, its bare, sun-bleached crown there in that kitchen window every day, whether shrouded in mist or mantled in snow, burned like a visual equivalent for the word *home* into whatever indelible storage vault in the brain contains this kind of information. Where the mountains are, that is where I am, even years and miles away—shaken and exhilarated, companioned and changing, sunlight blazing down on me like beaten gold.

At the Bottom of the Ocean

Psych Ward, 1986

There is a crack, a crack in everything,
that's how the light gets in.

—Leonard Cohen, "Anthem," *The Future*

The day I admitted myself to the psych ward at Baldy View Community Hospital, I spent the morning writing out bills. After that I phoned my health insurance company one last time, to ensure that their policy covered my hospitalization. I got an agent I hadn't spoken to before. "Are you going to be confined?" he asked. My mouth opened and closed, like a fish breathing air. I must have said something, stuttered some broken words. But what I remember is silence and the roar of biochemical static in my head. And that word, *confined*, hanging in the air like an accusation. Then my hand, placing the phone gently back in the cradle. *Confined*. As in committed, incarcerated, crazy. *Confined*, as in point of no return.

At the hospital, which is private and one of the best in Southern California, I look down at the weave in the rose-carpeted hallway as I enter the psychiatric unit with David. When I look up, what I notice is that there is chicken wire embedded in all the glass and doors. What I notice is that the latch clicks shut like a metal mouth, locking behind us, even here, on the open unit. What I notice is that the nurses' station, its wraparound windows webbed with more chicken wire, floats in the exact middle of the unit, an always-open eye I will learn to elude by slipping around corners, leaving the door to my room ajar, shutting myself in the bathroom.

I am led to my room. White walls, white beds, white louvered shutters that are shut, casting everything into a permanent twilight. A nurse with white, permed hair stiff as starched lace searches through my one small suitcase to ensure I haven't brought any sharp objects into the hospital with me. "I'm not suicidal," I tell her. If anything, I am afraid that, in my disorientation, I will inadvertently hurt someone else. It's the truth, but she searches anyway, muttering something about hospital regulations. David says goodbye, promising to visit later that evening. I know he'll come, but at the same time I feel abandoned in this place from which I fear I will never return. The static I can't seem to turn off crackles in my head, preternatural, loud in this hushed place.

I've been like this for weeks now, ever since the afternoon when, after a year of progressively worsening fatigue, I felt something break in my head, snapping like the rubber bands that propelled the toy cereal-box submarines when we wound them too tight as children. Is this why they call it a breakdown? Unable to sleep, unable to eat, frantic with anxiety, I required so much attention I'd turned our house into a hospital, stressing David (who's trying to finish his dissertation) so badly he had a grand mal seizure. This is why I decided to come here, to this place where I spiral slowly downward, as if in the ocean, feeling unreal as a plastic toy, my propeller broken. Here at the bottom there is nothing but darkness within and the pervasive feeling that I am somewhere outside myself, separated from the rest of the world by an invisible barrier. Later I will learn that there is a word for what I am feeling. *Depersonalization.* A common symptom in clinical depression.

But I do not know that yet. All I know is I feel crazy. On the verge of psychosis. My thoughts are jumpy and jumbled. I'm afraid to drive, for fear I'll let go of the wheel and lose control. I'm afraid I'll hurt David or my beloved cats. Reading and writing, my twin forms of solace, are impossible because I can't concentrate. It all combines in a continual inner litany, which I hear as static, whispering that I am both bad and worthless. Although I am not suicidal, I feel as if I am about to disappear into a Mariana Trench, where all contact with the world I love—Southern California, the ever-present mountains, my job at an independent bookstore, my upcoming marriage to David, my writing—will end. I have never been so afraid in my life.

This is when I see Rachel for the first time. What I remember is movement caught out of the corner of my eye. A figure across the hall, a tall graceful woman in a blue batik-print dress, her auburn pageboy swinging forward in a curtain that conceals her features as she leans, attentive, toward the woman to whom she is speaking (her roommate I learn, big-bellied from decades of antipsychotics, ladders of scars inscribed on her arms). I focus on the woman in the blue dress. Like a figure in a Vermeer painting, captured in the midst of doing something ordinary—pouring water out of a pitcher or sweeping a walkway—she seems to emanate light. All she is doing is talking, paying close attention to something, to some-body else. But that is enough. Her focus and stillness pull me away from my obsessive self-monitoring, my constant checking to see if I am all right. Something about her soothes me, breaking through the confusion that clouds my mind the way fog lifts from the sea, sunlight spread beneath it on the water in a thousand shining islands.

Or do I merely glimpse her across the hall, in her room, brushing her hair, the movement itself so fluid and graceful, so ordinary it gives me—what?—a thread by which to reattach myself to the world? Do our eyes meet? Does she come up to me at dinner and introduce herself? I think she says, "Hi, I'm Rachel. Are you Katherine's friend? She told me to look for you. She said you were a writer too and that we'd have a lot to talk about. Welcome to Wonderland." She places her hands on mine. I seem to recall hearing her say the words, "I know. It's scary at first. But you'll get used to it. I've been places much worse. There's always hope." She presses her cool fingers lightly over my own for a moment. "Everything's going to be okay," she says. Rachel is bright with conviction, and I trust her right away. In the fast-forward, Tilt-A-Whirl world of the hospital, we are close friends by the end of my first day. Kind and comforting, she will become my lifeline, reaching out to me in deep water where I fear I will drown.

It's hard to hide in the psych ward. Something about the place dissolves normal social boundaries, insisting on an instant intimacy I am unaccus-tomed to with strangers. Patients talk about their diagnoses as if discussing the weather. Mine is as ordinary as they come: major depression, single episode, compounded by generalized anxiety disorder. Others are much more serious. I am surrounded by people with anorexia, psychosis, bipolar disorder, and schizophrenia, all of whom terrify me, filling me with an icy dread that I will become one of them. Misdiagnosed for years as manic depressive (what would now be called bipolar disorder), Rachel has more recently been diagnosed with multiple personality disorder (MPD). With what I will learn is her typical passion, she has thrown herself into learning as much about it as possible. Each day she appears with another thick journal article given to her by Constance, the unit psychotherapist who has helped diagnose her. Constance will be instrumental in my own recovery, directing me to the healing wisdom of my own dreams—a Navajo wedding jug, a mountain trailing chiffon scarves of clouds, a road leading through Oregon mist shimmering with sunlight.

Rachel pores over the articles about MPD, underlining things and annotating in the margins. Although I haven't known her long, I can see she's hopeful. She tells me the new diagnosis "explains everything." Two closets full of clothes she'd never choose for herself and does not remember purchasing. All the times she's found herself somewhere unfamiliar in the car, with no idea how she got there. The personality who tells her to hurt herself. The one who is a child, a small girl with no one to defend her. The one who remembers, she thinks, all the things she doesn't remember herself. How can this intelligent and articulate woman be so troubled? And how, in the midst of her own difficulty, does she find the energy to be so kind to me, reassuring me when I am frightened—which is almost all the time—calming me with her soft voice and gentle words?

Talking with Rachel, I learn the jargon of MPD, becoming familiar with her "core personality," whom she believes sustains her, and some of her "alternates." "Write that down," I say sometimes, when her insights about one of them seem special or important. But the shiny gold notebook Rachel carries everywhere remains blank. Sometimes she will sit for an hour or more in the atrium, notebook open in her hand, staring into space, unable to write a word. I wonder who and where she is then, in those long moments when she seems to drift as if on some distant sea, far away from those around her.

The hospital routine becomes quickly familiar. Breakfast. In-patient psychiatrist and therapist appointments. O.T., where we are expected to work on "crafts," modeling a substance that looks like Play-Doh into whatever shapes occur to us. Feeling demeaned, I refuse to do this, despite the nurse attendant's threat: "This is going to go in your record." Then lunch, followed by more appointments and "group," to which we are assigned by diagnosis. Psychodrama is the focus of the afternoon, followed by quiet time, when patients are supposed to rest or read, although many watch mindless TV, the air around them acrid with cigarette smoke. Finally there's dinner.

Each night, after we finish eating, Rachel and Pamela (another MPD) and I walk fast laps around and around the unit corridor to stay in shape. Sometimes Rachel and I go outside, standing in a cobbled courtyard graced by a single live oak and breathing in the dry desert air, though she finds it scary. "Look at the mountain," I tell her, pointing to Mount Baldy, its summit still draped with a fringe of snow. And she does, her ardent gaze following it as if we are pilgrims, the peak our sacred destination. "I know we can both get well," she says, her voice so fierce I believe her.

Rachel is enthusiastic about her new psychiatrist, Doctor R. "He hugs me after each session!" she says, glowing. She is so elated by him that for a while I hope I'll get to see him too. Maybe he can help explain what's wrong with me, why I can't shake my pervasive feelings of unreality and dread. Then I see him hugging Rachel one day, just outside the cubicle consulting rooms where the doctors have their appointments. He presses up against her full-length, with what seems like more than professional concern, as she looks up at him, her face dreamy and soft. I hurry past, feeling I've witnessed something I shouldn't. When I finally do see him, pouring out my fear and confusion, he yanks out a silver fountain pen and scribbles his assessment on a prescription pad: "Dependence breeds hostility." I hold the small sheet of paper and study the crabbed words. What does this mean? I know my diagnosis. What I don't know is how his words can help. I study them in silence, sinking down with them like a stone, then put the paper in my pocket and turn it over and over between my fingers. I work hard and pull my share in my household, paying for half of everything. I've never thought of myself as a dependent person. But he's the doctor. He must be right, mustn't he? It takes me a long time to figure out that the main issue on the psych ward is authority and how one discovers one's own.

Of all the activities forced upon us in the name of recovery, psychodrama is the worst. Directed by Ed and Neva, two social workers whose knowledge of the psyche seems to begin and end with Psychology 101, the sessions are, to anyone with a modicum of experience in psychotherapy, a travesty, a circus where people are forced into "confronting" disturbing experiences but given no apparatus with which to contain them. Patients joke about psychodrama, but the process itself is frightening, and I dread the day I am up.

Rachel says with pride that they have never managed to make her participate, and she has shuttled in and out of the hospital more times than she can remember. But one day Doctor R. writes it up as part of his orders. "I can't do it," Rachel says over and over. "I can't do it. I know I'll have a rage attack." She proceeds to describe the nature of these attacks to me in horrifying detail. She rips her clothes, tears her hair out in clumps, hurts herself with any available sharp object, and tries to die.

But Rachel's doctor's orders stand. We meet in a small, darkened conference room made darker by the thick clouds of cigarette smoke that snake above the patients' heads into blackness. It's hot and close and hard to breathe. Ed begins the session by announcing that Rachel's psychiatrist has required her to participate. Rachel pulls back, trying to hide, first behind me, then behind a chair. "I can't," she pleads. "I can't. I'm too scared; I'll have a rage attack; please don't make me." Ed jerks her to the center of the room, says, "You're not going to get away with avoiding it this time."

Stiff as a wall, Rachel stands and weeps, silent tears spilling out of her eyes. Instead of nominating another patient as Rachel's partner (the usual procedure), Ed and Neva both begin firing questions at her so fast it's hard to keep up with them.

Crouched in a corner, my own mind hazy and slow, I catch only bits of what they say to her. Neva has walked Rachel back in her memory, with a singsong litany about going down a long corridor and opening a door to see what lies behind it. "I can't," Rachel says. "I can't. He's behind there. I can't; please don't make me." Ed is impatient. "Spit it out," he snaps. "Who's behind the door? What does he say to you? Where are you?" Rachel twists and turns, but Ed holds her tightly, jerking her arm up behind her back the ways boys attack in grade school. "You're hurting my arm!" she screams. "Let me go!"

This is wrong, I think. *I should do something.* But I don't know what to do. I consider running out of the room and going to the nursing station, where the nurses sit, gossiping as they write up their notes, but I know it wouldn't do any good. The staff, while not unkind, often seems a little annoyed when we ask questions, responding, "You'll have to ask your doctor about that." Who can I call for help when these *are* our helpers? My thoughts catch and hold for an instant, like an engine turning over. *This isn't right. This is wrong. Wrong, wrong, wrong.* The thoughts vanish, and the engine sputters and goes silent.

Meanwhile, Rachel has, inexplicably, begun to talk. Words fall from her mouth, running together in one long string. "It was my pediatrician," she says. "He touched me, he put his hands on me then in me and my mother was there and she said if I ever told anyone she'd wring my neck like a chicken, and now I have told and she is going to get me and so is he, and it's cold, it's cold, I'm so cold I can't . . ."

Just as suddenly as she's started, Rachel breaks off. She leans against Ed for a moment, limp as Raggedy Ann. The room is silent, cigarette smoke wafting around us like wraiths. Even Ed and Neva seem disconcerted by what has happened. Ed releases Rachel's arm. In a single, frantic reflex, Rachel springs free, leaps up, and runs out the door. Snapping to, Ed pursues her, with Neva trotting right behind.

Sensing that psychodrama is over for the day, the rest of us file from the room, quiet, eyes averted, afraid to look at one another. Rachel is nowhere in sight.

I don't see Rachel for the rest of the afternoon, and she isn't at dinner. When I walk past her room, the door is ajar, but something, some sense of respect for her privacy, keeps me from knocking. I can't even see if anyone is in there. It is as if Rachel has vanished, has been swept away from the unit like sea wrack from a beach. A terrible stillness emanates from the room, like the kind I remember before the thunderstorms of my childhood. I wonder why no one does anything, although I am not sure what I want them to do.

It's later in the evening and I'm on one of the four pay phones that line the wall between the open unit and the locked ward when I hear the scream. I'm talking to my best friend from college. Her steady Massachusetts accent tethers me to the world. I'm laughing about something with her, as we have since we were eighteen. But the scream breaks everything. "I'll call you back," I say. "Something weird is happening." I drop the receiver and leave it dangling. The scream comes again. Piercing, desperate, it cuts the air and reminds me of the time I saw a Cooper's hawk land in my yard and fly away with a baby rabbit or squirrel in its mouth, the shrill keening terrible in its helplessness.

Feet pound in the hallway, and the scream comes a third time. I see Rachel then, auburn hair streaming, running as if for her life. Her mouth is open, stretched around the sound she is making like in photographs I remember of plaster-embalmed residents of Pompeii, gasping for air from the pages of an old *National Geographic*. But what happens next occurs in slow motion, as if under water. I watch it, moment by wavering moment. Near the nurses' station, two burly orderlies from the locked ward wrestle Rachel down to the floor. She collapses beneath them and lies so still for a moment that I think that maybe they've killed her. Then one of the nurses emerges with a hypodermic filled with clear liquid. Thorazine. She jabs it into Rachel's exposed thigh and the orderlies drag her away, into the locked ward, where every door is solid metal and has its own key. The one at the main entrance clangs shut behind them.

My trance broken by the sound, I rush to the nurse, demanding an explanation. No matter how many times I ask her what happened, she can't—or won't—tell me the whole story. All I can discover is that Rachel did have a rage attack. Then she'd taken a piece of broken mirror she'd hidden in her room and tried to slash her wrists.

The open unit is eerie and still after she is taken away. Everyone has vanished, almost as if they fear contagion, frightened they'll be swept away as quickly as Rachel was, vanished behind that locked door. I lie awake for hours, replaying the sound of her scream in my head.

Astonishingly, Rachel appears at breakfast the next morning. Pale and shaky, she is led into the dining hall by the nurse from the locked ward and left there, as if nothing has ever happened. She stands completely still in the middle of the cafeteria at first, seeming unsure where she is. Then she moves toward the food carts. Her wrists are wrapped in gauze. Her forearms are chafed raw from the leather restraints, and her hands shake so much the items she puts on her tray dance as if on fire. Seeing her difficulty, I go and hold her tray for a moment, placing my hands over hers the way she did over mine my first day on the unit, as if touch and the presence of corn flakes and orange juice can anchor us to all the possibilities waiting outside, in the ordinary world. I'm doing it for myself as much as for her, trying to reassure us both that there is something stable in this place, even if it is so small a thing as a breakfast tray. Rachel smiles and says, her voice weak, "I guess I caused some excitement last night."

I look into the ocean of her guileless blue-violet eyes and say, "I guess so, Rachel. I guess so. But it's funny how they try to help you around here."

&

After her rage attack, Rachel was no longer forced to attend psychodrama. My situation changed, too. The tricyclic antidepressant I was on, my self-imposed exercise program riding the unit's dusty stationary bike, Constance's thoughtful psychotherapy, David's support and that of my friends—like Katherine, who gave me a lapis lazuli egg as a talisman, and Jackie, who visited every few days, sitting with me under the live oak in the courtyard, and Holly, who made the long drive out from Los Angeles, and David's mother, with whom I later spent time drawing, putting my fears on paper—or some combination of all these things had begun to work. I was getting better, at least enough to leave the hospital after the two weeks my insurance covered.

Rachel wasn't, although her serene appearance had returned. She spoke of Faulkner one minute, then sometimes said "I'm switching," and disappeared into one of her "younger personalities," the little girl who said nothing, or the infant who lay curled in a place where there was not even any language. I was curious and wanted to ask her about her experiences. But whatever had broken in Rachel and made her this way seemed to live in a country beyond words, a place where memory vanished down the long, black mine shaft of forgetting, where we send things too terrible to bear. All I knew to do was sit beside her, murmuring comforting nothings until the dissociative state passed and the Rachel I knew was back. I tried to be kind, but she scared me witless when she switched. Guilt-stricken, all I could think was, "At least I'm not like that." I still wonder, given the level of her own distress, how she was able to help me hold on.

The day I left the hospital, Rachel was wearing the blue batik-print dress she'd had on the first time I saw her. When I complimented her on it, she said she had stolen it from her daughter. "But at least I knew I'd done it!" she laughed, referring to the several wardrobes at home her alternates had selected.

"Rachel, how can I thank you?" I started to say, but she stopped me, putting her arms around me and whispering, "Easy, you don't need to. Listen, you are going to be fine." And then, looking right at me, her eyes blue pools of tears, she said, "You are going to write wonderful poems and have a book. You are going to get married, move to Oregon, and blossom!"

Her words, which felt like a prediction, shored me up within, for while in the hospital I had felt uncertain of my future, worried that my mental state had jeopardized my relationship to David and our plans to marry.

Rachel hugged me again, hard, then walked as far as the main door with David and me, stopping there to let us enter the fierce sunlight of mid-July together.

Momentarily blinded, I looked back to where I thought Rachel stood, waving from the step of the open unit. But I couldn't see her. I couldn't see anything but the dense, black rectangle of the open door. It seemed to have absorbed her the way Rothko's last, black paintings absorb the light. There was nothing there but darkness.

◦◦

I never saw Rachel again, though, like kids making a pact at camp, we had sworn to keep in touch, promising to send one another our writing and to provide updates on our health, as if our respective mental disorders were a secret sisterhood that would bind us forever. Two weeks after I was discharged, David and I married under a palm tree in our backyard, our decade-long partnership reaffirmed by our ordeal. A week after that we moved to rural western Oregon. I loved California and would miss my friends. But this particular leave-taking was leavened by hope, underscored by dreams I'd had about Oregon while hospitalized, their details so vivid I could feel the rain. Once there, I started running again, began teaching, returned to writing poems and essays, and slowly healed, David's support and the beneficent northwestern landscape more a factor in my recovery than therapy or medication.

I kept meaning to write to Rachel, but somehow I never did. I needed to plant myself in my new life, not look back at the most terrifying experience I'd ever had. But Katherine gave me news. Rachel was still seeing Dr. R. as an outpatient, which concerned me, given the disturbing embrace I had witnessed in the hospital. Rachel, too, had started teaching, at a local community college. She, too, was writing, or trying to, although she never sent me anything. It sounded as if she was beginning to put her life back together and I was happy for her.

But even as Rachel seemed to stabilize, more ominous reports filtered through. She had "accidentally" set her house on fire with a cigarette. She was okay, but suffered rug burns after paramedics dragged her from her living room. Then she started disappearing, finding herself in places she had no memory of driving to. One day, her daughter came home and found Rachel hiding in the closet, unable to speak. And then the phone call came from Katherine. Rachel was dead. "They said her heart just stopped," Katherine told me. "She was on quite a combination of medications."

There was a long silence, our thoughts loud between us. We would never know for sure what had happened, would we? Rachel had wanted to die so badly. Perhaps it didn't matter how it had happened, just that it had.

∾

I went out on the deck and listened to Oregon's beautiful Marys River, running cold and clear along the edge of the meadow behind my house, and then gazed toward the Coast Range, so much softer and greener than the stark, desert peak Rachel and I had studied with so much hope from the hospital courtyard. I wept then, for Rachel, for my own tentative recovery, for the cracks in the world through which she had fallen, never to be retrieved, and for the help she had given me, with such tenderness, even when in great trouble herself. I wanted to believe that wherever she was now it was a world filled with light. But I wasn't sure anymore. She'd traveled so far away from the place where we'd sojourned together, dreaming of getting better, that it was hard for me to imagine her anywhere but in enormous darkness, like the blackness she'd often described surging inside her body, an ocean within, trying to pull her under. "I get so tired of struggling," she said to me once, as we walked the corridors of the unit together. "Sometimes it seems easier to just give up and let go."

Did you give up, Rachel? Or did you just get too tired? It scared me to try and imagine what she might have felt or to think too much about the power of the dark arms—the only ones, it seemed, that could finally hold her—that had yanked her under and taken her to the bottom of her personal sea. For though our diagnoses were quite different, her darkness touched mine. I understood something of what it meant to break down, to lose control of one's mind. I had surfaced, but I remembered all too well what it felt like going down. It could as easily have been me at the bottom.

I thought, too, about what it meant to be the one who made it out of the psych ward and back to her own life, the one who went on, telling the tale of what was, after all, a brief chapter in Rachel's story. There was so much about her that I did not know, and we lock the dead in place, making them mythic, sometimes in ways that suit our own needs. I wanted to be true to who Rachel was. Although I didn't know her whole story, what I had witnessed told me enough. A creative woman trying desperately to hold on to her core self and survive the constant splitting off of other selves, Rachel had, through accidents of birth, circumstance, and biochemistry, slipped loose from whatever fragile lines moored her to the world. It mattered that I speak about the places where our stories intersected and resonated, as well as of her silences, for that was what I knew of her truth. Even partial, fragmentary, and incomplete, it seemed a counterbalance to all those blank pages in her beautiful notebook.

But of course it wasn't that simple. Standing there on the deck in Oregon, my arms wrapped around myself for comfort, I felt both very far away from Rachel and as if she was standing right beside me. *This wasn't supposed to happen,* I said to her. *You were supposed to get better too, remember?* Even though I knew it was irrational, I felt as if there was something I could have done. *Why didn't you write me?* I asked her, imagining, against my will, the darkness and pressure she might have felt, going under. But then I hadn't written either, had I? I stood there for a long time, my chest tight, my questions answered only by the stillness of the mountains and the sound of running water.

Then there was nothing else to do but go inside and begin making supper. I chopped up a butternut squash and apples for a casserole with a sense of purpose I did not feel. I knew only, in some dumb and inchoate way, that I had to weave myself into the details of daily existence. I moved mechanically at first, talking myself through my tasks, the very act of doing them more than it seemed, ballast that kept me steady and moving forward. Eventually, as the room filled with the scent of cooking and the cats wove around my ankles, meowing for their supper, I breathed more easily. But my heart ached for Rachel, about whom there would never be any clear answers. *Goodbye, Rachel,* I whispered, until the words ran down in my head. *Goodbye, goodbye, goodbye.*

༄

I would have my ups and downs after that, my life shadowed intermittently by depression's dark wing, although it was never again so severe as during the summer of 1986, when I committed myself, when I was, in the insurance agent's terrible and insensitive words, "confined." Something, I am not sure what—call it strength or stubbornness, fear or faith, or perhaps a simple trick of biochemistry—has enabled me, even during difficult moments, to remain in the land of the living, my face turned toward the light. It has not been easy, but I've been lucky, blessed for the many ways that the beauty of the world and the people I love hold me up, giving me buoyancy I don't always realize I possess.

Rachel was right. I did publish a book, and more than one. I became a professor and have had a rewarding career, helping young writers find their voices. I have, for the most part, been fine, prey only to the sadness and uncertainty that seem to go with the territory of my life as a writer. But I have never forgotten how it felt, adrift on a bottomless ocean, no land in sight. Sometimes I return to the psych ward in my mind, striding the corridors there again as if they will explain something I still do not understand about the way my soul bumped up against Rachel's, or take me somewhere other than where they always do, which is the door where she and I parted company, each of us going toward very different futures. Always her blue ghost stands beside me for a moment, so brave and tremulous I can almost see her in the clear California air—a sister, a reminder, a spur to keep going. And so I do, even though it means walking away from her again, these words my entry on her blank pages, my story of who we were in our brief time together, my stay against loss.

The Landscapes inside Us

There are places that don't belong to geography but to time.

—Saul Steinberg, *Reflections and Shadows*

One rainy fall afternoon, while searching through a box of memorabilia for letters from an old friend, I ran across a homemade birthday card David gave me in 1977, when we had lived together for about a year. Cobbled together from magazine photos featuring various California mountains, Mount Rainier, Alaska, and even Nepal (complete with hikers and Sherpas), the card opens like a book to reveal a close-up shot of a pair of Vasque Sundowner hiking boots, his gift to me. Turning the card's stiff, still-glossy pages, I smiled—a bit ruefully, as one does when confronted with a younger self—remembering how thrilled I'd been to receive it. At the time, I'd been making do with a pair of serviceable but worn boots borrowed from the Claremont Colleges' outdoor program, all the while yearning for my own. Besides being an extravagant present on his graduate student–adjunct salary, the boots felt like an official welcome into the world of hiking David loved and was introducing me to, one mountain at a time. "You're ready for them," he said, grinning. "After all, you're a veteran of Half Dome."

Oh, memory, I thought. What does one do with keepsakes like this, decades after they were given, when one is busy living a whole different life? I dropped the card back in the box, my mind leaping to a recent email exchange with David. I had written an essay that mentioned the San Gorgonio Wilderness, a pristine treasure seventy-five miles east of Los Angeles, where we used to cross-country ski in the late 1970s and early 1980s. Fact-checking the essay before submitting it for publication, I realized that I wasn't sure if the forests mentioned in it were ponderosa or lodgepole pine. Searching online, I was presented with such a variety of trees—Coulter and Jeffrey pine, white fir, incense cedar—that I decided to contact David and ask him, confident he would know the answer.

Each happily remarried for more than twenty years, we don't communicate often. When we do, I often come away feeling irritated and unsettled, as is possible only with an ex-spouse, the person who once knew more about you than anyone, but with whom intimacy has been replaced by distance. Always I am reminded of everything that led to the constant turmoil in our marriage and, years later, our soul-scorching divorce. And always I am saddened by the way connections between people who once loved one another are never severed completely, even when both parties have cut their losses, grieved, healed, and moved on, making better lives for themselves.

I knew it was a mistake to write David. Based on past experience, I knew my simple question about what type of pine forest we'd skied through over thirty years ago would probably precipitate a cascade of attention and personal information I neither wanted nor needed. So I braced myself. I was gratified that David knew exactly what type of pine I was talking about—lodgepole, he replied with certainty. But I was astonished that he did not recall the time a coyote ran beside us through falling snow as we skied up the fire road among the pines. When I thought about it though, it seemed typical of David, so busy skiing uphill as hard and fast as he could, always in a race with himself, that he had missed what was for me most important.

Former spouses can still push our buttons, even if unconsciously. I find David's amorphous way of filtering through my boundaries and into my emotional geography maddening. As I skimmed the email, I tensed, armoring myself against him in the way I've learned I must. But I wasn't prepared for what my question elicited in him, unleashing a string of "Do you remembers?" at the end of the email, that, against my will, pierced my heart and brought tears to my eyes as I sat before my computer screen in the early November darkness.

After answering my question about the pine trees, he mentioned places in the San Gorgonio Wilderness that I had not thought about in years— Jenks Lake, Baton Flats, Horse Meadow. With each name I was there again, skiing through a snowed-in wonderland of closed-up summer cabins we called the Russian village, along the fire roads, and through the pines, where the coyote he does not remember loped beside us. Those places took me to others we'd explored together, like the Central Coast, where we vacationed, camping our way up California's rugged shoreline. I was there again too, running at low tide on the beach at Morro Bay, or sitting mesmerized on the bluffs at Montaña de Oro State Park, watching seals and sea otters, so close it seemed we could reach out and touch them. I slept again on the beach in the blue and gray Sierra Designs backpacking tent I gave him one Christmas. And I woke again to the sound of surf, salt mist tangled in my hair, coating my skin in a fine sheen that mixed with sweat as I jogged along the ocean's edge near lush Fern Canyon.

All these memories seemed (probably inaccurately) to be bathed in the golden California light that is for me like no other in the world. Because it shone on me in my twenties and thirties, when I was figuring out who I was and where I belonged in the world, it will always be a home to me—and if I am honest, to who I was with him. David, proud in the way only a native can be, gave me the American West, opening the landscapes he cherished and sharing them with me like items in a treasure box until they became my own. They still draw me and sustain me within, though a different life has kept me in the Upper Midwest for over thirty years.

On our first trip together, in May 1976, David took me to Yosemite, his favorite national park. After a day of warm-up with short strolls in the Valley, taking in the famous waterfalls, our initial hike was the eighteen-mile-round-trip Half Dome hike. Climbing to an elevation of 9,000 feet, 4,800 feet above the Valley floor, and taking anywhere from nine to fourteen hours, this iconic hike goes from the top of Nevada Falls, through deciduous and coniferous forest, then chaparral, to the opening below Half Dome, where rugged Tenaya Canyon plummets a dizzying mile to the valley below. Then comes what seems like the hard part—a series of endless, granite-step switchbacks up Half Dome's hot, bare shoulder. Just when you think you can't go on, you are confronted by something worse—the famous steel cables, anchored into Half Dome's slick side, two-by-four boards attached every ten feet or so in a rickety-looking ladder, by which you must haul yourself up the last thousand feet at a forty-five-degree angle. A sign warns that travel on Half Dome is dangerous during and after thunderstorms. In the thin air, it proclaims, the Dome becomes a "giant lightning rod." Every year people die on this hike. People have fallen on wet, slick rock, tumbling to their deaths. Vulnerable on such bare terrain, others have been struck by lightning. Still others panic, necessitating difficult rescues. Terrified of the heights, not daring to look down, I only made it up with David wedged tight behind me every torturous step of the way, as if he could block my fall with his body.

On the top of the Dome, palms blistered and arms shaking, I lay down in the middle (which was "bigger than a football field," just as David had promised, though all I could visualize beforehand was the Pomona College soccer field where he ran), tucking my body flat against its reassuring surface and pulling my blue down jacket up over my head. Nimble as a mountain sheep, or one of the golden marmots we had glimpsed earlier in the hike, David scampered to the edge to peer down over the Half Dome's inscrutable face, where rock climbers inched their way from one crucial piton to the next. I knew he wished he was with them.

When I recovered enough to look around, I lay there for a moment, marveling as a hawk flew overhead, so close I could see its yellow eyes studying me intently, as if wondering what I was doing there. I had never climbed so high under my own power. Sitting up, I was dazzled, confronted with John Muir's heaven, which David had told me he'd called "the Range of Light." All around me lay what the hawk saw every day—a panoramic view of Merced Canyon, Yosemite Valley, Tenaya Canyon, and the toothy wedge of the Sierras where they tumble and unfold eastward toward Mono Lake in jagged undulations that capture every shade of blue. Here were Clouds Rest and Cathedral Peak. And here I was among them. Surveying what we had come through, I was terrified and elated. And I was hooked. "Going to the mountains is going home," David told me Muir had declared, referring to the Sierras, adding that it captured how he felt too. Looking out over wave after blue wave of mountain, feeling as if I were swimming through an ocean of air, anchored by sunlit stone, I knew he was right.

It seems madness to me now that David took me on a hike like this. What was he thinking? How could he make such an error in judgment? I'd spent my girlhood running around in the woods and fields of rural Pennsylvania and New York State. But I'd never climbed higher than the modest heights of the Poconos and Catskills, where my family hiked on occasion, and the Green Mountains in Vermont, which I claimed as my own when I went to college there. It seems even crazier that I agreed to do the Half Dome hike, though in my own defense, I had no idea what I was getting into. I loved mountains, but in my borrowed boots, carrying a borrowed daypack—which I threw off at one point, in a fit of exhausted pique, worried I wasn't hiking fast enough—I had no real concept of elevation in the West. I also had no idea that, on our way home the next day (after another, only slightly less arduous hike), I would lie shaking on a picnic table at Fish Camp, nauseated and chilled from altitude sickness and exhaustion. But just as when, inspired by David, I decided to take up running and set off and ran three miles without stopping, so did I set off into the Sierras, protected only by my ignorance and trust.

How many adventures were there after that? Back home in Southern California, I scrambled several times across the relentless glare of Devil's Backbone as David and I hiked the back way (which was, of course, the hardest route) up Mount Baldy, its naked pate snow-capped even in July. Once, fighting heatstroke, I clambered for hours over boulders in a box canyon below neighboring Ontario Peak when David took a short cut, a mistake that could have cost us our lives. We made it out and I recovered, slurping ramen soup and watching *Infamous Woman*, a movie about George Sand, an irony not lost on me. And there were always those mythical bighorn sheep that had appeared before us on the trail like spirits made of mist, having made their silent way up a steep scree incline. Speechless, we watched them go down the other, equally precipitous slope, disappearing one by one. It was an encounter I returned to many times in my mind, one I'll remember the rest of my life as emblematic of that time.

We went further afield too. Only with David would I have plunged into and then out of the Grand Canyon's variegated centuries of light and stone and time in a single day, a feat that still astounds me. Only with David would I have hiked Hermit's Peak (also 10,000 feet, like Baldy) in the Sangre de Cristo Mountains of New Mexico in an afternoon, the ghosts of flagellant Penitentes and fringes of the standing rainbow swirling around me. We did the same with Marys Peak, highest point in the Oregon Coast Range, hiking hard and fast to stand surrounded by the fir-mantled mountains I'd come to love best and call my home, the Pacific unfurling its blue bed to the west and the Cascades punctuating the eastern horizon across the Willamette Valley.

Only with David would I have returned to Yosemite in winter, skiing twenty-one miles round trip from Badger Pass to Glacier Point and back in a day. Always there was a point when it felt like a mistake, each excursion a little too much for me, stretching me past my limit. And always I loved it, my sense of myself and what I could do enlarged by these experiences and David's belief in me. My deepest understanding of who he was when at his best was informed by his intimate relationship with the landscape.

With my poet's eye, I slowed him down and made him look; with his ceaseless, restless energy, he dragged me forward into things I didn't think I could do, things that were bigger and older and wiser than either of us.

Perhaps it's that simple. We were young together and invincible in that youth, and no matter what other, improved lives we have built for ourselves, that will never go away. It is in me the way those mountains are in me. After David and I divorced, I traveled to California a number of times, and then to Oregon, intent on reclaiming the West as my own, not realizing until I got there that it already was. No wonder that, when hiking in the mountains that rise around Squaw Valley, near Tahoe, my friend Robin had remarked, "You look like you've come home." I had, though it was a different homecoming than I expected, the landscape alive in me, but singular now, mine, not ours. This is, I suppose, what it comes down to, and why I found myself snagged, in tears at David's insistent "Do you remember?" Encounters with David never fail to irritate me. But the problem is, I *do* remember. And the memories matter to me, as I think they do to him. If they don't matter, why ask?

Thinking about these things made me recall a conversation I had with David after the death of his mother, Helen, in 2010. I'd been close to Helen, a talented visual artist, printmaker, and art therapist who helped me find my way as a young writer in L.A. and referred to me as her second daughter. Following her memorial, when the family (including me) scattered her ashes with white rose petals from the Duffy boats in her beloved Balboa Bay, off Newport Beach, California, we stood in the kitchen at David's brother's house, making polite but awkward conversation over plates of food. David recalled a hike up Bear Canyon from Mount Baldy Village, where we'd house-sat several summers during our first years together. "Remember where you cross the stream?" he asked me. "Remember the house built on the rock you could only get to via the swinging bridge? Remember Bear Flats and how after that it was serious business, nothing but switchbacks all the rest of the way up the mountain?" I was uncomfortable with all these questions, wondering why he was bringing up these memories of our life together when Tom was standing right there beside me. Trying to include David's second wife, who didn't seem like the outdoor type and didn't look happy about this conversation, I asked if he dragged her off on these kinds of excursions. "Oh, no," she said, so abruptly I thought it best to leave it at that.

But as she spoke, my eyes met David's for an instant, the miles we'd hiked together passing wordlessly between us. It broke my heart. Out of loyalty to and love for Tom, who'd had the generosity of heart to accompany me to this gathering, and with whom I have created a happier and more fulfilling life than the one I had with David, I looked away. But I do not think I misread what floated, fleeting and unspoken, between David and me in that moment, or what it encompassed of youth and possibility, time and loss. We were the ones who were there together, and no matter who we are now, that landscape is inscribed within us, part of who we are, the way the mountains and ocean are a part of California, the blue and brown and green and gold of it a melding impossible anywhere else. There was no way I could deny or regret that.

∾

I'm a more moderate hiker now, tackling distances within my range and ability, following trails my sixty-something body that has endured multiple injuries can manage without breaking down. I still love it. But I've come to agree with John Muir, who said, "People ought to saunter in the mountains—not hike! . . . Now these mountains are our Holy Land, and we ought to saunter through them reverently, not 'hike' through them." When I hike now, shod in lightweight Merrell boots, I try to remember to saunter, something I am not sure David will ever do. Sauntering better suits both my inclination and my temperament. I ponder this as Tom and I explore a large county park we've discovered at the edge of the Driftless Area, the unglaciated part of Wisconsin. Nearly every week this summer and fall, we've wandered the rolling terrain, hiking up and down high ridges, passing through oak woods, pine groves, and restored prairie, bright now with goldenrod and asters. Near the end of each walk we often sit for a while on the bench beside a pond, watching dragonflies and swallows dip low over the surface of the water. The peace of the place seeps into me, and I am calmed in a way I'm not sure I ever was when I was young and scrambling up mountains, worried about proving myself.

But on a shelf in the garage I still have those heavy, leather Vasque boots David gave me the year after that first hike in Yosemite. Weighty as concrete blocks, they are impractical by today's standards, their thick Vibram tread almost indestructible. If I look very close, I can still see traces of red dust embedded in places from wherever I wore them last. Sniffing the soles, I imagine I can smell sage and bay laurel, the scent of summer distilled in the California chaparral, manzanita raising its red tangle around me, a faint trail switch-backing just ahead. There are so many miles in those deep treads, so much sweat and life and learning and trial that I can never quite make myself throw them out.

And so when David asked if I remembered, I wrote back—still a bit irritated, but honest—and said, "Yes, I remember. I remember everything. And I am grateful for it." Then I turned off the computer and walked back into my current life, recalling my favorite passage from among John Muir's many beautiful words: "I only went out for a walk, and finally concluded to stay out until sundown, for going out, I found, was really going in." David was the one who accompanied me out in the beginning, providing the impetus for our many walks and serving as my guide and companion. But I was the one who went in, companioning myself, as one does on pilgrimages to holy places. I thought of how I might not have gotten *here* had I not gone *there*, had I not taken all those California hikes, each one leading me deeper and deeper into what became one of many home grounds mapped inside my body, the places we love part of who we are after all, alive within us always.

Coyote Crossings

I saw the animal on my way home from the dog park. It was crossing the ice on the marsh along Rutland-Dunn Townline Road. At first, I didn't understand what I was seeing. The long bushy black tail, the pointed ears, and the narrow, pointed face all looked doglike, resembling my two collies panting in the back seat. *Is it a German shepherd? Or maybe a small Alaskan husky? What is a dog doing out there, alone on the ice?* I could feel my mind twist and turn in its traces, as it does when we attempt to register exactly what lies before us. *Who would let their dog run loose that way?* Then I noticed the tail again. It was carried down, not up and waving or straight out behind like that of a dog or wolf. I noted the creature's rich, rust-colored coat and the smooth efficiency of its loping gait. It was a coyote. A coyote, in the middle of the day, though they are diurnal, active primarily at dawn or dusk. *What is it doing out there?* Worried, I slowed the car, straining to see more clearly. The ice looked thin. Farmers shoot coyotes around here. It was on Department of Natural Resources (DNR) land, and there isn't a single hunting restriction on coyotes in Wisconsin. Then, as if it knew all these things, the coyote covered the rest of the white expanse in a few quick steps and was gone, disappearing like smoke into the woods.

One day early last fall, as I set out for one of the long walks that have, with midlife and injuries, replaced running for me, I encountered a dead coyote. I was less than a quarter mile out when I saw something large, brown, and motionless at the side of our road. *Dog,* I thought, my mind conducting the same riffle it had over the coyote at the marsh. Looking closer, I took in the lean torso, the slender, vulpine muzzle, the long legs and lanky build. It was a coyote. A perfect, beautiful, dead coyote, with the thick cinnamon-brown plush of its winter coat just coming in. The tire tracks leading to its body through tall grass suggested that someone had swerved, hitting it deliberately, as I have heard some in this state do for sport. Although I have seen coyotes many times, it was the closest I have ever been to one. And it was dead. I stood beside the body for a long time, memorizing its shape, color, and dimensions, one hand over my heart, saying a prayer for its spirit. The walk ruined, I turned back home.

But as I headed up our hill I couldn't stop thinking about the coyote, lying there alone, so close to the asphalt, left to rot and perhaps be struck again until it was nothing but another indistinguishable fur pancake so common on Wisconsin roads. Rushing into the house, I summoned Tom. I'm not a wimp. I've touched plenty of dead animals and held numerous domestic pets in my arms when they had to be put down. But for some reason I couldn't touch the coyote. "We can't just leave it there," I said to Tom. He pulled on the torn, gray ski jacket he uses for dirty jobs and walked back down the hill with me. "Oh, the poor thing," he murmured. "The poor, sweet thing." Then, without a word, he lifted the coyote in his arms and bent over the scraggly hedgerow and barbed wire at the edge of our farmer-neighbor's field. He laid the coyote down there gently, just out of sight, in the tall grass alongside the field. "That's better," he said. "That's a greener place to rest." It seemed to me that I hadn't ever seen anything as tender as the moment when he held the coyote in his arms, cradling it against his chest.

We hear coyotes often where we live, in the tranquil farm country stitched together with patches of woods and prairie, about fifteen miles outside Madison. There is nothing I like better than the sound of their uncanny, ululating yip. It is primal, essential, and utterly wild. Some people say it gives them a chill; when I told a citified friend about it she shuddered. But it pleases me to hear their barks, shrieks, and howls. I love to think of them, running through the fields at night while we lie sleeping. The sound reminds me of California, where I saw coyotes often, so there is an element of homesickness it salves for me, as is the way with things that move us. But it goes deeper than that. The sound of the coyotes' cry is more than just a reminder. It is something more powerful that echoes in my bones, as if my whole body becomes a flute in its presence. When I listen to them, I vanish, lost in another creature's world. That's the most important thing. They do not even know it—and wouldn't care if they did.

Once, when David and I were cross-country skiing up a snowed-in fire road in the San Gorgonio Wilderness in Southern California, a mountain coyote veered out from the thick cover of lodgepole pine and ran beside us for a good three-quarters of a mile, her yellow eyes blazing. She moved with ease, gracefully limber, glancing at us occasionally but not afraid. I don't know what prompted her to accompany us that way, as if we were all going somewhere together. Much better than we were at navigating the terrain, the coyote seemed to be playing a game, keeping the pace up with no apparent effort. Coyotes are both intelligent and playful, much like our domestic dogs. They are, in fact, the smartest member of the canine family. I could almost see that coyote's grin. I've never forgotten the lamps of her eyes, turned deeply upon us, or how, when she moved off into the forest again, she looked back at us over her shoulder for a moment, as if to tell us something. Then she was gone, as if she had never been there.

I saw coyotes all the time when I lived at the eastern edge of Los Angeles County. There, where wilderness slams up against the city in closer conjunction than any other place I've ever known, coyotes were and remain ubiquitous. Smart, adaptable, elusive, they have adjusted well and even thrived. Some of the highest coyote population densities ever recorded have been logged in Southern California. Coyotes are strong, agile, and versatile, quick to make themselves at home in changing ecological habitats. Homeowners with the chutzpah to build in the foothills know (or should know) not to feed coyotes and to keep their small pets inside. A house cat is an easy meal to a coyote. A friend who lived in the foothills told me once about finding a tuft of fur and one brown paw—all that remained of her beloved cat.

My coyote sightings were always at the edges of things. For a number of years, when I ran at Puddingstone, that still wild recreation area my refuge, I did so with my senses tuned for their lithe shape. As I looped through the rolling hills that were alive with wild mustard and purple lupine in California's brief spring, then burnt to the golden brown that looks like velvet from a distance in summer and fall, I often saw lone coyotes trotting briskly along, going about their business. Recent press about coyote attacks notwithstanding, they are wary of humans. I wasn't scared, knowing a single coyote would not hurt me. If I happened to encounter one face to face— which I did from time to time—we always passed one another respectfully, like two strangers with a mutual agreement not to mess with one another. Walking up on their toes, as coyotes do, they were silent and golden. They were a part of the landscape, like the western meadowlark singing its heart-breakingly beautiful song—one I have never heard anywhere else—or the San Gabriel Mountains that rose just to the north, their jagged outline piercing the sky as if the world had just been made that morning. As I ran, I rested my eye first on Mount Baldy, then on Timber, Thunder, and Telegraph peaks, comforted by their massive presence. It's hard to be frightened with a mountain range at your side.

There was just one time when I felt afraid. Running in the early morning instead of in late afternoon, as I usually did, I saw a pack of seven coyotes cross the road a half mile or so ahead. Their movements sinuous and efficient, they trotted together in a small, tight group that flowed along in one fluid loop, clad in every shade of the brown, gold, and gray fur that allows them to blend so well into the landscape. Unlike me, running for my physical and mental health and the dream time summoned by my body in motion, the coyotes ran with raw purpose, nothing on their mind but safety, food, and survival. They were lovely in the sunlight, their weave of golden brown bodies sprung from the foothills around us. They were also achingly thin. I froze, considering what to do. They paused and looked back. There were seven of them, one of me, and no one else around for several miles. I decided to reverse course, retracing my steps the way I'd come. Although I didn't think they would follow, I glanced back to reassure myself that they were not. But they were already gone. I stopped again and scanned the hills. What was it like to vanish that way? I couldn't see them anywhere. But I felt their gaze on me, seven pairs of golden eyes watching me until I disappeared.

A good friend during my California years had a cabin in Big Santa Anita Canyon, in the San Gabriels, where we sometimes hiked together. A few old-timers who still lived in the canyon year-round had taught a young resident coyote, nicknamed Snooper, to beg for food. Female coyotes can be as light as twenty pounds (as opposed to males, who weigh in at up to forty pounds), but despite her handouts, Snooper seemed especially small. Her coat was pale, almost buff-colored, so she stood out, leggy and vulnerable looking against the greenery along the stream that rushed through deep, narrow canyon. "Here, Snooper," my friend called, tossing bits of meat and cheese to her across the creek, remarking on her cuteness. Back and forth she paced, darting in for the food, and then darting away to gobble it down. It was a nervous ballet that I found painful to watch. I've fed birds my whole life and have a wildlife feeder in the backyard of my house here in Wisconsin, where I've seen deer, foxes, skunks, raccoons, and opossum (though it's mostly ground-feeding birds and wild turkeys that avail themselves there). But something about feeding Snooper didn't feel right. It was as if, to get the food, she had to step too far outside her wildness and into our world. She wasn't there for entertainment. And she wasn't safe. I knew my friend meant well, but I couldn't help feeling that the young coyote might lose in the end, shot the minute she came too close or snapped at a child. I hope that wasn't the case.

Not long after finding the dead coyote on our road, I had a mysterious dream. I was turning David's 1967 Volkswagen Beetle around, backing up from a bank ablaze with golden poppies and purple owl's clover the likes of which I had not seen since I left California, when the coyote appeared. It was panting heavily and looked as desperate as I felt, trapped in a grid of city streets that resembled Los Angeles. I felt concerned about the coyote, but when it jumped on the roof of the car I knew something was wrong. "Roll up the windows," I shouted to my companion. But I didn't move fast enough. Flecks of saliva showered me like rain, still warm from the coyote's mouth. Had I been cursed or baptized? Coyote is the trickster, after all, master of change and transformation. For a number of Native American tribes, especially in the Southwest, Coyote is both creator and destroyer, a wily shape-shifter whose unpredictable actions almost always have unexpected results. His elusiveness makes him the perfect symbol of psychic permeability and changeability. Coyote is there, then not there; visible, then invisible. Coyote always vanishes just when we think we have him in our sights. The Navajo call Coyote "God's Dog." I cannot imagine a better name.

When I was coming of age in rural New York State in the late 1960s and early 1970s, a couple of the coolest kids in our school dropped out and hitchhiked to Arizona, where they lived for a while, along with their lab-mix mutt. I wanted to be like Debbie, with her mane of wild blond hair and her Indian print skirts that always seemed prettier than my own. I envied her boyfriend, Billy, with his curly red hair and androgynous ease in his body, a cascade of blue and green beads spilling down his chest. I was a good girl, on the Regents track, college bound. But I had a rebel heart and wished I was them, coming back from the wilderness with their dog that had, it was rumored, mated with a coyote. I yearned to see those pups, rolling and tumbling at Billy's parents' ramshackle farmhouse, where kids said his father would offer you dope. My father, ever the scientist and interested in animal behavior, was curious about the so-called coy dogs too, though I could tell he had deep reservations about that kind of cross-breeding (which was rare at the time and results in a sterile litter). But somehow I never got to see those pups. Years later, when I first saw a coyote cross the Glendora Ridge Road before me on a summer morning in the San Gabriels, I thought of the coy dogs for some reason, wondering what had become of them. Here was the real thing. The coyote turned the yellow fire of its eyes upon me, holding me in its gaze for a moment as I looked deep into its bottomless spirit. I looked away first, and the coyote melted down the hillside.

If asked, I could describe exactly where the pair of foxes that live on our hill have their two dens. But I have no idea where the coyotes that we hear at night bear their young (though I know they will move the pups immediately if disturbed) or how it is that they survive, living so close to humans' unfriendly territory. I have never seen coyote skins hammered up on fence posts here, the way I have in New Mexico, where the rest of my family lives. But farmers are not coyotes' friends. I know coyotes make their dens in rocky crevices, on riverbanks, in hollow logs, under rocks, and in the dens of other animals, which they sometimes enlarge for their own purposes. I know they eat everything from grasshoppers to bird eggs to snakes to small rodents to rabbits and deer. They love fruit, and in the desert West they will eat cactus and mesquite beans. They have excellent vision and a strong sense of smell, and they can run up to forty miles an hour, covering up to eight square miles in their home territory. But I cannot tell you where they live, and if I do discover their den, I will try my best to forget it. Coyotes are a mystery, their yips like the aurora borealis made audible, a wordless green conversation I will never understand, a keen plainsong that pierces the darkness of a winter night.

This afternoon, walking across the snowy fields near our house and into the DNR land beside Island Lake, Tom and I saw coyote tracks. Smaller than our collies' prints, larger than the foxes', they ran in nearly the same straight line as the latter, the hind paws falling close or directly into the forepaw tracks, in one perfect row. They looked like the coyotes were balancing as they walked, and the tracks were beautiful, pressed like the shadows of flowers into the white expanse. I could have followed them forever, watching how they parted and met, crisscrossing over the ground the way their voices do at night. "They're here, aren't they?" I asked Tom in what wasn't really a question. "Even when we can't see them, they're here." "They are, indeed," he replied, tucking my arm under his in the way that always makes me feel cherished. And we walked on, the snow blowing in our faces, our prints mixing with theirs, braided briefly into the fabric of what Tom calls the more-than-human world, then vanishing, lost in the mystery of it all.

III

The Persistence of Rivers

The Persistence of Rivers

All water has a perfect memory and is forever trying to get
back to where it was.

—Toni Morrison, *What Moves at the Margin*

I. Wisconsin River, Mazomanie, Wisconsin

I'm sitting on the front porch of a cabin on the banks of the Wisconsin
River, watching the morning hours slide past on the river's silver back. The
water is somehow still and moving at the same time, as wide rivers often
appear to be, its surface reflecting a blur of trees, sandy islands, and sky
that, if I stare at them all long enough, become a dream the river is having about itself. What is it like to reflect things that way, one element of
this world showing others to themselves? I read a book once in which the
author posited that water possesses consciousness. This morning, staring
early into river light, it is easy to believe the river is aware. It glimmers back
at me through the mist, illuminating everything the way memory sometimes does—the present infused by the past—as if from down a long blue
corridor where we recognize ourselves. "Sometimes there are rivers," I said
many years ago to a man I once loved, "that tell you who you are." I was
writing about a tangled stream that rushed out of Big Santa Anita Canyon
in the San Gabriel Mountains, as different a channel of water from this
placid-looking waterway as you can imagine. And yet it too reflected the
landscape around it. It too dreamed.

The best thing about the cabin where I now sit is the fact that in the
impromptu, hodgepodge manner of cabins everywhere, the bed is on the
front porch. Because of this, the river is the first thing I see in the morning
and the last thing I see before going to sleep. Even during the night, when
I wake up, I can see it out there, sliding silently by on its watery business,
shining with the dull glow of old silver, reflecting clouds, stars, moonlight.
I love being able to sit up in bed in the morning with my journal, a mug

of tea, and three pillows at my back, watching the river to see if I can understand what it has to say, a landscape of possibility open before me.

I have a friend who grew up nearby, and I've found myself thinking of her while I've been here, imagining her as a girl on these banks. Although I was raised in landscapes where mountains—or at least hills—served as the primary physical and emotional frames of reference, I can see how living beside a river such as this would imprint one with both stillness and fluidity, the ability to be in motion and to be aware of it at the same time. Although the Wisconsin is different—and bigger—than rivers I have known well, watching it takes me back to my own origins in water. I think of rivers that began me, like the Perkiomen in eastern Pennsylvania; rivers that raised me and helped me endure, like the Titicus in rural New York State; rivers that healed me, giving me back to myself, like the Marys River in western Oregon; and finally, rivers that have taught me something I didn't know about myself, like the Yahara in Wisconsin.

I think of larger rivers, too. The Schuylkill River defined my early girlhood, marking the way in from the country to my grandmother's house in Philadelphia, single sculls flying lightly across its surface, like the print of rowers in a Thomas Eakins painting that hung in our living room. I think of the Hudson, which my family crossed on the Tappan Zee Bridge as if it were the River Styx, moving to New York State at the beginning of the end of my mother's life. I think of the Rogue in western Oregon, where I hiked wild and precipitous banks in my early thirties, still fragile from a nervous breakdown and weeping at the sight of salmon as they leapt again and again up a waterfall, their battered silver bodies driven by instinct to return, against all obstacles, to the home stream. To have seen such a thing even once is to have stood in the presence of miracles, filled with what, in a children's book my aunt gave me after my mother died, Rachel Carson so aptly describes as "the sense of wonder."

Just listing the names of the rivers I have known or spent time beside, I realize that, although I think of myself as a mountains and ocean person, my life has been laced through by rivers, as if I had been born with their courses inscribed in my palm. Large and small, they have defined me in the way they define a landscape, cutting through it, changing it, determining what happens on its shores. I once spent an entire semester in college studying the role rivers played in the settlement of this country. But I had not thought about what rivers might mean to me, or what those more intimate lanes of water called creeks or streams had to tell me about how we come to be who we are. It is as if their bright music was so much a part of my life that I hardly heard it unless I stopped to listen. But even now, walking beside a creek or stream, I pause and incline my head, as if hearing a familiar language in its swirls, splashes, and riffles. If I just listen hard enough, I think to myself, it will tell me how to live in this world. But of course I never understand its message completely.

II. Perkiomen Creek, Pennsburg, Pennsylvania

I am not romanticizing or being poetic when I say the sound of running water began me. It was the first sound I knew, its ripple and babble present in my consciousness before I ever saw it, for my parents brought me as an infant to an old fieldstone farmhouse right on the banks of Perkiomen Creek. We lived there for the first few years of my life before we moved to another old farmhouse at Wild Run Farm, the true paradise of my childhood. But perhaps because I had a brush with death during those first years, I have a number of crystalline memories of the Old House, as we came to call it. Some are snapshots, involving my parents' faces, or glimpses into rooms, like Vermeer paintings. But most of my memories involve the Perkiomen, which tumbled beside our house in ceaseless conversation with itself and the land. Much more than a background sound, the creek was a voice that lulled me, perhaps because, as my father told me years later, he and my mother walked beside it almost every day, me strapped against one of them in a blue, Snuggli-style baby carrier. "It always calmed you down," my father said. "It was like a lullaby." And how could it be anything else? The sound of running water, both echo and source, is a reminder of the rivers flowing in of all our mothers' bodies.

The room where I slept faced the creek, and in the summer my mother rolled my crib up against the window so I could look out across the water. Though I had no name for the creek, I thought of it as a liquid path one could follow forever, to the fields beyond, where a nearby farmer's Holsteins grazed, tiny figures in an enormous green landscape under puffy clouds. My zoologist mother had an extraordinary affinity with animals, and she fed Eastern bluebirds from that window. (This was the early 1950s, before DDT brought the species to near extinction.) The sound of her voice calling, "Here bluebird, here bluebird," wove itself into the music of running water with grace and authority, making an impression on me. In the family mythology, "bluebird" was the first word I uttered. I wish I could claim to remember that moment when I matched the bird with sky on its shoulders to its name, but of course I do not. I question the myth instead, wondering whether, as with so many family stories, that is how things really happened or how we wish they had.

I have no doubt about the way the Perkiomen (which means "place where the cranberries grow" in Lenape) imprinted me with its velvety murmur as it tumbled over amber stones, sorting them by size so neatly they seemed arranged at its bottom like a beautiful mosaic. I liked to dabble in the water, as all children do, watching the current swirl around my starfish hands, turning over stones. Moving even a single pebble altered the creek, though it did not stop its flow. I have a vivid image of crouching at the water's edge with my father, who liked to sit beside the creek, watching as it sinuously and effortlessly rearranged itself. Although I had no idea we were engaged in contemplation, I learned something about its power and value in those moments.

I learned something similar from my mother as I stood in the crib pushed up against the window. In my first memory, I gaze out over the creek and the fields. I have arranged all my stuffed animals along the window side of the crib so they also regard the landscape. Holding myself up by the bars of the crib, I stare at the scene. The creek is a sparkling line beneath me, one that seems to demarcate the world of the house, my parents, my mother's twenty cats (each one beloved), from the world beyond. I watch the cows drift across the green grass. I watch the wooly clouds. I watch the creek, laid down before me, and then look up to see its undulating patterns reflected on the walls and ceiling in waves of moving light. As I watch, something happens. There is a *here*—a place I know well, one that forms the limits of my small world—and a *there*—places I know nothing about, enormous lands waiting to be discovered. The vista seems endless, as if I could gaze at it forever, the stuffed Scottie dog and panda watching beside me. I am alone, but I am not lonely. All I want to do is look.

That experience at the window is something I've thought about during times when loneliness has been my predominant emotion. If, as some psychologists say, our first memories are important templates, offering us patterns by which we can better understand our lives, mine is a good one, given to me by people who, each in their own way, understood the importance of looking. Writer Barry Lopez captures this psychic imprint when he recalls something Wallace Stegner once said about place: "Whatever landscape a child is exposed to early on, that will be the sort of gauze through which he or she will see all the world afterward." Lopez enlarges

on this experience by describing it as "emotional sight, not strictly a physical thing," which makes sense to me. To this I would add sound. For the
background of my beginning is alive with the sound of running water.
The Perkiomen purls smoothly over stones, the landscape around it illuminated by streamlight, by water into which many voices have fallen and out
of which many voices emerge; it is a thread of silver pulled through my
earliest years, my parents' gift to me, everything since stitched with the
memory of its music.

III. The Perkiomen, Again

We left the house beside the creek in 1955 and moved to Wild Run Farm.
I almost died that spring, ill with a fever of unknown origin that sent
me to the Children's Hospital of Philadelphia for a number of weeks, so I
have no memory of leaving the Old House or arriving at Wild Run Farm.
Instead, a number of indelible images of the hospital are burnt into my
being, primary colors outlined in shimmering bursts of light, as if illuminated by the popping flashbulbs of that era. In one, my parents try to
distract me with a bowl of chocolate ice cream while the pediatrician makes
a venous cut down into my left ankle for an IV. In another, I awake at night
in a white iron crib to see my mother leaning over me like an angel. I am
burning up, then packed in ice. They are changing the IV in my ankle.
I fall asleep, watching the gold of city lights, no creek sound anywhere.
Finally, I am on the mend, "helping" a nurse fold a little pile of nubbly,
white, institutional washcloths, wondering why I am not yet well enough
to eat Easter candy.

And then I am home, though in a strange place, one I do not recognize,
waking up from an afternoon nap in my father's study to the sound of a
pine branch scraping the window. It's a cloudy day and everything seems
gray, pearlized by some trick of early summer light. Nothing stirs after the
pine branch falls still, and as I look out the window I am aware of something missing. The creek is not there. I cannot hear its music or see the
distant cows grazing on the horizon against which I have always mea-
sured my small days. I am filled with a silence so immense that I seem to
blur around the edges, running into it, merging with it, as if I have
been absorbed in its fabric. I don't know yet, of course, that this particular
country silence, this green world dreaming deep around me, is something
I'll seek my entire life when living in other, noisier places. All I know is I
am held by it, adapting to its shape as water fills a pitcher, and this silence

fills me with something that, though I have no name for it, I recognize as peace.

The sound of running water has vanished as mysteriously as the Old House. At various points throughout my childhood, my father will explain that we had to move away from the Old House because the land where it stood was flooded to make Green Lane Reservoir. Did that mean, as I reasoned at the time, that the Old House had drowned and was covered in water? Did fish swim through the windows where my mother had sung and we both had watched the bluebirds? I imagined the ghost house, white beneath the water, its walls wavering and shining. When we drove over the causeway across the reservoir into Pennsburg village, I gazed out across the water, looking for signs of the Old House, the stone chimney perhaps, or the tip of the red roof peak sticking out of the water. I saw only the flat expanse of shining silver-gray that seemed to stretch on without end, ominous in its vastness.

One summer—during a drought so bad it brought the neighbors up the road to our door with jars for water when their well went dry—the reservoir's levels dropped so low the crumbled foundations of houses appeared like beached ships on the dry lakebed. Was one of them the Old House? Was that all that was left of it? The fading outlines on the striated shoreline haunted me. *Someone lived there once. Someone lived there, and it was us.* Where had the silver creek that ran beneath my window gone? Where were the bluebirds? Where was the house I did not remember leaving? Regarding it all as we passed in the car, I understood something about the meaning of time passing.

Fortunately, the creek, which twisted and turned around Pennsburg and through Montgomery County on its way to the Schuylkill, wasn't far away at all, but just down the road from Wild Run Farm. It wasn't close enough that my brother, sister, and I could play in it unsupervised. But on hot summer afternoons we walked down to it, accompanied by my mother and our corgi-beagle pups, Megan and Tina. The road was dirt, hot and white, little puffs of dust erupting beneath our feet. But the creek, which ran under a chunky, moss-covered WPA-era bridge at the bottom of the road, was cool and sweet, a million shifting strands of silver twirled together, then pressed flat in a shimmering bolt of water. Sometimes we stood on the bridge, playing Pooh-sticks or fashioning small boats from leaves. We'd drop them into the water on one side, then race across the bridge, looking not so much for whose was ahead but for where they were going. Resting my cheek against the rough aggregate of the bridge, tracing my fingers across its surface, I'd stare down into the creek, wondering where it led, until I lost sight of my boat around a bend in its leafy shadows.

Other times we slid like otters down the path at one end of the bridge. Paved with many rocks, like a cobbled underwater road, the river ran wide and shallow here, the color of pale tea. It was good for wading, and we spent hours beside its glancing, golden light, building fairy houses and miniature villages or exploring the shallows in cut-out Keds my practical mother turned into summer sandals. Poking around without apparent purpose, we were pulled into the creek's reverie, held in a daydream that unfurled before us, lulling in its movement. My mother sketched. We splashed in riffles and pools, feeling the gentle tug of the creek's current. I stretched full length on the bank toward it, trying to lap from the creek as I imagined an otter might. The water was cold and clean, and tasted of minerals. Bracing and eternal, it seemed like water from another time. I slurped quickly, and then plunged my face into the creek, its current brushing my skin like invisible hands that pulled me away from the solidity of the green bank, my mother and her pastels, the sounds of my brother and sister playing.

Lifting my face from the water, I stared down into it. The otter was gone, and someone who looked like me but wasn't quite floated among the trees and clouds and leaves, reflected among them like a peculiar island, everything still, but also moving. As I watched, something twisted and turned in my body and seemed to drift away, merging with water and sky. Was it my spirit? Was it the otter? I felt as tiny as one of the flecks of pollen that floated like gold dust on the creek's surface. What was an "I" anyway? What did it mean that I was alive, human, a girl with wet braids, trailing her fingers in the water until they were wrinkled and pale? The feeling, which I could never summon voluntarily, made me feel thin and insubstantial as petals of the trilliums we looked for nearby in the spring. It was defined by such a heightened sense of reality that I felt unreal. It came upon me as a waking dream, both thrilling and disconcerting. I rode the feeling out in waves, until it dissolved around the edges, like a fraying maple leaf caught under a stone and worn away by the water until only the skeleton remained, and I was returned to who I was, an ordinary girl, the creek running beside me.

The pups loved the water too, and they bounced and splashed beside us until the day Tina, the one with orange eyebrows who made my mother laugh, was struck and killed by a blue pickup as it roared past on the road. I still remember my mother holding the dead puppy in her arms and saying over and over, "He didn't stop. He didn't even stop." We returned to the house, and after my mother dug a hole at the edge of the hayfield, my brother and sister and I helped her wrap Tina in a length of blue calico. She let Megan sniff at her before lowering Tina's still-warm body into the ground. My mother was crying so hard she could barely speak, snot running down her face the way it ran down mine when I cried. It was as if the creek had broken inside her. In that moment, I realized that my mother, who had seemed invincible, couldn't do everything. As I sat there in the sweet-scented summer field beside her, the torrent seemed to well up inside my chest too, and I felt an enormous tenderness for her. Did I place my small hand over her work-roughened one, or did she reach out and take mine, as we walked with Steve and Jenny back to the house?

We didn't go down to the creek for many weeks after that, and when we did, it was with caution and sadness. Megan was tethered to us by a bright red leash, and my mother insisted on walking on the outside. But the road, rarely traveled by anyone but the mailman, was silent. When we got to the creek, it seemed darker and sadder, tinted deep copper in the long light and late summer shadows, running and running and running. Dropping my stick in the water that day, hanging over the edge of the bridge, all I could think of was Tina, there and then not there, and the sound of my mother's weeping.

If the creek was sweet relief in the humid Pennsylvania summers, in the winter it was a brilliantly etched, crystalline world of blue and white, an illustration from *The Snow Queen*. Several times during the winter, and always on a weekend, when my father was home, my parents took us on excursions to the creek. On those days, instead of walking down the road, we cut through the woods across from our house and followed a tiny stream downhill to the creek. Frozen over, rimmed with ice in fantastic formations, the stream was a world of its own, one where blue caves shimmered, crystal chandeliers tinkled, and delicate goblets shone, all at the edge of water so dark it was almost black.

Fascinated by the miniature worlds and snow palaces the ice revealed, I ran ahead, entranced by what I saw, looking and looking. Interested in the science behind beauty, my biochemist father explained how the ice formed. But my mother was quiet, looking closely as well, holding his hand in her red-mittened one. Everything sparkled, spangled with light. The stream was a bright voice, whispering beneath its frozen surface, then rushing down the slope to join the creek's larger one, where we stood for a while, awed by its winter velocity and power. Watching the frigid water surge past, I clung close to my mother, steadying myself against the familiar contours of her body, amazed that this was the same creek I had stuck my face into the summer before. How did things change so fast and so completely, from one season to another? Did I change that way too? Did anything stay the same?

We left Wild Run Farm and the Perkiomen a few years later, when I was nine. My mother was already dying of breast cancer, though it had not been confirmed, and my father had been offered an excellent job at Geigy Pharmaceuticals. The position was so much better than the one he held at Merck that (as he told me years later) he couldn't afford not to take it. With no understanding of what it means to leave a place that has made you who you are, my brother and sister and I were caught up in the excitement of the move, thrilled by the van with a painting of the Mayflower on its side and the enormous boxes the friendly movers gave us to play in. But as we drove away on a hot August afternoon, leaving Wild Run Farm empty and echoing, I turned and reached over the rear seat to comfort my Dutch rabbit, Babe. As I stroked her soft brown and white fur, I gazed back down the road, filled with a curious feeling. It didn't last long, but it was there, the shape of loss lying down inside me, a quiet presence that would inhabit me forever. I watched dust glitter in the sunlight before it settled behind the car. I watched the dark green hollow at the end of the tunnel of trees, where the creek ran, going about its silvery business, oblivious to our departure.

As the car rolled forward, I looked back. *Perkiomen, Perkiomen*, I said, turning the word, which was then—and always has been—beautiful to me, over and over in my head, as if to engrave the sound of running water in my consciousness. I wanted to tell my father to stop the car. But we turned the curve onto Bowers Mill Road, and Wild Run Farm and the lane down to the creek were gone. I would not see either again for forty years, until the summer my father died, when I'd lean over the WPA bridge—which stood firm, as if no time had passed—my tears falling into the creek, like minnows loosed in the home stream. As I traced my fingers across the pebbled surface of the bridge and gazed into the amber water, everything was exactly the same. And everything was different—and haunted—as is the way of things when one revisits the ur-places of childhood. I was not sure it was good I had returned, except that I was reassured everything was still there, like a parallel world, another family with three young children living at Wild Run Farm, the creek running on without me. I did not stay long that day, sensing my time there had passed, as it had for others before me, swift as creek water gurgling over stones with a bright, glancing sound I will always remember. *Perkiomen, Perkiomen*. Even now, the word has the power of a spell or incantation. Like a secret code only my brother and sister and I know, when repeated over and over it evokes a vanished world. "I bring you some water lost in your memory," says poet Patrice de La Tour du Pin. "Follow me to the spring and find its secret." The Perkiomen holds mine. I will never plumb its secrets completely.

IV. Styx-Hudson

We crossed the Hudson to get to our new home in New York State. We crossed it, and I did not look back. It was the biggest river I had seen after the Delaware, and as we sped along the dizzying gray lanes of the Tappan Zee Bridge, I held my breath, looking out the car window at the blue vastness that swirled below, afraid the bridge cables might snap and we'd plummet to our deaths. That winter I'd feel the stiff winds blow up and down the Hudson in Dobbs Ferry, the town in lower Westchester County where we lived for a year, but the river itself was an invisible presence, its cold breath huffing over us like that of an enormous, dangerous animal. A few years later Pete Seeger would spearhead a famous—and very successful—effort to clean it up. The tall ships would sail up the Hudson during the bicentennial, their white sails billowing out like wings of enormous birds, so lovely that I wept, a pride in my country that I rarely feel welling up within. Decades later, when birds clogged an airplane's engines, the plane would land in the Hudson, as if descending over liquid tarmac, all the passengers surviving. I wrote a report on the river in eighth grade for my New York State history class, marveling at the role the Hudson had played in shaping the place where I lived. It's a beautiful river.

But for me the Hudson was also the River Styx. My mother died. My father remarried just six months later, trying to fill a loss that tore him open like a shot to the heart. I felt the Hudson's cold breath on the nape of my neck, closer and closer. It caught me. It held me in its cold arms. It woke me, screaming and inconsolable, in the middle of the night. It swept me under, swallowing the story of a loss so enormous it silenced me for many years. River of death. River of darkness and dread. River of sorrow. River from which, having crossed over it into another country, one does not return. The Styx-Hudson washed childhood away.

V. Titicus River, North Salem, New York

I did not live in close proximity to running water again until I was twelve, when my family, which now included two stepbrothers, moved to North Salem, a small town in northeastern Westchester County, where I spent the rest of my girlhood. There are many stereotypes about Westchester, all of which irritate me, for none describe the town where I grew up. Located fifty miles from New York City, at about the farthest distance commuter fathers like my own were willing to travel by train, North Salem was dotted here and there with orchards, small dairies, and horse farms. Densely green and rural, the town seemed to float in its own pocket of time, a bit out of step with the rest of the world. There were wealthy properties in the town, yes, where small influxes of folks we scorned as "city people" took up residence during holiday weekends and summers. But the kids I attended school with were the children of ordinary people—mechanics, nurses, farmers, the local postmistress. The North Salem I knew was a place characterized by its lakes, rushing streams, wooded hills, fertile valleys, pastoral views—and a river, the Titicus, which wound through the township like a snip of blue ribbon.

Titicus, Titicus. We learned in school that the name, like so many in the Northeast, is an abbreviated form of a Mahican word, *Mughtiticoos*, which translates as "place without trees." But when I say "Titicus," the word unfolds in my mouth like a rare spice, its spiky consonants punctuating my breath. I see the river where it ran under the bridge at the end of our road, dark copper as a tarnished penny, shaded on each side by dense stands of oaks and sugar maples. Its banks were tall there, and the river ran swiftly, headed toward a small dam and a waterfall just downstream. I crossed the bridge twice a day, walking the half mile between the big white house where we lived at the top of the hill, in one of the town's original homesteads, and the school bus stop at the flagpole on the triangular village green.

The bridge was high, and the river, at least at first, seemed to me dark and secretive, as filled with mystery as the inside of my changing body. Although I'd often stop and gaze down into the river, something about it—its shadows, its depth, its pace as it quickened toward the waterfall—

made me anxious. If I stared down into the dark, honey-colored water for too long, I began to feel a seductive vertigo that made me pull back, afraid of falling, or perhaps even of climbing over the bridge to see if, in some weird test of fate, I could fly. Once while I was in the grip of those feelings, a man who had been fishing startled me, stepping out from behind the trees like a figure hidden in a Currier and Ives puzzle picture. Native brown trout ran in the Titicus, which was also stocked with rainbow trout, so it wasn't uncommon to see people from out of town fishing along the river, silent sentinels watching the water run by, waiting for a tug on their line.

But this one spoke to me, asking me about myself in a manner that suggested I was an adult, not a young teen with dots of Clearasil on my face and a humiliating tendency to turn scarlet whenever I opened my mouth. The man had brown eyes and hair almost the color of the river and carried an old-fashioned creel and willow basket. He asked me about the town, the Titicus, and what I was doing there, and he seemed genuinely interested in my responses. As we spoke, something I had never felt before seemed to catch and flutter between us. I felt as gripped by his gaze as I had been by the river a moment before. I don't believe the man meant me any harm. In retrospect, he seemed to be one of those adults who possess the rare gift of treating children as seriously as they deserve. But his attention cast a spell over me. Something about the encounter unnerved me, and I finally burst out with an inelegant, "Well, I have to go now," and ran up the road, clutching my heavy blue introductory French textbook against my chest.

As I moved from the green chill that always hung over the bridge and into the sunlight of open fields and stone walls that had stood for two hundred years, I had the distinct sense that something momentous had happened. I'd had an experience I didn't even begin to understand, and somehow it all had to do with the river, which both mesmerized and frightened me. The river was just doing what rivers do, running with its braided amber strands through the dappled light, but it provided me with a reference point in the landscape, one whose swirls and shadows showed me things I couldn't articulate. I didn't tell anyone about meeting the fisherman. But I thought about him for a long time that night as I lay in bed, remembering how the rhythm of the Titicus, echoing under the bridge until it seemed to vibrate up through my entire body, had thrummed into my cells when he spoke.

The river was shadowed at the end of our road, but true to its Indian name, it wound through the sunny fields that surrounded our neighbors' houses. One of these neighbors was a family of freckle-faced boys, the Feeners, who jumped into the river from a rope swing in their backyard, swaying out across the deep coffee-and-cream colored water before letting go with a whoop. My brothers swam there on a regular basis, but it was definitely boys' territory, and I never wanted to join them. I wasn't the strongest swimmer, and the thought of flinging myself out across the river on the rope terrified me almost as much as the oldest of the freckled Feeners, who was in my class and so good in algebra—which I was failing—that he was rumored to be some kind of genius. He had bright blue eyes and interested me in an abstract way. But it did not occur to me to try and infiltrate this realm, where boys' pale bodies swayed, dappled with river light and tree shadows, strange as another species, before disappearing into the swift water.

The next neighbor up the road had a daughter, Nan, a year younger than me. Walking back and forth to the bus stop every day, Nan and I became friends. Drawn together at first by our love of horses, we turned our attention, like the sunflowers lining the edge of her mother's garden leaning into the sun, toward the idea of boys. Nan's parents' place had a farm pond, created by a small oxbow, which the river ran through at one end. Nan and I paddled there on hot summer days, stepping gingerly through the muck toward deeper water, the boys' shouts echoing from around the bend. Although we were secretly fascinated by them, and aware, through the scrim of trees that separated our world from theirs, that they were trying to impress us, we had no real desire to join them. Ponds are private places, and ours, shining caramel in the sun, felt like a separate country, one where we could be ourselves. We did strange little dances in the water to the faint sounds of my prized transistor radio, 77-WABC echoing down from the banks where we'd spread our towels. Sometimes we dared one another to wriggle down the tops of our bathing suits, letting the shimmering water, glittering with mica, stream down over our faint beginnings of breasts.

Nan and I tended, at least at first, to confine our swims to the placid, unruffled pond. But if we moved to the edge, where the river ran through, we could feel the irresistible tug of its current, trying to draw us downstream. Holding on to the bank, we'd stretch out full length, delighting in the tug and sway of the water, moving us even as we stayed in place. Only our hair, which we both wore long (mine straight and hers curly), surrendered to the current, streaming out behind us like liquid capes, caressing our backs and shoulders, light as river grasses. The pleasure of the moment lay in the possibility of letting go, of being almost swept away. Now and then one of us would lose our grip, at which point we'd cling to the other, laughing and shrieking, the stillness broken as we wrestled like the girls we still were.

If the area downriver from the pond, dominated by the boys' exploits, felt off-limits to us, the area upstream, with its entrancing twists and turns, pulled at our attention, exciting our curiosity about what lay around the next bend. On languid summer afternoons when everything seemed to stand still, Nan and I pushed her parents' old rowboat, its blue paint chipped and fading, into the pond. After some maneuvering, we headed upriver, in the direction of Connecticut, where the Titicus begins. Connecticut wasn't far away; I grocery shopped with my father at the Grand Union in Ridgefield every Saturday morning. But small towns are worlds unto themselves, and Nan and I were thrilled with the idea that we were, as we called it, "rowing to Connecticut."

Once we left the pond, the water ran clear and deep. Gazing down through it, we could see large flat rocks, coated in silt and slippery to stand on. Every now and then a speckled trout flashed past. Jewelweed and pickerelweed, bulrushes, thistles, and milkweed crowded the banks in a low hedge that made us feel both cut off and sheltered from everything around us. We rowed, sometimes in tandem, our damp thighs brushing against one another as we sat, crammed into the splintery seat, and sometimes singly, the girl who wasn't rowing perched in the prow of the boat like a figurehead, calling out what landmarks lay ahead. Every now and then, when we got hot, we would take turns lowering ourselves into the water and hanging on to the back of the boat as the other rowed, savoring the flow of the river as it sluiced around us, stroking us with cool, invisible hands. When I was the one towed, I'd close my eyes, tilt my face up to the sun, and give myself over to the moment in a way it is only possible to do when you are still half-child, without any conscious thought of what you are doing. The oars creaked. The water streamed past my body. If I opened my eyes, I could see Nan, looking at me as she rowed, her upper lip beaded with tiny pearls of sweat, her damp hair curling around her shoulders. We could spend an entire afternoon that way.

On one of these excursions up the river I had an experience I have never fully understood, perhaps because I cannot remember it all, time and the river having silted it over so only the outlines linger, like those broad, flat rocks at the bottom. The same kind of rocks jutted out from the banks at one bend in the river. They formed natural sunning spots for bullfrogs, which often startled us with their galumphing splash, and yellow-and-red-striped painted turtles, which slid into the water silently, with a grace belied by their awkward-looking bodies. It was on these rocks that something happened. We met a boy, not someone we knew, coming downriver in a boat like ours where the channel was narrow enough that we had to pull aside to let him pass. Or was the boy already there, alone, without a boat, fishing or swimming? Or was I alone in the blue boat, Nan left behind for some reason? I dip my net again and again into memory's water but cannot come up with a clear picture.

What I do remember is the boy—strong, slender, tanned, his brownish hair bleached blond by summer—and me standing there on the rocks beside him, talking to him after he'd helped me from the boat, his fingers firm and cool against mine. We weren't flirting exactly. But something about him exerted a mysterious pull, real yet invisible as the currents of the river itself. He seemed outlined in light, and I felt on equal ground with him. If I had to give it a name now, I might call the feeling that infused those moments on the rocks with the boy *yearning*. I yearned for the boy as I yearned for what lay around the next bend of the river. I longed for him as I longed to let myself go in the water's pull. I ached for him as we can only ache for things we have not yet experienced, but which our bodies somehow already know.

And that was all that happened. Some sort of mysterious exchange or understanding passed between us as we stood on the rocks together, the river swishing past. Then I stepped back into the boat or slipped back into the water and returned to Nan, changed from who I had been. "What was that about?" I remember her asking. "Nothing, it was nothing," I said, wanting only to be alone with the feeling, away from what felt like her poking and prodding. Instead of showering that night, I slept with the scent of the river, sun-dried on my skin and hair, puzzling over what had happened. Although Nan and I paddled our slow way upstream several times that summer after the encounter with the golden boy, I never saw him again. Sometimes I wonder if he existed, or what would unfold within me if I could untangle the knot of memory that contains him, a knot tied tight as those in the rope swing the neighbor boys swung out from over the river.

Nan left for boarding school at the end of the summer, while I entered North Salem High, and our lives flowed in different directions. I saw her sometimes when she came home on breaks, and I even slept over at her house once or twice. We smoked our first joints together, and I remember consoling her over a hopeless crush on an undeserving boy. But things weren't the same. We never swam together in the pond again or went up the river, paddling to Connecticut. When I wanted to swim, I rode my bike seven miles to Mamanasco Lake, just over the state line, or snuck into Titicus Reservoir, where swimming was forbidden because it was part of the New York City water supply. But sometimes, during later summers, when my siblings and I hiked up Hunt Mountain at dusk, I'd gaze down at the Titicus River as it wound, silvery slow, through the fields far below. I'd think about Nan and wonder about the boy, who he was and where he'd come from. Did something of our conversation linger in the Titicus? Does the river remember what I have forgotten, as water is said to contain all conversations.that happen beside it, and if so, what would it tell me?

Several years ago, visiting North Salem for the first time in almost forty years, I stood on the bridge at the end of the lane where I'd met the fisherman, looking down at the river and listening, as if the girl I had been there could recount her story. But all I heard was the river as it echoed under the bridge, its reverberations rippling up through my body, familiar yet incomprehensible as they had been the first time I felt them. There was no voice there but that of the water itself, running on as it always had over the copper-colored stones, the spell of gravity pulling it forward and away from me, no matter how hard I tried to hold it.

VI. Day Lily: Interlude with Colonial House and Stream

The spring I was fifteen, the property where we lived in North Salem was put up for sale, for a sum far greater than anything my forever-strapped parents could afford. We left the big white Georgian-style house, perched like a ship in full sail on the hill behind its picket fence, and moved to the other end of the township, into another old place on 150 acres, part of it in Putnam County, which might as well have been another country, as far as I was concerned. The farmhouse, which my parents were lucky to find, had been built in 1753 and is the oldest home I have ever lived in. Owned by an absentee landlord, who lived on Prince Edward Island in what seemed to me romantic isolation, the house was beloved but rented out because of some mysterious sadness his wife associated with the place. Long, low, and white, with green shutters and a porch that ran its entire front length, the house, as I would discover while writing a paper about it in college, merged two architectural styles—Dutch colonial and New England salt-box. One entered through a massive oak door, many inches thick and held by iron hinges, its wood pocked here and there by holes the landlord claimed were made by Revolutionary War musket balls.

Stepping inside, we were in another century. The beams and rafters that held the house up were massive, hand hewn with an adze. The floors were wide oak planks, polished to a buttery sheen and darkened by the passage of time. A fieldstone fireplace dominated the living room, its chimney so big the narrow and dangerous stairs to the second floor unpleated up around it, accordion style. The hearth was a single, massive slab of stone, which we wondered about, marveling over how settlers could have maneuvered it there. Staring into the fire on cold winter nights, I tried to imagine what it must have been like to cook at that hearth, a pot dangling from the enormous iron hook that still hung above the flames like a soot-blackened claw.

I had lived in old houses before and would do so again. But I have never inhabited a dwelling imbued with as deep a sense of previous residents as the one on Fields Lane. My sister, my stepmother, and I all saw ghosts there. When I wrote the paper about the house for my American art and architecture class in college, I corresponded with the landlord's sad wife and learned something of its history, enough to corroborate that the ghosts we saw—one of mine was a young woman in an eighteenth-century dance dress—matched her descriptions of ancestors. Thinking about ghosts, I wondered where my mother's was, and if she perhaps haunted Wild Run Farm, roaming its rooms, which stood empty for five years before the house sold. The sorrow our landlord's wife felt had opened a window on my own.

It was impossible to live in a house as steeped in history as the one on Field's Lane and not feel immersed in times much bigger and deeper than mine, my small life part of a stream of others that had passed before. Lying in bed at night, my resentment at having to share a former side parlor with my sister tempered by the fact that we had our own small fireplace, I'd muse about all that had happened in those low-ceilinged rooms, the house breathing around me. It had seen everything, and it took us in and protected us, even as our family unraveled after my stepmother had an affair with my father's best friend at Geigy. At times it seemed only the house held us there, deep in the country, where the world still seemed safe. We never locked the front door except at night.

Our new home was marvelous, but what lay outside was even better. Rising behind the house, the sunny meadow, where a neighbor's old horse browsed, edged upward into woods of oak, beech, and sugar maple. Bisected by stone walls and seldom-used bridle paths, this was a private realm, one that provided us kids with a refuge from the unhappy adults in our lives. We claimed the woods as ours, establishing a rough camp at the top of the hill in a clutch of conifers that we called the Pine Forest. We spent many summer nights bedded down under the stars, glad to escape from the house, where our parents' arguments echoed down the heating vents. To get there, we had to cross the stream that ran behind the yard. In the nomenclature of rural places everywhere, we referred to it simply as the Stream, as if there were no other. But because I secretly named it Day Lily, for the thick stands of orange flowers that grew along its banks, I will call it that here.

Day Lily Creek did not begin in the Pine Forest, but somewhere farther uphill, where a spring bubbled up from the ground. Still, it seemed to start in that place we'd made our own, spurting from between tumbled granite stones with a sound like many tiny, muted hoof beats. Bouncing and spar-kling, twisting and turning, Day Lily tore down the hill until it slowed and wound behind the house, more sedate now, at the edge of the terraced garden my father referred to as the lower meadow. If, as Gretel Erlich has written, "a stream is an expression of its watershed; that is, liquid . . . liter-ally 'expressed' from an ecological matrix, the green breast of Earth," it seems right that our stream began near the spot where we slept so many evenings, at a sweet remove from our parents' turmoil and trouble. Flowing as it did between the yard and the woods, Day Lily marked a line, dividing the world of home from the world where we kids were on our own, step-ping through a forest that, though it was second-growth hardwood, felt as if it had been there forever.

We built a stone fire ring in the Pine Forest and slept rayed out around it like spokes in a wagon wheel. We had no proper equipment, no tents or sleeping bags, just blankets and pillows we'd pulled from our beds. Rolled up in my blue flowered quilt, I learned that, to get comfortable, I had to let my body relax into the ground until I could feel what I thought of as the bones of the earth holding me in their hard embrace. But even then I lay awake, listening to the stream's clear voice long after my sister and brothers had fallen asleep. Had the Mahican people given a name to this creek? Had the ghost of the young woman I'd glimpsed in the house ever walked up here, listening to it as I did? Did Day Lily Creek recognize us kids as we arrived on summer evenings, a ragtag band of explorers and escapees, making our way through the dark to our place of refuge? The murmur of running water filled my consciousness until I felt a part of it as it glimmered there beside us in the night, like a black scarf shot with threads of silver, moonlight reflected on its wavering surface. Why did the sound of the stream make me feel both full and lonely as I lay beside it?

I listened and listened, until discomfort gave way to fatigue and I slept. Although I've slept outside in many places since, I do not think I have ever slept as deeply as I did on those summer nights in the Pine Forest, my siblings and stepbrothers piled around me like puppies, the stream's shimmering and sibilant mystery carrying me into the darkness. In the morning we woke, cranky and stiff, the magic of our night in the Pine Forest countered by the reality of having to return to the pain and confusion in our lives. Still, we were filled with the sense of having gone somewhere special. Trooping back down the hill, we were quieter than usual, holding the sound of the stream and wind in the pines inside us, careful not to spill a drop.

The Pine Forest and the source of Day Lily were our escape and refuge. But the place where we interacted most frequently with the stream was where it curled around the lower meadow, then straightened out to run alongside the yard behind the house. I spent hours sitting next to it, trailing my fingers in the cool, clear water, watching water striders cast their four leaf clover–shaped shadows on the surface and sandy bottom, daydreaming about a future I could not fully imagine but knew had to be better than what I was living. Sometimes Day Lily was a mute witness as I paced beside it, fuming, filled with adolescent storm and outrage about everything (from my stepmother insisting I wash the kitchen floor every day, to being grounded for a month for having dared to cross her, to being given a detention at school for acting like a smart-ass in class) until the sound of running water brought me back to myself.

One spring morning I glanced out the kitchen window to where the stream, full of rain and snowmelt, had overflowed its low banks, spreading across the yard in a shallow lake that reflected the house, perched on the rise, like a dinghy. We were never in danger, and the water went down a day or two later, having revealed a fiercer face of our gentle companion. But it was disconcerting to realize that something so tranquil could become a force of destruction.

Almost every day after school, over endless cups of Tetley or Constant Comment tea at the battered kitchen table, I'd glance up at my sister, noticing how her face, our hands, the room itself were held in the reflection of the stream's wavering light. *Don't ever forget this*, I thought, looking into her thick-lashed hazel eyes, so like our mother's had been. I picked watercress in the stream, reveling in its sharp green scent, and I wept there when a cement mixer from the gravel pit down the road hit and killed one of our kittens. One blistering August afternoon I burned a love letter to a boy and threw the charred bits into the clear water, watching them float under the bridge and away. I splashed Day Lily's cool balm over me as I lay beside it, tanning myself with a makeshift cardboard reflector covered with tin foil. Once I lay down in the stream full length in my homemade paisley bikini, letting the water wash around me as if its gentle touch could smooth out all my rough edges. It almost seemed it did.

Apart from the tiny streamlet running into the Perkiomen near Wild Run Farm, Day Lily was the smallest thread of running water I had ever known. Intimate, familiar, and domestic (as the tumbledown springhouse across the road attested), the stream was so much a part of my landscape I sometimes barely even saw it. But it defined everything around me. I missed the sound of Day Lily when I was away at a friend's house overnight and had to imagine the sound of the water turning over itself, mixed with the breeze in the big maple outside my window, and the horses cropping alfalfa and timothy in the field.

One could cross Day Lily's narrowest places in a single running bound, but the three quick steps needed to get across the board bridge to the woods are still alive in my body, instinctive as breathing, familiar as home. The step in the middle, suspended over the water, always sounded hollow, resonant with the possibility of falling in. I think I could pace it out perfectly even now, were I returned there to the sound of the little stream shushing down its sandy channel—running I know not where, pulling me back into my life the way the future pulled me away—and to the house that echoed so, filled with history, possibility, and sadness. I left Day Lily behind when I left home for college. But the sound of its water runs within me yet, cold and pure as the springs that fed it.

VII. Marys River, Wren, Oregon

In the first story I ever wrote, when Mrs. Wilson allowed us to choose our own topic in third grade, I told the tale of a pioneer family traveling by covered wagon on the Oregon Trail to what I described as "a deep green place of plenty, beside a silver river," a landscape I imagined as a promised land. I was in my pioneer phase, having torn through the Little House books the year before and moved on to titles like *Heroines of the Early West* and *The Oregon Trail,* which influenced my literary efforts. Mrs. Wilson had me bind the story between green construction-paper covers—decorated with an awkward-looking Conestoga wagon—to hang on the bulletin board. I have always wondered if the story wasn't prescient, anticipating something I would discover only when I moved to Oregon in my thirties. From the minute our yellow Ryder rental van began descending out of Ashland toward the sun-bleached, green-gold that is the Willamette Valley in late summer, I felt as if I had found a real home, arriving, after a long journey, in the place where I belonged. Oregon lay before me, as I imagined it had before the pioneers, matching up with an internal vision like no place had before it.

If we are lucky there are landscapes in our lives that work on us as if we are part of the land itself, shaping us, scraping us, refining us, making us into more of who we really are. Some do this by imprinting us psychically, the way eastern Pennsylvania imprinted me, its clear rivers, fields, and hardwood forests so much a part of my inner geography that it became what nature writer Susan Shetterly describes as the "standard of comfort by which you measure whatever else is real in the world and whatever else is beautiful." Other landscapes work on us by being so different from anything we have ever known that they require us to create a whole new set of internal and external reference points. California, where I lived for over a decade in my twenties and early thirties before moving to Oregon, had been like that for me. With its Mediterranean air, sharp-etched mountains, and implacable sunlight, California demanded change. It knocked me down with its heat and vastness. It pummeled me with its backyard sea. It burnt me brown and limber as I hiked its foothills, the scent of sage and California bay laurel baking in sunlight, an incense possible only in that place.

Still other landscapes shape us by being so familiar that they seem a country we have always known, a place we can step into and feel part of right away. Not native—that would presume too much—but accepted, the way the shoots of lilac that pioneer women brought west with them in their wagons were by the Oregon soil. When I moved to Oregon, I felt as if I knew where I was. It was not so much that I recognized something in the landscape (though it was indeed beautiful to me), as that I felt welcomed by it, taken in. Bounded on one side by the Cascades and on the other by the Coast Range, the Willamette Valley in western Oregon is like an enormous cupped hand that holds its residents as gently as Mrs. Wilson had held my hand, her fingers around mine as we pinned my story on the bulletin board. This was earth I could grow in, a place where I could imagine sinking my roots deep and staying forever—the dream, perhaps, of every pioneer.

At first this awareness was subliminal. I was still broken when I came to Oregon and encountered the Marys River, which rushes like a wide silver path, twisting and turning from its headwaters in the Coast Range toward the Willamette River, which in turn flows north, toward the Columbia River and the Pacific. It was 1986, and David and I had moved to Oregon so he could take a position at Oregon State University. "Major Depression, Single Episode, Recovered" it said in red ink on my medical chart, packed deep in a box in the yellow van. But I knew depression was still with me. I was also beginning to understand that it had lived inside me my entire life, the blue fingerprint of something deeper and more terrible than ordinary sadness pressed into my being after my mother's too-early death. Winston Churchill, who suffered from depression too, described it as his black dog. I only wished mine, which had receded but still haunted me, the memory of my separation from the world still strong, could be given as tangible a label.

I had been cracked into pieces. But Rachel's prediction when we parted at the hospital had come true. I arrived in Oregon tentatively reassembled. Continuing the combination of medication, therapy, and exercise begun in the hospital, I had pulled myself together enough that, at least on the surface, I seemed to be who I had been before. David and I had married, celebrating with cake under the apricot tree we both loved. A few days later, we'd packed the van and headed almost a thousand miles north with our three cats. "We're going to the promised land," I joked, as we chugged up I-5 through California's blistering Central Valley. I was kidding. But after what I had experienced, Oregon did seem a promised land, a place where I dared to hope I might begin again, the way the pioneers had, making a new life and reclaiming the more confident self I felt I had lost along the way.

Because my illness delayed our move, we arrived in Corvallis, which means "heart of the valley," without housing. Although we'd planned to live in town, an ad about a place for rent on seven acres along the Marys River, twelve miles west of town at the edge of the Coast Range, piqued our interest. And so we found ourselves heading west on Highway 20, toward the coast. Just before the road began to rise, darkening into a winding green tunnel shadowed by fir trees, we turned north on the Kings Valley Highway, crossed the bridge over the Marys River, and turned left. In minutes we were walking around the property at Priest Road.

I still remember the sense of having stumbled into an enchanted realm that fell over us as we got out of the car. A mix of oak savanna, Douglas fir, noble fir, and open pastureland, the property was bounded on one side by the Marys River and on the other by the quiet road, which was named for the pioneer family who'd settled the land and from whose ancestors we would be renting the house. From the beginning it was the land that claimed our attention. The house, built over the foundation of the original homestead, which had burned down, was nondescript. Painted pale green, its best features were views of the mountains and a wide back deck facing the river. But the land took us in and seemed to hold us in a way I had not been held in a very long time. California had taught me a lot about the West, but I sensed Oregon would take me even deeper. I took a deep breath and exhaled slowly. Standing there in that narrow valley, bounded on three sides by mountain foothills and cut through by the river, trying to absorb the many variations of green, I felt safe, as if I had been tucked inside a pocket lined with emerald moss.

No one seemed to be about. Feeling like intruders in a secret garden, David and I stepped around the property. Stone-edged flower beds filled with bush fuchsias and roses were scattered through the backyard. There was a small pond, where I'd watch the delicate, aqueous dance of rough-skinned newts mating the following spring. A grape arbor bearing five kinds of grapes ran the width of the property, down to the river. Blackberry brambles lifted their lanterns of purple fruit everywhere. Marys Peak, the highest mountain in the Coast Range, floated just to the south of us like a humpback whale, gauzy clouds trailing behind it like torn chiffon scarves. Wind sighed through the fir trees, green spires that would imprint their shape on me, altering my frame of reference in such a profound way that ever after, when out walking, I would look up, searching for their conical shape and the shape of the mountains behind them. The sound of the river, which bore my mother's name and was visible through the trees along the bank, ran through everything, its liquid burble and thrum the heartbeat of the place. After living for many years in a desert place, the river sounded like a voice I'd once known well but had not heard for a very long time. I recognized it right away, as I have always believed I might recognize my mother's voice were I ever to hear it aloud again. The river called out to me, taking me back to my beginnings beside the Perkiomen.

The house was empty, but the caretaker had been there, watering the yard. He had gone home for lunch, leaving on Rain Bird sprinklers that hissed here and there, spangling everything with what we'd learn was water pumped straight from the river. It flicked across us, wetting our faces, soothing us with its cold sweetness. "It seems too good to be true," David said, turning toward me, weeks of tension draining from his face. "Yes," I replied, feeling the same sense of relief. "I think we should take it." And so we did, moving into the little green house along the river on the land that matched so closely what I had imagined in my childhood story.

What is it that makes us fall in love with a landscape? What makes a place a home, even if it is somewhere we have never been before—like the acreage along the Marys River in the unincorporated hamlet called Wren was for me? How do certain places align themselves with something in our spirit in such homefelt ways that they exert an almost physical pull upon us? A poet, not a geographer, I can only speculate. Perhaps certain landscapes satisfy some sort of yearning within us, one we don't even know we have, bringing us comfort and ease. Although I had grown to love California during my years there, taking pride in being a latter-day California Girl, on some level the Golden State had always been a place of temporary sojourn. Like so many others, I had reinvented myself there, finding my voice in writing, discovering who I really was. But home? That was a different story. Home was wetter, softer, greener, infused with what, after living in Oregon for a while, I joked was the ancestral British-Celtic pull of ocean and rain. I had not thought about the fact that it also meant living beside a river so like the one I had known as a child.

On the afternoon we looked at the property, I did not yet know that the Kalapuya name for Marys Peak, *Tca Timanwi* (pronounced tcha-TEE-man-wee), means "Place of Spirit Power" or that the tribe sent their adolescent boys and girls to the mountain on vision quests to hear the voices and stories of their guardian spirits. I did not know the stories claiming that the river was named for the first white woman who crossed it in the early 1850s, and I never have learned why the name isn't possessive. I did not know the names of common things—twinberry, snowberry, Oregon lilies, salal—I would come to love, learning the lexicon of that place to express what I hadn't known before. I knew only that the river had my mother's name and that something about the spot was so comforting I never wanted to leave it. Perhaps it is enough to say it eased my longing. Perhaps it is enough to say I sensed in the land an awareness or attention I wanted to make my own. Perhaps "where we are interacts reciprocally with who we are," as poet Reg Saner says, making us into something different and bigger. Perhaps the river called me home.

Following the grape arbor down to the river that first day, I came to a break in the undergrowth, a natural sitting spot next to a wide shelf of rock, shaped like the Indian head on old nickels. I stepped out on the rock and stood, surrounded by water on three sides. The river was wide and shallow here, its bed an intricate cobble of amber stones. Green-gold light filtered through firs and alders, dappling the surface of the water as it spilled downriver toward the bridge, beneath which cliff swallows flitted to and from their nests, slicing the air with their blue flight. Hunkering down on the rock, I dipped my hands into the river, lifting the water and spilling it over my face. It smelled of moss and stones and time. Even as it evaporated, I felt as if it blessed me, washing through me, welcoming me to the place.

I needed that welcome. Although I looked—and in many ways was— well again, with the tricyclic antidepressant nortriptyline playing its serotonin trick on my synapses, the brokenness of the experience went deeper than even I knew. I was functioning, but my connection to what I called the normal world felt tenuous. I watched myself unpack boxes from our move, place dishes in cupboards, hang pictures, take walks, follow the river. Many days I felt as if all that held me to the earth were the fragile ropes of my new routine, part of which involved giving myself over to the natural world in a way I hadn't since I was a child. After writing—or attempting to do so— in the morning, I'd go out for a long run, then come down to the river and perch on the Indian rock for a long time, staring into the water as it flowed past. Sitting so still I felt a part of the landscape, I gave myself over to observation. I watched as a doe and her fawn bent their graceful heads to drink, studied the slow fan of a blue heron unfurling its wings, stared into a pool filled with minnows the length of my little finger, followed a steel-head as it finned its way upstream. Everything was holy; everything required my attention. The act of looking took me outside myself and my own obsessive concerns about my illness, filling me with the world around me until there was no room for my problems. If I contemplated the river long enough, I became the river.

If I was having a shaky day—and there were more of those than I would have liked—I engaged in a practice I called river walking, which involved stepping slowly upstream, moving against the current. Although the river was deep in places (there was a swimming hole downstream, on the other side of the bridge, where the water was over my head), it was broad and flat where it ran along our property, never more than waist deep. One day, having waded into the river to cool down after running, I was struck by the way the water first touched my body and then parted around me, as if I were solid as rock or fallen snag. And so I began walking through water. Something about the ritual soothed me, as if the pulse of the current against my body washed all fear and anxiety away, dissolving it, sending it downstream and away, into something larger. I'd wade upstream for what seemed like hours, caressed by the river's invisible hands, moving through the ever-shifting, flickering reflections of the alders and fir trees that grew along the banks and my own body that blurred then grew still behind me, until I felt steady enough to go back into the house again.

From the beginning of my time beside it, I understood the river had things to tell me. But it offered comfort in ways that both preceded and transcended language. Whether I was sitting on my Indian rock, still as the deer I watched drinking there, wading across glinting pebbles flecked with mica, or swimming in water the color of honey, the river held me in an embrace that was both soothing and indifferent to my human struggle. No matter what I did, the river flowed around me, its ceaseless, sibilant conversation washing me as clear as it was. It was a time without words that led me back to words, a mysterious parallel to my early childhood beside the Perkiomen, when all I'd heard for hours was the sound of the water talking to itself as it slipped silkily over stones. Listening, I imagined I could hear the voices of pioneer women and children who once lived on its banks, raising gardens, washing clothes, tending animals. Sometimes there were other voices, murmuring in a tongue I did not understand, and I wondered if they were the Kalapuya, who had used these waters. I was aware, too, of pools of silence that had fallen into the water miles away, traveling toward me like small oases of calm that held me. I gave myself up to them and they eased my sadness. And always the river purled along, familiar, but at the same time constantly changing, never the same from one day to the next.

When the rains began in the early fall, I watched as they filled the river and were swept away, as it seemed my own tears were. Though logic suggests the wet Pacific Northwest winter, with its long, silver-gray days, might be hard for a depressive, it wasn't like that for me. I felt invigorated and rejuvenated by rain. I loved learning its many varieties, its subtle language, and how it came and went, now a deluge; now a sparkling beaded curtain; now diaphanous, sun-shot mist. Most of all, I loved running in it, my legs pink with cold, my yellow Moosehead beer T-shirt soaked through, logging trucks honking as they barreled past when I turned onto Highway 20. I loved the feeling of rain on my face and how it licked me gently, everywhere, like a thousand tiny tongues.

One spring, when the river ran high in its banks and spilled over into the lower yard, creating an extended shallow pool, I felt a little afraid, watching as it churned, dense as muddy coffee, filled with froth and broken branches. It wasn't the gentle sun-dappled creek of summer then, and it seemed dangerous, capable of sweeping me away, the way anxiety sometimes still did. But the waters receded, and the next summer David and I bought an inflatable yellow raft, in which we explored areas downstream, expanding our understanding of the river. As I got to know the area, running and riding my bike, I found a place nearby where a covered bridge like the one from my childhood spanned the river. When my father visited, I took a picture of him before the bridge, then tucked it into an old scrapbook next to a deckle-edged snapshot of him standing beside the bridge over the Perkiomen, holding me as a baby. Always the river was familiar, its sound taking me back to my origins beside water, beginning me again. Like the wild foxgloves that bloomed in pink spires everywhere, reappearing every year, perennial, I wanted to stay there forever.

We knew when we moved to Oregon that our time there was limited. David's salary was paid for with a grant from the Environmental Protection Agency. It was due to run out in a couple of years, and was perhaps renewable, though there were no promises. But life in the beneficent Oregon landscape beside the Marys River was so healing for me that I could not imagine leaving, and I forced any thoughts of doing so into the background. I found a writing group and began teaching at both the county

community college and through a community education program. I began
to find my way and built a small local reputation for my women's writing
workshops. One wild March day as I walked around the backyard, cooling
down from a four-mile run, the blackout window blind of depression
rolled up in my head with a sharp snap, and the world, indeed my entire
being, seemed flooded with light. I was myself again, back from the underworld I had stumbled into two years before. I fell to my knees, and there
among primroses and mud I gave thanks, watching as Marys Peak sailed
through the clouds, the sound of the river running through everything. Did
my soul somehow know my time at Marys River was running out, that I
needed to be well to carry on?

David's funding wasn't extended. I would have done anything to stay
and had already lined up more teaching and work in the local independent
bookstore. But David was unable and unwilling to jettison a nascent academic career. He liked Oregon, but it didn't mean the same thing to him
that it did to me. We began making plans to move, following yet another
job, this time to Denver. It was the beginning of the end of us, though
neither of us saw it at the time. I knew only that I was leaving something
so much a part of me and so crucial to my well-being I wasn't sure I could
survive without it. In the months before we moved, I dreamed my flowerbeds were uprooted, Marys Peak disappeared, and the river itself overflowed, washing the little green house away.

The day we left Oregon, I ran around the backyard, taking photographs
while David waited, impatient, in the truck, the cats' carriers piled high on
the seat beside him. Afraid I might forget something, I snapped random
glimpses of it all—the mossy oaks, the grape arbor, the fir trees, the mountain, and the river, glinting that day like broken silver between the trees.
Every leave-taking I had ever experienced seemed conflated into this one,
and I felt frantic, panic stricken, as if, like a small child, I might have to
be pried away from the place, kicking and screaming. The last thing I did
was go down to my Indian rock and stand there, the water swirling past,
rill and stillness mixed together. I couldn't bear the idea that it was all
going to go on without me, and yet of course it would. I belonged to the
river, but the river wasn't mine. I thought again about the folk belief that
rivers remember every voice they have ever heard. I knelt and splashed my
face with water as I had that first day. *Remember me*, I whispered, dropping
my voice into the river with all the others it carried. Then I turned and

walked away, as I had from so many other places. My heart was broken over leaving, but I was stronger from my time there.

Over three decades later, having learned with difficulty to love another place, I still cannot look at the pictures I took that day. I know the river lives on within me, the persistence of running water in my life the source of memory, recovery, and dream. But that is not the same as living beside it, and I have never completely reconciled myself to its absence. The Marys River taught me to again regard the world the way a child does, crouched down and staring, alive to every swirl and reflection. The river taught me to move as it did, letting the simple pull of the current hold me as I returned to myself, one shining fin of light at a time. Where the river meandered and slowed in stands of camas and cattails, it taught me to relax, merging with "the line of beauty" that Thoreau says dwells "in the curve." Most of all it brought me to a place of healing. Though it was on the other side of the country from the place where I began, it was such a close echo of my beginnings beside the Perkiomen that it seemed my whole life was contained there, a channel carved deep between bright green banks. Perhaps I would not know any of these things had I never left it. Or perhaps I would know them more deeply and truly, a "semi-native" Oregonian as the green T-shirt I bought proclaimed I was. I cannot say. All I know is this: I left the river, but it has not left me. Like water, which is restless even when contained, I am still searching for my level.

VIII. Yahara River, Pleasant Springs Township, Wisconsin

It's been many years since I've lived with a river running through my back-yard, decades since the claims of love took me from the Marys River. On the north side of my hill now, I look down across farm fields to Island Lake, a spring-fed, glacier-sculpted beauty that shimmers among the fields, reflecting every change of light and weather. The lake, with its bristly, tree-covered island, is a focal point, and restful to the eye. It has become a spiritual compass for me, a place where each day I take my bearings. The waters of Island Lake are a constant backdrop, shining among the cattail marshes like time's own mirror.

I love the constancy of the lake, but I miss the sense of possibility offered by moving water. Lakes invite contemplation and inner stillness. Rivers, while mesmerizing and hypnotic, are mutable, one thing forever becoming another as the water slides past, always on its way somewhere else. As Oregon writer John Daniel notes, "We don't tend to ask where a lake comes from. It lies before us, contained and complete, tantalizing in its depth but not in its origin. . . . A river," he speculates, "is a different kind of mystery, a mystery of distance and becoming, a mystery of source."

I'm not sure I agree that lakes, especially spring-fed ones like mine, don't tantalize us with their origin. Springs are, after all, mysteries of their own, bubbling up from earth as they do, and the lake has its own magic. But I think Daniel captures an essential truth about rivers when he says they are each "a mystery of distance and becoming." For what do rivers speak to in us but our own insatiable curiosity? Curiosity about what comes next, what lies around the curve, what fish or bird or animal or aquatic insect the next riffle might divulge. Where has the river come from? we wonder. And where will it take us if we surrender to its currents, savoring how it reveals itself to us by taking us somewhere, showing us to ourselves as we ride its silver back, the river in endless motion, just like us?

These days, when I spend time beside a river, the one that companions me is the Yahara, within whose watershed I reside. Named after the Ho-Chunk word for "catfish," the Yahara originates north of Madison and flows through the area's famous chain of four lakes—Mendota, Monona, Waubesa, and last of all, windy Kegonsa, which lies closest to where I live. From here the Yahara heads south, toward its confluence with the Rock River (along which Tom spent his boyhood), which in turn joins the Mississippi, flowing on, like all rivers, toward the sea.

Tom and I have canoed almost all of the Yahara and love best the winding, wooded section south of where we live. Here I have learned the difference between canoeing on rivers and on lakes. Here I have learned to paddle in tandem with Tom, so that sometimes it seems we and his yellow canoe, Good Medicine, are one being. Here I have heard the raspy *skyew* of a startled green heron and held my breath as we watched a deer drinking, her brown eyes reflecting the river's wild wisdom as we slipped past.

A still-ambivalent transplant to Wisconsin, I am surprised to realize that I have spent more time canoeing the Yahara than any other river. How did this come to be? And what has this unprepossessing river taught me when I wasn't aware of anything but the pleasure of moving upon it, my paddle lifted, dripping with water weeds and gilded by sunlight? I realize that, like the river, I have been in motion the whole time, my life running with a power and momentum I only sometimes understand, each of us a mystery to ourselves after all, until the moment of final reckoning. "Shall we gather at the river?" the old hymn asks. Perhaps that is when I will grasp all of what rivers mean.

Certain moments canoeing on the Yahara stand out in my mind, like the bright beads of rain I once saw, strung on a storm-drenched spider web spun across a fallen tree, or the row of basking painted turtles I glimpsed, lined up on a log in the sun, their shells shining like lacquered boxes. But I've spent most of my time with this river on foot, strolling beside it at the local dog park as our two tricolored collies lope ahead. There's a play area for water-loving dogs, who fling themselves with abandon off the dock built for this purpose, chasing sticks and balls (an activity I am secretly glad our dogs disdain). But for the most part the river serves as a liquid fence, keeping dogs safe on the isthmus of the park. I stroll beside the water, measuring my steps to its cadence, listening again for voices I might recognize, the water, as always, speaking a language it seems I once knew.

As I walk, I am seduced by the Yahara's cattail marshes and sedge meadows, its sandhill cranes and snowy egrets, its kingfishers and great blue herons, its ever-present flocks of honking Canada geese. I watch the way tree swallows dip over the water, the blue-green sheen of their wings like delicate scissors cutting a path through the air, and admire hordes of red-winged blackbirds as they twist and turn in complex skeins, their voices a thousand creaky screen doors flung open on spring. The Yahara is neither as beautiful nor as beloved to me as rivers I've known in the past. Often a soupy gray-green in high summer, clouded with algae whose growth is abetted by the agricultural runoff endemic to this part of the Upper Midwest, it's not always appealing. In winter, whether frozen over or clogged with chunks of broken ice, it's gray and foreboding. But there are times when, standing on a sheltered, half-moon beach where the water moves more slowly, I can see through to the river's sandy bottom and am reminded that nothing stays the same. Everything—the river, life, me—changes. And after that, it changes again.

I love the way the Yahara links—and makes possible—the four big lakes, running like a silvery umbilicus between them. I love how it swallows the sky so that, walking beside it, I almost lose perspective, the reflections of oaks in the water as real as the trees they mirror, and I feel I am walking on clouds. I love the way the river pushes against its few small dams, and I am happy one of them has been taken down, allowing the water its natural momentum. Most of all I love the way the river seems to dream in early

October, its deeper currents hidden beneath its still face. Staring into the depths, I almost grasp something in the mystery in all rivers. Simultaneously here and there, behind and ahead, moving and calm, rivers take me deep into my own past and beyond the present into an as-yet-unknown future.

Once, standing alone on the Yahara's small sandy beach, I had the urge to dip my hands in the water. Cupping my palms, I was startled to see my own lifeline, sharp and visible in a way I hadn't noticed before, glimmering up at me even as the water slipped between my fingers. Was my life a river, too? Despite all my years watching rivers, it was a story I hadn't thought to tell myself. If, as Ursula Le Guin says, "story is our only boat for sailing the river of time," this moment was one of my tales, a liquid page scripted by ripples, eddies, and whorls.

Which is perhaps rivers' greatest mystery and what keeps me coming back to them, despite my love of mountains and oceans. I am caught and held by rivers, pushed and pulled by them, sung into being by their very riverness, as incapable of resisting their flow as I am of not breathing. Each river I encounter changes me, baptizing me with its wildness into who I am at the moment—a source, a channel, a pair of grassy banks, a flood—allowing the promise of rebirth as surely as if I have been hallowed by total immersion. As sometimes I am, gathered with my many selves beside the river of *then* and *now*, listening and watching for what comes next, my life remade by moving water as it quickens, gathers, and falls, rushing always toward the next bend, around which the shining path seems to go on forever.

IV

A Wisconsin Book of Hours

Four and Twenty

Once upon a time, when women were birds, there was the
simple understanding that to sing at dawn and to sing at dusk
was to heal the world through joy. The birds still remember what
we have forgotten, that the world is meant to be celebrated.

—Terry Tempest Williams,
When Women Were Birds: Fifty-four Variations on Voice

It's leap day in Wisconsin, wet and muddy, and a south wind whirls
wildly around my hill in dervishes that seem intent on driving winter
away. With the wind come red-winged blackbirds, one our earliest arrivals—flocks of them, hordes of them, thousands of black bodies that wheel
and turn as one through the sky in great, undulating clouds, wind-whipped
and singing at the top of their lungs. *Onk-la-ree, onk-la-ree, onk-la-ree.*
We're here, we're here, we're here. Their feathers shiny as anthracite, epaulets
flashing like crimson silk shoulder pads outlined in daffodil yellow, they
dart and flash among the trees, rising and falling together like fishing nets
tossed out by a giant. Their wild voices fill my heart with hope.

I've been listening to blackbirds since I was a child beside Perkiomen
Creek, my bed pushed up next to a window by my enterprising mother,
who taught me to look at things so hard you feel yourself become part of
them. Along with the sound of water lapping over stones, the song of red-
wings is stored in my cells, each voice like our green door, its rusty screen
flung open on spring. Decades later, I fell in love with Tom when, not
knowing my history with blackbirds, he nicknamed me Redwing, setting
loose a multitude of wings in my chest.

How is it they rise and fall so beautifully together, these sleek, black swim-
mers, navigating effortlessly in the clear sea of air? The flock assumes

shapes so fast, one bird after another, that, if I wished, I could read them as portents of some divine purpose, as ancient people might have. Here a teardrop, there a book opening, there a long fluttering sleeve from a magician's robe. And always the twisting cylinders that condense into lengths of shimmering rope strung across the sky, the birds moving as if they are one body and being—fluid, sinuous, organic. It's easy to see why early twentieth-century scientists thought such flocks navigated by some sort of "natural telepathy" or "group soul" we call a murmuration, a description I love for its poetry alone.

I've learned there's also a technical word for what these sky dancers do: *allelomimesis*, from the ancient Greek *allelo*, mutual relation to one another, and *mimesis*, imitation or mimicry. Biologists speculate that "each bird tracks the movements of just seven neighbors, which leads to the domino effect" of thousands coordinating without accident. But that doesn't explain the mystery of this avian-wave maneuver. The birds swoop down in a perfect wedge, landing in the yard. Something about the wind and their many voices, raised together in a choir, fills me with a desire to go outside and join them, as if my human body might melt away and be transformed, like a woman in a fairy tale. How would it feel to lift and turn as they do, ecstatic, the one surrounded by the many, my voice a liquid burble, my bones filled with air?

If I were afraid of flocks or had bad memories of Hitchcock's *The Birds*, I'd stay inside, watching from a window. But I am not. So out I go, dashing around in a bizarre outfit—a thirty-year-old, jade green ski jacket thrown on over my pajamas, blue gardening Crocs on my feet—to sling handfuls of wild birdseed mix on the ground. My hair stands on end, and the wind half blinds me, blowing seed back into my eyes. The birds erupt into the air, the huff of their many wings like the hand of God passing briefly over my face.

I step back, and in an instant the blackbirds are on the ground again. They strut and jostle, a sea of stalking monks, all officious black feathers and probing beaks. Landbound, they look travel-worn, even weary, and I am glad I put out food. Where were they yesterday? I wonder, knowing only that they are here to claim territory, seeking out nesting sites in the cattail marshes around Island Lake. Meanwhile, the blackbirds pick the yard clean. Then, in a breath, they explode up and away, as if yanked on a string, one entity again, settled in the bare branches of the oaks.

I walk around where they have feasted, not sure what I'm looking for. A claw print? A jet feather I can cherish for its sheen and the many miles it has traveled? Maybe it's something like the trail they left earlier in our woods, flipping leaves over with their beaks, rucking up the dappled brown floor, spots of damp gleaming darkly, like doors to the underworld. In the end I find nothing, just walked-upon earth, faded yellow grass. But the hill vibrates with their presence. In the oaks, black wings slice the air, rising and falling, like surf or love or wonder. All I can say is that I have seen blackbirds arriving, sketching ephemeral drawings in the sky the way my mother used to dash off studies in charcoal, pages in her notebook flashing past. Spring is coming. I stand there staring, as snow begins to fall, wondering where these many souls will roost come evening.

In the Presence of Water

If there is magic on this planet, it is contained in water.

—Loren Eiseley, "The Flow of the River," *The Immense Journey*

Any day now Island Lake will slide open, the ice that sealed it shut all winter disappearing, molecule by sullen molecule, as if it had never been there. It's March at last, when winter begins its slow release in the Upper Midwest. When I stand on the back side of our hill and gaze out across the fields where hay, corn, and soybeans grow in summer, toward the wilder circle of land owned by the DNR and used for "waterfowl production" (otherwise known as hunting), and partly by our farmer-neighbor, John, who still farms eighty acres that abut the lake, there is a tangible difference in the color of the ice. Paler now, mushy on the surface, it reflects the sky differently than it did in the heart of winter and has turned a softer blue.

Only a few weeks ago it was a steely indigo, beautiful in its own way but forbidding in its depth, clarity, and coldness. At sunset, dusted with snow, it soaked up pink like bloody fabric, which it then surrendered to dusk, when it lay mute and unreflecting as a sheet of hammered pewter, only a memory of light sealed in its depths. In this winter of record snow there were many days when the lake stretched, an untrammeled version of the fields that surround it, like a patch of tundra too dangerous to traverse. Though I've contemplated it, standing at the edge in the Vermont Tubbs snowshoes I've had since college, I've always decided against it, the thought of falling through the ice into the spring-fed depths too terrifying to risk the thrill of walking on water.

Once, several winters ago, when we had less snow, the lake was so clear you could gaze into the underside of this world beneath its frozen surface. Another time it looked as if some giantess had dropped her compact while hurrying across the fields, leaving it to gleam there with the luminous sheen of old mirrors in shadowy hallways. That day, when I noticed the lake from the window in the house where I most often look upon it, I saw several small figures sliding back and forth across its reflecting surface, like skaters from a child's music box. Though I knew they must have been kids from down the road, or perhaps the people who own the mysterious and private island that gives the lake its name, I felt granted access to another time, as if I had fallen through a thin spot to a previous century when, with fewer entertainments to distract them, people skated here on a regular basis.

Gazing out the west-facing window, my eyes squinted against the brightness, I watched the small figures glide and twirl, her black frock coat flying out behind her, his red sweater like a spot of moving fire, while their doubles danced beneath them. And though skaters must have spun across the ice down there since then, I never saw them again, their presence so ethereal and dreamlike that I wonder if I imagined them or if they'd bled through from the days when people from the surrounding farms cut pale blue blocks of ice from the lake to store in sawdust in ice houses and barns.

In warmer seasons they baptized believers here, immersing them in the lake's silty stew, to be reborn with a name that stuck, marked forever by the presence of wild water. How much more dramatic than having a few drops from a church font sprinkled on your forehead. Like everything in the past, I imagine it to be sharper and clearer, a more visceral and immediate experience, perhaps because it was closer to something wild.

Though I am not a churchgoer, choosing to practice my own eclectic hybrid of Quaker/Buddhist/nature-mystic spirituality, I can imagine being overwhelmed by spirit when dipped in the lake, white robes billowing out around me like the water lilies that bloom here in the summer, dotting the surface, their petals like sails. I can imagine being taken, shaken, submerged, and cleansed. Like all untamed bodies of water, the lake, though small, has its own logic and spirit, which impress themselves upon you whether you're walking beside it (my practice in autumn with the dogs), gliding over its surface in a canoe, or as I do most often, gazing at it from the top of the hill, as if it is my job to watch the water's ever-changing surface. Radiant, animate, it is a resting place for the eye that reminds me where I am each day.

What is it about an aerie that lifts the soul? Looking out from our sunroom windows, or in summer, from our tiny deck—balanced on the back of the house like a crow's nest—Tom and I remark yet again that we would never have bought this place without this room, perched in its grove of oaks. And of course the view across the fields that daily draws my eye, pulling me outside myself and into a distance that is never the same, and that changes me even as I look.

Sometimes the scene reminds me of other, unrelated landscapes, connected to this one only by mood or tone. A photo I saw once of English marshlands. A painting that hung in my grandmother's Philadelphia dining room, of a stream, burnished with sun, flowing into a glowing pond. Or South Pond in Vermont, where I spent that enchanted twentieth summer, a female Thoreau, happy in my cabin without electricity or running water.

More often, however, the view of the lake reminds me of a painting I fell in love with my freshman year in college, while taking a seminar in American art and architecture. It was George Inness's *Home of the Heron*, which captures a dreamy scene of water and trees, its composition broken by the shape of a dark bird flying up, just as I have seen herons fly up from our lake. Our textbook, Daniel Mendelowitz's massive *History of American Art*, characterized Inness as an "Independent," which I liked, as I felt myself an independent too, an outlier stepping to her interior music. His dreamy transcendental scenes appealed to my romantic sensibility. Staring at the painting as it flashed before us on the screen—this was in the day of slide projectors—or poring over the tiny image in my book, I felt I recognized something in it. Although I had grown up with art, watching my mother sketch and accompanying her on many sense-drenched trips to museums, I think it was the first time I realized that paintings have the power to tell us something we might not have realized about home, by preserving an encounter with an actual place.

I had been captivated by landscapes before. The pastoral beauty of eastern Pennsylvania had imprinted itself so deep in my psyche as a child that years later, watching the opening credits of *Witness*, a film made near Lancaster, unroll in a movie theater in Southern California, I surprised myself by bursting into tears at the sight of tall green grass waving in the fields. The forested hills of northern Westchester and Putnam counties in New York State had shaped my adolescence. And I had chosen to go to college in Vermont because I loved the Green Mountains. I had spent my girlhood in rural places, wandering freely for hours in the woods and fields. But I had not understood what that meant. It took a painting to explain the connection between home and landscape, though perhaps Gerard Manley Hopkins's "inscape" is more apt here, capturing as it does the "thisness" of a place and how it enters us, making a home in our soul.

Home of the Heron is beautiful, a shimmering gem of luminism, all light and shadow, glowing from within. I have read that Inness was deeply mystical in his later years, and the painting captures something of the feeling of awe that still seems to me beyond words, an emotion I feel but cannot articulate as I gaze at my own landscapes. "The aim of art," Inness wrote, "is not to instruct, not to edify, but to awaken an emotion." I could not have articulated what I felt when I first gazed upon *Home of the Heron*. But this is what it was. In this painting, Inness captures something of the experience of both looking at a world and being looked *back* at by that world, held for a time in nature's great and implacable gaze. In such moments one hangs suspended inside an enormous *other* presence that allows us to experience, as poet Mary Oliver describes, being "vanished . . . into something better." At eighteen, cloistered in the stuffy dark of a classroom in Dalrymple Hall, a nineteenth-century barn converted into classrooms at my tiny and unconventional college, dust motes floating in the projector's beam like fine snow, I could not have said this. Homesick without realizing what I was experiencing, I knew only that *Home of the Heron* gave me solace. It seemed like a place where I too might find a home. I never imagined that I might someday, many years later, live near a lake that, during summer in particular, reminds me of the moment when the slide of the painting clicked into view and something in me lined up with it.

It is this sense of resonance and recognition that draws me to Island Lake, the scene asking for my attention simply with its presence. And of course there is also the mystery of islands, which, whether large or small, are always worlds of their own. Tom and I have paddled the edges of the island, admiring how it rises to a hill in the middle, speculating about paths that come down to the water, and watching everything from kingfishers to flocks of cedar waxwings to deer drinking, but we have never set foot on the place, always observing it from a slight distance. Though surrounded by DNR land, which is open to anyone, the island itself is private, part of a farm along Rutland-Dunn Townline Road. Hunched at the northern end of the lake like a great furred animal, the island bristles with No Trespassing signs. And since last summer, when the water rose with heavy rain, the island, which much of the time is connected by a narrow marshy isthmus to the mainland, has been true to its name—its own place, cut off from the shore. Like a small continent, it anchors the lake, holding the whole watery world in place with its presence. Longtime locals say they've never seen the water so high.

Islands, in their isolation and privacy—part of the solid world, yet separate from it—capture our imagination and invite exploration. The high water levels held out the possibility of circumnavigating the entire place, a temptation impossible to resist. So one June afternoon Tom and I set out in our yellow canoe to explore. All seemed well as we rounded the north side of the island, enjoying the sun on our shoulders, trying to identify the dragonflies that landed and sunbathed on our arms, and noting the wood duck nesting boxes and a flooded dock, standing upon flimsy pilings, that made the island appear inhabited, though we knew it wasn't. But as we circled the island, we heard a small outboard motor. Hunters sometimes ply the lake in canoes or rowboats, but as far as we knew, motorboats weren't allowed on a body of water this small.

As we rounded the north end, there one was. The people who own the island were ferrying what looked like the makings for a barbecue out from the mainland, a makeshift outboard engine wobbling on the back of their rowboat. I felt outraged, wishing I could pull a plug in the lake and strand them on the isthmus. None the happier to see us, they asked in a distinctly unfriendly manner what we thought we were doing there. We explained that we were curious to see the other side of the island, only to be told that we were outside the DNR boundaries.

"We own the island, and the water you're in too," the driver said, flicking his cigarette over the side of his boat as if to emphasize his point, while an older woman with a washed-out perm watched silently from the stern, gripping the gunwales hard. "You really shouldn't be here at all."

"Well, we'll just paddle on then and get out of your hair," Tom, always a peacemaker, said, as we headed south and back into the DNR portion of the lake. As shocked by the way they were violating the stillness of the place as I was by their attitude, I couldn't resist saying, "Oh, by the way, we're your neighbors. We live over on the other side, up the hill." This seemed to mollify the grizzled boat driver a bit.

"It's just that people go on the island and leave trash and stuff," he muttered as we paddled away.

"Well, we won't leave any trash," Tom called back, dipping his paddle firmly into the green water as our canoe shot away.

I thought that encounter—which, like my glimpse of the winter skaters, was never repeated—might change my relationship with the island and the lake. But the island was there before the farm, and the lake is bigger than whoever happens to think they own it. Later, friends who work at the DNR explained that what the people had told us wasn't true. The DNR, who subsequently bought the island, owned the water. It seemed a funny concept to me, as ownership does in general. How can anyone own the water? But don't I cling to my four acres of prairie and oak savanna with just as much ferocity? If the island were mine and I feared people intruding on it, mightn't I act just as suspicious? I hope not, but you never know. Islands are their own worlds, after all. Private and reclusive myself, I could imagine feeling touchy about outsiders.

As with so many things, time passed and the island reassumed its mystical role in the landscape. Sitting on our hill at dusk on summer evenings, surveying the lake from the Aldo Leopold–style bench Tom built as a winter project, we watched the island fade into the dusk, its edge blurring with the sky. Perhaps we aren't ever intended to set foot on the island. Perhaps we are only meant to observe it, loving it with our gaze as it floats above its own blue reflection in the dusk, looking back at us—whatever goes on there mysterious, inviolable, blessed.

Just as I have never walked on the island, I have never swum in the lake around it. It is beautiful, surrounded by white oaks and cattail marshes, full of white and yellow water lilies in summer. But like many bodies of water in Wisconsin, it has felt the taint of agricultural runoff. It has a thick greenish color in summer. Lake weeds grow from its depths thick as kelp forests, rooted in mud our neighbor John tells us is at least a foot thick. John grew up down the road and has seen everything in the sixty-plus years he has farmed this land, including the loss of his heritage (our house stands where his cows once grazed). "Ayep," he says, rocking back on his heels, smiling, and sounding more like a Vermonter than a Wisconsin farmer. "It's not to be fooled with, that little lake. There are a lot of hidden springs in there. It's twelve feet deep in places."

Perhaps what John describes is shorthand for the essential mystery of the lake. Slipping over its surface on a hot day, gazing into the murky depths, I see that it's not an appealing place to get into, though when I dip my arms in up to my shoulders or dangle a leg in over the edge of the canoe, I am always surprised by how cold the water is. I lick my finger, and the water tastes surprisingly sweet. Even in summer, when the lake is a rich stew of an ecosystem, the air above it threaded with red-wings' raucous calls, it has its secrets. The chill takes my breath away for a moment. I think of researching town records, trying to find out more about events that happened here. But I don't, more interested in learning the lake's own language. "Water is always trying to tell us something," says nature writer John Jerome. If I live enough years beside this body of water and listen with enough care, perhaps I will understand what it has to say.

Here, now, on the hinge between seasons, I incline my head toward the ice, listening for what's going on beneath its blue surface. Once, walking beside the lake around this time of year, I had the privilege of listening to the beginning of breakup, thousands of pieces of ice chinking against one another, blown by the wind in a mysterious and otherworldly music, like crystalline chimes or champagne glasses breaking. Although on a far bigger scale, it took me back to my family's wintertime walks along the stream leading down to the Perkiomen. Were my parents' spirits walking beside me now, invisible but present, telling me where to look? As I gazed across the lake, I noticed that even then it was thinning in places, infused with a translucent blue that promised to return the sky to itself. And not long after that, when I least expected it, gazing down from my hilltop I saw that there was a spot the color of lapis lazuli embedded in the broken white. Open water sloshed and glowed within the hole, like a portal to another world. My eye caught by the water's reflective prism, something in me that had been shut tight all winter, sealed up just like the lake, breathed a sigh of relief. I felt as if I too could let go of my winter burdens, allowing them to melt away and disappear behind me, vanishing like the ice on Island Lake. And one night, before the frozen water was even gone, we heard the sandhill cranes that nest there every year returning, their beautiful, primordial cries echoing through the darkness and growing more urgent in recognition as they approached the familiar water, home again.

High Wind Warning

This morning the wind woke me, roaring and booming around our glacial knoll with a sound like ocean waves, crashing and shushing. It surged up through the bare limbs of the oaks, crested the back hill, and swirled against our little brick house, wrapping us in ragged shawls of noise one almost needs made-up words to describe. I sat up in bed, listening as the wind's many untranslatable voices tangled in the trees for a moment, only to be drowned out by the next gust. What gives wind its wild music, and who would we be without it, calling us out of ourselves and into the whirl of the world?

"The wind's out of the west today," Tom announced. "They're warning of gusts up to fifty miles per hour." Like magic passwords in my magpie mind, *west* and *wind* conjured the sixteenth-century lyric: "Western wind, when will thou blow / The small rain down can rain? / Christ if my love were in my arms / And I in my bed again." Encountering the poem for the first time in college, I was entranced by the way experience—weather, yearning, the lover, home—is all one thing for the poet, everything connected, as it so often is for me. Even in its longing, the poem seems to suggest that, like beads on a string, every instant is sensuous and beautiful, like life itself if we surrender to it.

The poet probably meant the westerlies, those winds that undulate across the northern hemisphere. Today's blast is local, the result of a low pressure system off Green Bay, yanking wind across the state. It's not cold outside, but the turbulent air has a bite. I pulled on a down coat and headed out to see what was happening. I was met by a din, the agitation of air like the voice of creation. Spruce trees shimmied. The branches of the white oaks dipped and surged and creaked. Excited by the commotion, blackbirds chortled madly, bobbing on branches like obsidian carvings. A red-tailed hawk skirled, attempting to fly straight into the wind, a wisp of straw for a nest dangling from its mouth. From the marshes around Island Lake the sandhill cranes called over and over, as if excited, weaving their prehistoric yodel through the watery burble of Canada geese.

It had rained during the night, and the yard looked like the site of a stampede. Water-soaked and squishy, everything was raw and exhausted, ugly with the sheer effort of renewal. Mud season we called it when I lived in Vermont, the time of year when water runs out of the hills. But Tom says he never heard that term used in Wisconsin until the last few years. Whatever one calls it, earth is rebirthing, thawing from the surface down. Melt that couldn't percolate the still-frozen ground dotted the yard in small, grass-filled ponds, each one a tiny Sargasso Sea, winking in the sunlight. At least the wind was drying things out.

Headed down the west hill, my feet sliding on the muddy trail, I lifted my head to the wind's broad hand, sniffing like our collies and wishing I had their olfactory acuity, every inch of ground an adventure in mice, voles, squirrels, foxes, skunks, opossums, raccoons, and deer. In the distance, I could see whitecaps scudding across Island Lake's normally placid surface. The air smelled damp and pungent, of wet grass, old leaves, and manure blowing up from fields. Here and there moss burned in bright patches, its emerald fire the only green in the world. I stopped to watch the gusts tug at a piece of loose bark on a dead tree, peeling it away like a shingle, and I was almost blown over. Removing small branches from the trail, I felt like a peasant gathering kindling in a painting by Bruegel. Would old age be like this, my spirit walking four ways into the wind, until one day it disappeared?

At the bottom of the hill, after making my way through a copse of saplings, their dead leaves rustling like taffeta, I clambered up behind the shelter of our oldest tree, the red oak we call Grandmother. Over ten feet in circumference, some of her roots visible above ground like higgledy-piggledy stairs gripping the hill, the Grandmother oak stands sentinel, guarding the hidden rear flank of the property. Once, in a difficult season, I leaned into this tree and felt her lean back, absorbing all my fear and anxiety. I do not tell many people this, just as I do not tell them that I have on occasion spoken with angels. It's too hard to explain. But it happened, and even creaking in the wind, the Grandmother oak possesses mysterious stillness and presence, her branches sieving the sky. I don't know what I will do if she ever blows down while I live here.

Standing in the tree's protection, shielded from the cold currents, I pressed my cheek against her rough, gray bark and thought about wind. I remember being sick in bed as a child and reading Christina Rossetti's "Who has seen the wind? / Neither you nor I" while watching a willow tree thrash the air and musing on invisible things. I understood that wind is air in motion and that it's caused by differences in temperature and air pressure. More difficult to grasp was the religious aspect of wind, something I found a bit suspect even in Sunday school, though I loved the mystery it embodied. "In the beginning God created the heavens and the earth," the Bible tells us in Genesis. I imagined the world existed as a blank, a liquid black pearl, nothingness filled with potential. Then the spirit moved over the face of the world, wind over the water, beginning everything, as we all do when we take our first ragged breath, the air itself animate, the tiny wind of our own lungs animating us. Spirit, breath, wind. No wonder the Greeks had one word for it: *pneuma*, the divine exhalation that muses over all creation.

Tucked behind my tree, I pondered winds I have known. The bitter nor'easters of girlhood stung my cheeks with snow everywhere from Pennsylvania to Vermont, while in Wisconsin marrow-chilling Alberta Clippers make northeastern weather seem mild. The cooling blue northers—was there such a beautiful name?—I experienced during a brief time in Texas wring humidity out of the air like a washrag the color of sky. In Southern California, Santa Anas scrub smog from the air during fire season, wiping everything clear and sharp as a scene etched on glass. And the Catalina eddy, responsible for late-night and early-morning low clouds and fog, followed by sunshine and sea breezes in Los Angeles, is the gentlest wind I've ever known, the perfect embodiment of a zephyr.

My daydreams interrupted by a crashing branch, I stepped out from behind the oak. The tempest hit me again, full force, as if blown across the entire continent. Where had it started? Where would it end? Wind shrieks and whooshes and squalls. It blasts and booms and buffets. It screams and whispers. It sneaks through cracks in our houses and seams in our clothes, weaseling in with icy fingers. It roars, then falls still, pausing for a moment, all its swagger gone in a sigh, exchanged for silence that pools out around us like prayer, reminding us we are small and human.

I toured the prairie, where the dull gold of big bluestem and Indian grass was blown sideways by the ruckus. Then I stood again at the top of the back hill, in the open space under the bat house. Were they up there, those little brown mice with wings, those endangered ones, still sleeping in all that clamor, their shelter swaying like the mast of a ship or a cross? I hoped so.

Possessed by a sudden desire to let the wind take me, I spread my arms and stood, like a figurehead of a woman at the front of a ship, my coat blown out behind me. I lifted my face to the wind, letting it scour my face with its rough tongue, like a giant cat. What *are* you doing? I wondered, recalling a friend who had confessed to running across the moors at Haworth, in Yorkshire, calling out "Heathcliff, Heathcliff!"

Dropping my arms, I tore around in the swirl of it all, the way I ran through wind and rain as a child, when my spirit, like the world's millennia ago, was still forming. As it still is. I could feel the wind's heavy, invisible body pressing against me, like the angel Jacob wrestled, or even God, appearing with his usual bluster, ordering Mary to bear love and mercy into the world. I thought again of the nameless poet, yearning for the western wind strong enough to fill his sails and bring him home. The wind was all-powerful, exultant, almost too much to take in. I could understand why it can drive people crazy. Later in the afternoon I watched a bald eagle struggle to land on a branch, its tail feathers spread open like an ivory fan, and I was summoned again to wonder. But at that moment my nose was running and I'd had enough weather. I went inside, made a cup of tea, and sat down to think about it all—the wind still drumming against the side of the house—thrumming with questions I will never be able to answer.

Window Tree

On the last day of the world
I would want to plant a tree

—W. S. Merwin, "Place," *The Rain in the Trees*

Summer mornings when I wake, the white oak tree outside my window is the first thing my eyes fall upon. If I have nothing pressing to do, I sometimes spend a while in its presence, staring into the leafy green swirl that rises and falls, for all the world like waves in the ocean, though here in Wisconsin I am thousands of miles from any salt water. All spring I've watched its chartreuse leaves grow, deepening toward the bottle green they assume in summer, shade spread in an ever-lengthening carpet beneath it. Early in the season, the carpet is dappled, punctuated by the shiny green parasols of mayapples, lit here and there by trilliums, their pristine white petals fluttering like fine silk handkerchiefs. A little later on, lilies of the valley also illuminate the edge of the woodland floor. Although they can be invasive, I planted them because they are my birth flowers, and because several other houses where I lived before this one had them, their intoxicating perfume one of the many small ways I have attempted to find a through line in a life that's taken me all over this country. "White coral bells upon a slender stalk," I sang as a child at Wyndcroft School, thrilling to the idea of those bells being my personal flower as I bound up small bouquets for May Day.

But the lilies of the valley are gone now, nothing left but their faded leaves, and it is the oak that holds my attention, the one I see every morning from my window, and other trees I've studied in the past, learning their shape and movements as intimately as one learns those of a lover's body, in houses and places before this one. For although I have lived in this house for twenty years and the oak is the first thing I look at every morning, it is only in the last few years that I have come to truly know this tree, attending to it deeply enough to glimpse its spirit. Although it is not the oldest tree on our property, the oak's trunk is close to four feet in diameter. Tom estimates that it's 165 years old. It is a part of the savanna that covers the hill, though it's such a battle against honeysuckle, buckthorn, multiflora roses, and wild grapes that we'd need a herd of goats to keep the invasive species fully at bay. "Bit by bit," I say, reminding myself that restoration is a slow process. I try to content myself with maintaining an acre or so of prairie and doing a little bit more each year on the savanna, hoping that this oak, which abuts a field too steep to plow, still experiences something of the openness it once knew.

I see the oak every day because when we moved into this house we rejected the larger master suite on the more public front side of our property for a small back bedroom that faces north and is completely private. There are no other houses visible from here, nothing but the tree and the fields beyond it, reminding me of the secluded farmhouses I grew up in. When I look out the window on sharp winter nights I can see the stars tangled in the oak's branches like bits of sparkling ice. The branches seem to spiral even when still. They remind me of Georgia O'Keeffe's painting of the tree D. H. Lawrence loved to gaze at during his time in New Mexico. I know my tree so well that I look for certain stars between certain branches as the seasons pass, my own spirit heartened and guided by the familiar sight.

That's part of what I'm looking for, the intangible thing I seek without even meaning to when I stare into the lustrous green of the oak that shines like an inverted bowl. A sense of the familiar, something recognizable and unchanging. Staring at it, even at the break of day, when my identity is still tentative and newborn, heaved up on the shores of waking from sleep, something in my spirit is anchored, then flies free, taken outside itself to become a part of the tree, lost in dappled light. Deep within the green, I am held in the safety of my domestic interior and released into the oak's depth and fullness, almost the way one is in a tree house as a child—the pleasure of being hidden away from the world something we don't experience enough in the rush and bustle of our adult lives. Slow down, the tree seems to say to me. Pay attention. Take heed.

And so, when we arranged this room, we defied feng shui by facing our bed north in order to see this tree. "Tree at my window, window tree," I think to myself, the words to a poem I memorized in childhood rising unbidden in my mind, so vividly that I see the fat blue volume of poetry, its covers threadbare, the front one falling off. It had been my mother's book when she was a girl and was passed down to me. I turned to the book often, memorizing a poem a week from it for recitations in second grade, practicing aloud as my mother braided my hair in the mornings. Over fifty years later, forgetting who wrote this poem, I am surprised when perusing the bookcase where I shelve poetry to rediscover that it is by Robert Frost and, like so much of his work, filled with dark undercurrents. "I have seen you taken and tossed," the poet writes, adding that the tree has "seen me when I was taken and swept / And all but lost." The poem seems a sophisticated choice for an eight year old and I wonder what sad or disturbing glimpse of the adult world prompted me to pick such a piece.

There was a tree at my window then too, an enormous weeping willow I loved for the way it filtered the light gold, its long branches making it a Lady Godiva of trees. My mother worried about the willow, fearing its shallow roots might cause it to topple in a storm. But it never did. I knew every creak and sway of that tree. One of my most vivid sensory memories of childhood involves taking a nap in my antique spool bed, wrapped in the golden light of the willow as if in a transparent comforter. As I lay there, falling asleep, a small plane crossed overhead and faded away into the distance, the mechanical sound comforting because it began in a time before loss or sadness. My mother was not yet sick, and her death from cancer was still several years away, a rent in the world's fabric I could not have imagined as I lay there wrapped in dappled light and shadow. Even now, the receding buzz of a plane in the distance summons a flicker of recognition, and I feel again perfectly safe. Such is the story memory writes in our senses.

"The story of my life is the story of trees I've loved," writes California poet Deena Metzger. "Some were standing, some fell down." I, too, can map my life in terms of trees I've loved, those that have stood visible from different bedroom windows. After the willow of my early childhood came the giant sugar maple with its whirligig helicopter keys; its leaves turned the purest red I have ever seen in autumn. Later there was the scrim of conifers in Vermont's Green Mountains, broken here and there by chalky birches, standing out like ghosts.

When I lived in Southern California, my bedroom window also faced north, framing a view of Mount Baldy, doyen of the San Gabriel range, where snow often lingered until July. A cypress curled beside my window, as frenzied as one by Van Gogh. But its deep green was a solace on hundred-degree days, as was the shade cast by the leathery leaves of the live oaks, their polished sheen coated with a layer of dust that was only washed away in the January rains. Accustomed to leaf fall in autumn, it took my north-eastern eye a good five years before I got used to seeing oaks with their leaves on year round. I loved their grit and prickly edges, made to with-stand a harsh climate.

In Oregon, I lived on seven acres also dotted with oaks. On summer mornings, one cast its shadow through the white lace curtains in my bed-room, encouraging me to get up and head out into a landscape that healed me from clinical depression. Draped in moss, the tree, like those in my present life, was a study in opposites—deep-rooted yet never completely still, it anchored me at moments when I feared I might fly off into madness or slip away into death.

Perhaps their combination of stability and motion is why my Celtic ancestors thought of trees as spiritual presences. Musing on this, I read in Caitlín Matthews's *The Celtic Spirit* that trees were seen as "sacred powers, mediators between the worlds, with their roots penetrating the depths of the underworld and their branches . . . scraping heaven . . . straining at the ceiling of the apparent world." And, too, there is the World Tree, promi-nent in so many cultures, which connects the underworld, earth's surface, and heaven. Does my tree do this for me as I contemplate its mystery, perhaps without my even realizing it? Is there a word for it? What kind of tree is the World Tree, anyway? Does it have a common name?

I have always loved common names best (white oak, not *Quercus alba*), because they summon the familiar and homely. Perhaps this is what learn-ing to live in and love a place is all about, a process of becoming ever more familiar until one can walk about in the dark without bumping into obsta-cles, as I now can on this land, with nothing but the texture of things to guide me. It hasn't always been this way. When I first moved to the Upper Midwest I felt too exposed. I was fresh from the velvety coniferous forests of the Pacific Northwest, and the land in Wisconsin felt too open to me. "There aren't enough *trees* here," I remember weeping, not yet familiar enough with my environs to know that forests had been razed by settlers to create farmland. "I feel so naked." I still experience that sometimes, walking the country roads. Something in me flinches beneath the bigness of the sky. Vulnerable in a way that's almost proprioceptive, it's as if, with-out trees, I am physically off-balance, the place where my body connects with the world gone awry in a way I find forever disconcerting.

This is perhaps why I feel so sheltered on this hill, with its patches of oak savanna, neither hemmed in nor too out in the open. The trees here, including the one outside my window, tether the hill in the landscape, their roots like guylines holding things down. Without them I might blow away, as unrooted as I sometimes feel, my travels throughout this country leaving me forever homesick for something I can't quite define. And yet here I've been, on this hill for all these years. It's possible, I know, to travel deeply by sitting very still, watching what you look at every day for the new thing it will tell you. If, as he claimed, Thoreau "traveled a great deal in Concord," a world really, so have I on this Wisconsin hill.

That kind of attention can yield surprising riches. "My job is to watch the palm tree," I remember my friend Holly reading from her journal many years ago in California. She called it "that perfect traveler," though of course the palm tree never went anywhere farther than her neighborhood in East Hollywood. I watched palm trees in California too, unnerved at first by their strangeness, and then growing to love them for their glitter and thrash, their ability to sway on long limber stems, moving with change as easily as they moved with the breezes that blew in each evening off the Pacific, the Catalina eddy always predictable. I never once saw a palm come down in an earthquake. Instead, they move with change, swaying through it. Would I were as flexible.

Outside my window the breeze lifts the leaves of my oak, turning them over like a thousand green fish. They rise and fall with a sound that is half rushing water, half air, though I wonder if I would think of it that way if I had not also lived close to the ocean. The leaves shift and whisper and rub against one another and the wind, reminding me yet again of something I seem to need to keep learning—that it is possible (and even good) to be still and in motion at the same time, rooted and flowing. Staring into the tossing green, I think of how many places this tree has taken me in the space of a single morning. Perhaps, as Caitlín Matthews says, "trees truly are mediators between worlds, living bridges between our apparent world and the unseen realms of the otherworld." Living as long as they do, most of them many more years than a human life, perhaps they also mediate between the present, with all its immediacy and blinding blur, and the past, which we like to think is unchanging, though as William Faulkner says, "it's not even past" but goes on happening in a way that makes me feel light and insubstantial inside if I think about it too hard.

And so I return my gaze to the tree, staring at it until I seem to breathe with it—my own being rising and falling, as if my consciousness has been painted on the green silk of its leaves. I am learning slowly, so slowly, how to keep still and grow at the same time. I haven't any idea how many leaves grow on a single white oak. And yet what strikes me, staring into the green, is how, taken together they make one thing, a canopy stippled here and there with stitches of light, all of it rippling, shining, whole.

Strange Angels

Encounters with Sandhill Cranes

And still the birds came, came in watery flocks
—Wallace Stevens, "Dry Loaf," *Collected Poems*

The cranes are gathering now. In the bronze green, late summer marshes where fuzzy brown cattail flowers begin to release their fluff, in the large undisturbed fields where the grass turns tawnier each day, in the ragged green collar of oak-studded land around Island Lake that our farmer-neighbor does not plow, the cranes are congregating. Although they won't begin their annual migration to their winter grounds in southern Georgia, Florida, and Mexico until September and October, they come together now in a loose fellowship that will tighten and consolidate as the days shorten and summer leaches out of the land. Like a group of pilgrims or spiritual seekers collecting before their journey begins and uttering preliminary prayers, the cranes seem to be readying themselves, preparing for the long flight they must make, some of them for the first time. In the heat and humidity–stunned marshes the distinctive, rattling *kar-r-r-o-o-o* fills the air as they call back and forth to one another, announcing their arrival, staking a claim in this watery world even as they ready themselves to leave it.

Sandhill cranes are large birds, close to my own height. They can stand as tall as five feet and weigh from ten to fourteen pounds, with an enormous wingspan—six to seven feet. The color of cinnamon toast after losing their yellow-brown baby fluff, they later turn the smoky, pearl gray of clouds on overcast days. But they often appear pale brown because they paint their feathers with mud, preening it in so they are better camouflaged among reeds and grasses. Looking at cranes in the marshes near my house, I've been struck by how effective this makeup is and how well it conceals them, embedding them in the texture of the vegetation they browse. In some parts of Wisconsin, ferric oxide in the mud stains their feathers rust brown, like a semipermanent dye. With their curious vermillion eyes, black bills, legs, and feet, and a scarlet cap-like patch on their head (the only color in an otherwise neutral palette), the males and females look almost alike. They don't mate until they are four years old, sometimes going through long courtships. But when they do pair up, it's for a lifetime. Cranes can live twenty-five to thirty years with the same partner, a fact I find both moving and inspiring. Families of cranes migrate together, the young birds that have outgrown their families hanging out in ragged flocks like unruly adolescents. The chicks (oddly known as "colts") are usually born by mid-May and able to fly by mid-July—a good thing, as they need a lot of practice for the journey ahead. Trawling National Geographic's website, I learn that cranes are one of the oldest known bird species in the world, their structure identical to a Miocene fossil ten million years old. Perhaps that is why their call is so evocative, why it seems to float across the millennia as it does, immutable and enduring.

We've heard them calling all summer, watching from the cedar love-seat on the back hill as they drift in over the corn, hay, and soybean fields toward the lake in the evening, their enormous wings first angled to decrease the lift, balancing their speed with the rate of descent, then tucked as they land. But we hear them more often now, especially early in the morning and in the evening when their calls ring out, clear in the quiet world. Beyond anything else, the cranes' cries epitomize for me the spirit of this spot in southern Wisconsin, with its scattered wetlands and prairie and remnant oak savanna punctuating the landscape in strokes of dark green that look oil-painted into the scene. In a landscape that has had wildness farmed out of it for over a hundred years, the cranes' haunting ululation seems to convey a message from the land itself—what it remembers and what it has forgotten, what persists, indomitable, unchanged. Although their call has been described as a rattle, a cackle, or even an iron wheel grinding on a dry axle, I find it both beautiful and strange, the voice of time itself, telling stories of wind and water and the distance between one homeplace and another. There is something both melancholy and comforting in their call, something that speaks of arrivals and departures. It is my favorite sound in the world, one that never fails to make me pause and lift my head, straining to hear more, as if by listening I might begin to understand something about home and migration, the cranes teaching me how to be more alive in my all-too-human skin.

The cranes are the first birds we hear each spring, arriving before even the red-winged blackbirds that appear out of nowhere to mob our feeders in raucous hordes. Obedient to the mysteries of changing light, celestial navigation, and whatever instinctual understanding tells them it is time, the cranes return before the season begins, when the cattail marsh is a maze of frozen still lifes and snow lies thick upon the ground. Locally, they begin to gather several miles away, near open water below the dam on the Yahara River, where it flows out of Lake Kegonsa, the smallest of the four lakes that define this part of Dane County. Every day Tom and I witness what appear to be scouting parties, ragged-looking groups of three to five cranes—why do they seem like males?—that drift in over the fields dotted with lines of last summer's cornstalks to see if Island Lake is open. Always we hear them before we see them. And always the sound makes something—hope, relief, the prospect of mercy and new beginnings—surge up in our chests. "I heard the cranes today," one of us will say to the other, our voice lifting a little in the telling. Though there may be weeks of winter still to come, and I worry about the cranes on cold nights, wondering how they survive in the rattling, ice-shrouded marshes, their return is the sign that winter's back has been broken. Like the messengers they are in most mythologies, the cranes know something we do not.

The day we hear them, Tom notes their return in the blue, leatherbound phenology journal where he records seasonal observations, writing down when things happen so he can observe patterns over the years. I stare out the window of the sunroom in the cold half-dark, comforted by the presence of these great and elegant birds without whom the land seems empty, as if it's holding its breath, waiting for something that's missing. Perhaps this is the release the cranes' return permits. Knowing they are out there, striding through the cold like gray-cloaked monks, already searching for the perfect place to build their nests, I can breathe again. Knowing this will happen—that there will soon be jumbled and untidy platform nests of grasses up to five feet wide in which each female will lay two olive eggs, speckled with brown—gives me comfort. Attending to the sound of the cranes, I feel less alone in the world than I often do, part of a domain that is infinitely wilder and wiser.

Once, farther on in the season, I stood at the end of our long dirt driveway late one afternoon, the mail clutched against my chest as I stared up in wonder. A flock of more than fifty cranes was flying over my head, homing in on Island Lake. They were flying so low I heard the rustling flap of their wings, the upstroke quicker than the down, saw their necks held out, straight as rulers, felt the blue shadows they cast over the restored prairie along the road. As they flew, they bugled incessantly, as if talking to one another about what lay ahead. They called and called until it was all I could hear. I stood, still as a deer, wrapped in a vortex of sound that lifted me up and pulled me with it, their calls taking me far from anything I had ever known. For an instant or two I felt as if something had flown out of my body, as souls are sometimes said to do.

Then, just as quickly, the air went quiet, the sound of the cranes fading away in the distance like a whisper as they landed and settled into the marsh for the evening. Once or twice during the night we might wake and hear them burbling to themselves. The gentle sound was broken now and then by small outbursts of single loud guard calls when the cranes were disturbed by a passing raccoon or coyote. But always they calmed down again, their quieting like the world falling back asleep. Drifting off myself, I imagined them clustered in scattered groups, their red eyes shining like small, strange moons in the darkness.

Several years passed on this hill before I saw a crane again as closely as the flock that flew right above me. I often watched cranes in the adjoining field, where, given their aptitude for probing the ground for corn, they are sometimes a nuisance to farmers. I marveled at the geometry of their flight as they floated in over Island Lake in raft after triangular raft of perfectly orchestrated motion. The cranes were integral figures in the landscape, arresting the moment with movement, making any scene in which they appeared the embodiment of Ralph Waldo Emerson's "concentrated eternity." But I always saw them from a bit of a distance, as if I had not yet rooted myself in this place deeply enough to be permitted intimate observation.

Then one day, as I sat at my study desk, struggling over a piece of writing that was not going well, my eye was caught by slow, deliberate movements in the backyard. I looked up to meet the shining crimson eye of a crane as she stalked methodically over the lawn, stopping now and then to poke for something in the grass. Cranes are omnivores. They'll eat tubers, grain, insects, worms, mice, and even snakes. Imagine being a snake caught in that long neck. While I couldn't think what the patch of domestic grass sandwiched between prairie and savanna offered, the crane had found something of interest there.

Yet the hunting itself seemed almost incidental, as if the crane was present for the sheer pleasure of the walk. There is no more elegant movement. Slowly, slowly she raised a delicate-looking leg, jointed like a length of shiny black rattan. And then, just as slowly, she lowered the leg, planting her foot with the practiced certainty of ballet dancer, as she bent to peck at something on the ground. Entire lifetimes of meaning and understanding seemed to hang suspended in the pause between each movement as the crane worked her way across the yard with great intention and economy of motion. Transfixed at the window, I felt as if I were watching an Oriental brush painting emerge before me on the page. Or as if I were part of one. It was the most perfect example of walking meditation I had ever seen.

I sat that way for a long time, my breath slowing, something in me aligned with the crane's deliberate pace and attention to movement, until, with one long glance back over her shoulder (could she see me?), she walked away, up the rise to the crest of the hill and down the deer path, leaving great stillness behind her. As I sat there trying to absorb the enormity of the bird's presence, the title of Tess Gallagher's poem "Each Bird Walking" floated into my head. The poem itself isn't even about birds, but the singularity and intention suggested by the words captures the spare beauty of the cranes. Each bird walking, I thought. Yes. Oh yes. That was the only way to describe it.

I've seen cranes up close a number of times since then. There have been several occasions when their appearance has been more than synchronistic, almost miraculous, as if the hand that now and then allows the human and the wild to align in meaningful conjunction was at work. The first time was when an F3 tornado swept through our small town of Stoughton in August 2005. Tom and I were out running that afternoon, loping along the White Oak Nature Trail in nearby Lake Kegonsa State Park. It was raining hard, harder than any thunderstorm I had ever been in. But we laughed as we splashed our way along, exhilarated by the wildness of the weather, unaware of the cyclone less than a mile away, touching down and kicking its hobnailed boot through over a hundred houses. It was only on the way home in the car that we saw downed power lines, hissing like snakes; trees that had been ripped out of the ground, their roots exposed, obscene, to air; and shivering families standing next to the piles of splinters that had been their houses. The downed power lines forced a detour that turned the usual fifteen minute drive into a half hour, every instant of it spent wondering whether we'd find our house intact when we got there. Half-remembered prayers from childhood rose up in my head, jumbled together with Buddhist phrases invoking loving-kindness and compassion. Indiscriminate, I gabbled them to myself, appealing to any benevolent energy that might protect our home.

As we cut down County N, through the marshes of the Roe Memorial Environmental Preserve, a pair of sandhill cranes exploded out of the cattails beside us. Drenched with rain, covered with mud so thick and brown they seemed to struggle against the weight of it, the cranes rose in unison over the tattered landscape. They looked as if they had been caught even closer to the knife edge of the storm than we had, perhaps even whirled up into it, like something from *The Wizard of Oz*. Cranes have been known to fly as high as 5,000 feet during their autumn migration, rising into the chilliest reaches of November to catch thermals that will carry them south. But what could it have been like for these two to have been thrown up in the air and then have their element turn on them, rolling and tumbling the great birds, then dunking them, dragging their long elegant bodies through muck?

Looking at the cranes, I wondered how they had survived, and what other animals had suffered that afternoon, their struggle unmarked and unnoticed, obscured by human loss. I will never know. But watching the cranes, backlit against a disturbing, violet sky, I was filled with the conviction that our house would be safe—as we found it was when we roared up our driveway a little while later. Rounding the curve up the hill, we saw the whole house illuminated by the setting sun, not even a leaf of the hundred-year-old oaks disturbed. Inside, the cats and collies greeted us sleepily, rising from the beds where they were when we had left. A great stillness lay over everything. Then from the marsh came the calls of cranes, reassuring in their familiarity, echoing up from the marshes, neighbors welcoming us back.

Only a few weeks later cranes once again rescued me from the net of worry in which I am so often entangled. It was a day or two before we were to leave on a three-week trip to England. A homebody at heart, I was nervous about my first trip abroad, and my anxiety was exacerbated by the recent tornado. I found myself in the backyard, messing around in a shady flowerbed I'd carved out under the mulberry tree. I had other, much more urgent things to do. But filled with the urge to anchor myself in the earth of home, I made an excuse to plant some fall perennials, telling myself it would be too late if I waited until after the trip.

Squatted on my haunches, my hands wrist deep in the black, beginning-to-smell-of-autumn earth, I heard the familiar, rattling *kar-r-o-o-o, kar-r-o-o-o, kar-r-o-o-o.* I looked up to see three cranes landing in the hayfield on the other side of the fence. I watched as they settled into themselves. Then, as if choreographed, the three began to dance, rising and falling in the green-gold field like something out of a dream. Although most well-known for their elaborate courtship display, cranes engage in many dances. As I watched, the three cranes bowed, jumped, and flapped their wings, rising and falling, exquisite and graceful as marionettes. Perhaps they were young birds; my notes from a visit to the International Crane Foundation in Baraboo, Wisconsin, tell me dancing is a "normal part of motor development for cranes." The dancing, which looks like an intricately planned and patterned ritual, "thwarts aggression, relieves tension, and . . . strengthens pair bonds." Would that our dances were anywhere near half as beautiful.

I value the Crane Foundation's detailed observations about crane dancing, but as I watched my three cranes dance, I confess these studies were the last thing on my mind. For as the cranes moved, their steps as deliberate and formal as dancers in a minuet that I knew had nothing to do with my world, I felt as if they danced for me. Or rather, as if some accident of circumstance—the need to plunge my hands into home ground before I left it—had granted me the gift of being present at this occasion. Once again, just as when I watched the solitary crane making its perambulation through our yard, I was caught in a spell, enclosed in the invisible circles of protection and peace that watching wild things can bring. As I watched the cranes' graceful movements, words from "Song of a Man Who Has Come Through," a poem I love by D. H. Lawrence, danced through my head:

> What is that knocking?
> What is that knocking at the door in the night?
> It is somebody who wants to do us harm.
>
> No, no, it is the three strange angels.
> Admit them, admit them.

I don't know who the three strange angels are whose presence so unsettles the speaker in Lawrence's poem. The cranes I saw in the September field were the opposite of threatening or frightening. Kneeling there with my hands in the mud, I *knew*—as every now and then one is permitted to know things of a larger and more beneficent order—that they were three strange angels. Everything was going to be all right. I would travel safely and learn from my time abroad. The house and the land I loved would be there when I returned. And the cranes would be there too, the sound of their calls crisscrossing the air above the fields, the lake, and the marshes as they always had, the sound of home welcoming me into the mystery of the familiar.

Flower Moon

A Wisconsin Book of Hours

The Book of Hours was a prayer book for the laity that developed in late medieval Europe and that was used for private devotion. These works were often personalized for individual patrons and illuminated. . . . The text included a calendar of liturgical feast days and a series of prayers to be recited eight times a day, according to established practice.

> —*World Digital Library*, a project of the Library of Congress and UNESCO

Lauds (Sunrise)

Before sunrise, the hill we live on hunches like a great beast, dreaming in the gray stillness that is neither light nor darkness. As the sky brightens, the drumlin lumbers awake. Its teardrop shape seems the embodiment of time, earth moved by the glacier as it scraped over Wisconsin, then back again, leaving behind gravel and till from as far away as Canada. Geographically dislocated myself, I take an odd comfort from living in this place. The land contains primeval memories of movement and changes that I can almost sense at times, layered beneath the surface where I lead my daily life. Thinking about all this at first light, I sleep and wake, sleep and wake again, so that the panoply of how this place evolved seems to be happening right now, the hill coming into being beneath me. Then the white oaks visible through my bedroom window swim into focus, gaining shape, definition, and sharpness, emerging from a child's spiraling scribble of gray, the way we ourselves do from dreams.

Prime (6 a.m.)

Every morning I watch as the sun paints the trunks of the oaks outside my window a pale blushing pink that turns red, then brightens and becomes gold, as if the world were beginning again. I could lie here all morning, letting the light deepen, bringing the world into being, remembering what my Quaker-educated mother explained about the concept of Inner Light, that seed of brightness the Friends believe every soul contains. I loved the idea then, and love it still for what it suggests of an individual relationship with spirit, as if the Light were a small flame each heart tends. As a child raised in a spiritually eclectic household, the Light my mother described seemed more accessible and friendly than a patriarchal God, more like a personal friend. I imagined it as a little fire I carried inside me, something I could share with others, like a settler girl bringing fresh coals to new neighbors.

Late in her life, the writer Colette, crippled with arthritis, her movements restricted to her Paris apartment, described the fire burning at all hours on the hearth as her friend. I love the passage for what it says about how we are never really alone, as well as the way it points out that whatever illness or difficulty we are experiencing is never the whole story. There is always so much more calling out for us to attend to things. I could live my whole life looking and never see enough, grateful for the visible prayers creation has strewn before me. Colette's words remind me that the light in the trees each morning is my friend and that studying it matters. From one of the oak branches a Baltimore oriole sings, its song as brilliant and beautiful as the fire burning in its sleek black-and-orange wings. Then all the other birds on the hill join in, stitching the air with sound.

Terce (9 a.m.)

I'm perched on the glacial erratic on our back hill with my tea. The pair of wrens that have taken over one of our bluebird houses flit and chatter and swirl, their brown feathers brushed gold in the sun, as if someone has dipped them in pollen. With its vantage point over Island Lake—which floats like a blue dream in the near distance, fringed in a ruff of oak and cattail marshes—this spot is one of my favorite places. Several years ago I bought Tom a cedar loveseat, and we often sit out here, our gaze resting on the water, no other houses in sight. Once, seated alone, musing, I gazed into the vertically slit amber eyes of a vixen fox that popped up in the slanting remnant meadow on the other side of the barbed-wire fence. We studied one another for a few minutes, companionable in our curiosity. Then she moved on through the tall grass, leaving me changed, a different woman than I was before our encounter.

This morning I chose the rock, running my fingers over the familiar rough-ness of its surface. Quartz and feldspar stripes ripple through the darker gneiss, like waves in the shallow sea that once covered Wisconsin. Gneiss is an ancient metamorphic rock formed some thirty kilometers below the earth's crust. Does our rock hold within it memories of being folded and refolded? Does it recall being heaved to the surface or, millennia later, being carried and abandoned by a massive white paw as the Green Bay lobe of the Laurentide Ice Sheet crept across this part of Wisconsin? Does the rock miss the place it came from, far north of here? Would it recognize it were it to be returned, changed by living far away from home, as I have been?

I used to spend time on this rock every day after I ran, meditating as my body cooled. The ancient stone possesses an energy all its own, and although it may have been endorphins, several times a mysterious force pulsed through me as I sat there, one that left my spine tingling, like a gold wire stretched toward the earth. I've since learned that feldspar can align our chakras, subtle bodies, and meridians, and is even good for astral travel, which may explain my experience. I was a bit wary of the rock after that—reverent, as one should be in sacred places. But this morning it's a welcoming bench, warm in the sunlight, steady beneath me, holding me balanced in time, its surface speckled by a thousand tiny white petals blown in, like snow, from the flowering hedgerow.

Sext (Noon)

I'm lying spread-eagled on an old, brightly striped Mexican blanket in my sunny yard, trying to feel the bones of the earth. Sick with an amorphous, ill-defined migraine, I am trying to return to my body in the only way I know how, pressing myself fiercely, even desperately into the ground, allowing it to hold me and tell me who I am. I must look like a nun, pros-trate before the altar in prayer, rooted in earth and aligned with the stars. The wind stirs through the white oaks in our savanna, many of them over a hundred years old. Down the hill, the Grandmother red oak, axis mundi of this place, stands guard, her gnarled, mossy roots gripping mysteries deeper than time.

I lie here in May, the greenest month, listening to a world that is all chirp and rustle and sun in the leaves, thinking about the importance of pausing. I flatten my body against the ground. I'm trying to think like a drumlin—

attempting to feel the shape of time and how it has moved, the weight of history and change and hours alive in the earth beneath me, my own life a late addition, layered over the traces of many others. Thousands of years ago the glacier stopped here. And here I am, a pilgrim soul, alive on one of the earthen teardrops it left behind. As I sit up, I am startled by brilliant flashes at the bird feeders—the deep blue of the indigo bunting and the crimson of the scarlet tanager—pausing to rest and feed as they pass through on their travels, pilgrims too.

None (3 p.m.)

It's humid and overcast, the air slicked to my skin like wet silk. A catbird, saucy in his black cap, rustles in the lilacs outside my study window, singing a long succession of astonishing and varied musical notes. He flings himself against the glass. I don't think he can hurt himself, but the soft taps are disturbing enough that Tom puts up strips of glittering scare tape to chase him away. They hang there, moving in the breeze like silvery virgas falling from clouds, or shining strands of dreams. The catbird mews from a nearby tree. Then a minute later he's back, burbling wildly. I stand eye to eye with him, looking straight into beady, black wildness, recalling a catbird that used to sing from the forsythia bush at my parents' farm in eastern Pennsylvania.

One summer my mother began carving a small statue of Saint Francis. She planned to attach it to a bird feeder. She wanted to create an altar or holy space, hoping to lure the catbird with the fruit the species loves. One year later she was dead of breast cancer at age forty-two. I don't know what happened to the statue, which was unfinished, still evolving into what she imagined it would be, the way I was when she left me. But her impulse to make the statue lives inside me, eternal, the way a meditation teacher I've worked with tells me all moments of love, care, and comfort do. "Think of yourself as a windowpane," he says, "with your spiritual benefactors standing behind you, their love and care streaming through you." I do so, and I see my mother and grandmother standing behind me, etched in light. Mary and Elizabeth. My personal saints.

On another day at this same hour, my mother saints arise from water. Tom lifts our canoe upside down over his head, balances the portage yoke on his shoulders, and carries it down the tractor lane between our farmer-neighbor's eighty acres of corn and soybeans to explore Island Lake. It's

Tom's sixty-fifth birthday and, happiest with a paddle in hand, all he wants to do is drift around on the water. Which we do, slathered with Coppertone that evokes childhood, laden with binoculars, camera, and notebooks. I wear a wide-brimmed straw hat, like the one my grandmother wore while gardening. *Am I her now?* I think of a photo I have of her as a girl paddling a canoe. She wears a long white dress and a strand of beads, and she has her hair piled up, Gibson girl style. Despite these impediments, she sits in the prow, hand firm on the paddle, as if certain even then exactly where she's going. I trail my arm in the shockingly cold, spring-fed water, reminded, yet again, of the baptisms that took place here in the nineteenth century, wondering why they fascinate me so. Might my life be different if I'd been plunged into water like this as my first act of faith? Then I remember my summer in Vermont, when South Pond baptized me every day. Yes, that counts. And my life was altered afterward, wasn't it?

The lake is as still as a prayer. We sluice silently through the shallows among fists of yellow water lilies about to bloom and reeds that look like ink paintings. All around us are cattail islands. A delicate chartreuse tracery of ferns we've never noticed before is woven into the dense green spears, which makes us wonder if the lake isn't filling in over time. Tom's in the stern, keeping us on course with his stronger arms. I'm in the bow, paddling too, the sentinel calling out what lies ahead. But if an emergency arose, a rock or a snag, we could work together, pivoting as a team. There are birds everywhere—sandhill cranes, great blue herons, kingfishers, Canada geese, green herons, mallards, mergansers, red-winged blackbirds, and the acrobatic tree swallows that skim the water, their flight etching the air with a trail of invisible messages. The lake is a quilt of sound, a psalm without words.

Vespers (Sunset)

Every day at sunset Island Lake turns pink. The sun appears to sink right behind it, infusing everything—water, trees, and sky—with rose. I know there's lots of life going on down there, geese and cranes drifting in for the evening after a day foraging in the fields. But from the hill it looks as if the lake pauses, held in perfect, blushing stillness that seems to reflect things more accurately than ordinary light. One year when Tom asked me what I wanted for my birthday, I replied, "I don't want anything but the pink lake." He took a photograph of the scene, and I look at a framed print of the pink lake every day as I brush my teeth. He also had the snapshot reproduced on a ceramic mug, enabling me to hold a miniature version of the lake in my hand as I sip my strong Barry's Irish tea. I love both mementoes, gestures of the love they represent. But I love the pink lake even more. As the sun disappears, the mourning doves coo in the blue spruce trees. The subtle iridescence of their feathers is the same pink as the water.

Compline (9 p.m.)

What I most delight in as we first stroll, then stride toward summer, are the lengthening days and the way they fill the soul with hope and expansiveness. A child of the northern latitudes, I love the long, light evenings. But it is only the end of May, and they are not here yet. By nine o'clock it's almost dark, something past dusk but not yet night, the time of day my father, who loved words, used to call the gloaming. Looking the word up, I see it is derived from the Old English *glōming*, or "twilight," and of German origin, related to "glow." Even at the edge of darkness there is light.

Matins (Midnight)

It's the middle of the night, but it's not truly dark because of the full moon, which shines in every window of the house, beckoning me to rise from my bed. I get up and walk from room to room in my thin cotton nightgown, savoring its touch against my skin. I pause for a moment in panels of light that fall before each window, looking up at our silvery sister, whose face I never tire of studying. According to the Algonquin, for whom each moon marked a particular moment in the year, this is the Full Flower Moon, also known as the Corn Planting Moon or the Milk Moon. I love the idea of keeping track of time by following closely the cycles of the moon. I've purchased lunar calendars for decades, attracted by their more organic portrayal of the passing days, hoping they might slow me down.

I wish I'd known more about Native American concepts of time—for which many tribes have no actual word—during the moonwalk in 1969. I was sixteen that summer, witchy and rebellious and full of trouble. My father insisted we kids watch the whole thing on our never-fully-functional, portable Sony TV. Crowded together with my four siblings in a hot upstairs room—where the reception was deemed better—I fumed in silence while my dad boomed, "This is a historic moment, kids." When Neil Armstrong planted his cleated boot on the moon's virgin surface, I teared up, becoming a bit hysterical, although I wasn't sure why. Later that evening I went outside and stood alone in the moonlight. I raised my bare arms high and lifted my face to her, reclaiming her as my own, calling myself home in her soft light. *Moon, moon*, I whispered, the very shape of the word in my mouth holy, like another name for mother. *Moon, moon*.

The first summer we lived on our hill, an impulse similar to the one that prompted tonight's perambulations made me get up and go outside in the middle of the night. Wandering through the backyard, I looked up and saw three great horned owls sitting in a dead oak tree. I stood there, washed by moonlight, looking up at them as they looked down on me. I didn't know yet that owls have always lived on this hill, that we'd watch a pair of owlets hatch in an old hawk's nest on the back hill, or that the sound of owls calling—their *whoo, whoo, whoo-whoo / Who's awake? You too?*—would come to seem as much the sound of home as the cranes conversing in the marshlands around the lake.

I didn't know any of that, but I knew it meant *something*, in the same way I know this moon does tonight. When I step onto the deck in my bare feet, night holds me in its indigo arms. I look out over the patch of meadow on the lee side of the hill, musing on my plan to enter it sometime and sit for a long while, listening for what the land there has to tell me. If I were less lazy, I'd do that now, lying down like a deer in the dew-silvered blue-stem, my nightgown soaked clean through, like those of the supplicants lucky enough to have been baptized in the wild lake that glimmers in the distance. "Often I am permitted to return to a meadow / . . . / everlasting omen of what is," Robert Duncan says in what is perhaps my favorite poem in the world for the way it embraces the mystery of creation. My scrap of meadow shines under the moon's glow as I step back inside, chilled now and ready for bed. The hours are alive inside me, their invisible pages illuminated, even as I sleep, with the Inner Light of this time and place. Our house floats like a small boat in the enormous, spangled dark, the hill dreaming beneath us.

V

The Kingdom of Ordinary Things

An Alphabet of Here

A Prairie Sampler

My time living at Deer Run has stitched me into this place. Let me thread my needle and spell out a few of the many ways the land has taught me its language.

A is for New England Aster

Purple stars fallen to earth, they bloom around the autumn equinox, shining out from the faded gold of prairie grasses. Delicate looking, but hardy, their rayed petals surround goldfinch-yellow hearts that glow like small lanterns. They comfort me as I walk up the dirt drive at dusk. Native Americans called them "the flower that brings frost," as if they were floral shamans, ushering in the dark season. They provide nectar for migrating monarchs, which I have seen balanced upon the blooms like chips of stained glass fallen from heaven. The prairie is hushed and still as butterflies sip sweetness, the stars for which asters are named coming out overhead.

B is for Big Bluestem

Quintessential plant of the tall-grass prairie, it is what the pioneers saw and thought resembled rippling waves, the famous sea of grass. It grows eight feet tall, with roots up to twelve feet deep, and has reddish-brown seed heads that look like gilded turkey feet. I have read that big bluestem once grew so tall and thick, it hid herds of bison or cattle. When I lie down in its rough, straw-scented gold, I feel as if I could vanish into something else entirely—time rolling through me like a deep, green ocean.

C is for Canada Geese

At dusk they drift in across the fields in great fleets, flying to the waters of Island Lake for the night. Their sleek black heads and necks are accented by a smart white chin strap; they look dressed for a formal party. But their honk is the sound of pure wildness. I've watched geese my whole life. Their V-shape has been etched into the strata of my psyche from the time I first lifted my eyes to their trailing black ribbons, stunned by the beauty of great migrations—how they make us stop for a moment, temporal, the skein of our own lives fluttering there in the sky. At night, with one male standing sentinel, the geese murmur, journeyers down on the lake, their voices an undercurrent in my dreams.

D is for Drumlin

The word means "littlest ridge," from the Irish Gaelic *droimnín*, and it is what we live on top of, our house settled into a drumlin's northern end. Composed of debris from other places, left behind like geologic midden heaps when the glacier stopped just south of here, then retreated, drumlins look like enormous earthen teardrops. I've read that they usually occur in groups called swarms, though ours is solitary, which makes me wonder if it is really a drumlin at all. They are the perfect landform for someone like me, who has lived too many places and feels forever displaced, pining for some-where else. When I sink full-length into the ground here, it whispers a story of uprootedness, memory, sadness, and—this is mysterious to me—home.

E is for Glacial Erratic

On the crest of our back hill lies a boulder the glacier picked up—perhaps as far away as Canada—then left behind as it melted, the lobe of ice that cov-ered this area like a great white thumb dragged across the map of Wiscon-sin and then slowly retreating. The glacial erratic is a stranger here, like me. Ribbons of quartz and feldspar undulate through the dusky gneiss, like the movement of time itself, preserved there to be touched and pon-dered. Always I wonder if the rock recalls being gouged out, dragged far from home, then left behind by its icy abductor. And always I remember the occasions when I was sitting on the boulder after running and a slender lightning bolt of energy ran up through my body from the stone. Both thrilling and unnerving, it told me in no uncertain terms that the boulder is holy. Sitting on it, that holiness touches me.

F is for Fireflies

Like tiny lamps held by fairies, their luciferin glow dips and bobs over the prairie on July evenings, many more of them here than above fields planted with Roundup Ready corn. Males in the air, females on the ground, they blink on and off in a code it seems I can almost understand, having studied it since I was child, watching them flicker inside a Mason jar with holes punched in the top. The night my father died, a firefly pulsed three times in the house, as if saying "I love you." There is nothing like fireflies' yellow-green light, their bioluminescence. Even their eggs glow in the dark. I was taught to always open my Mason jar in the morning, letting my captives go, that they might illuminate the next night with their sparks of cool lightning.

G is for Great Horned Owl

All night in the middle of winter, the great horned owls call around our hill. Their distinctive *who's-awake-me-too* call drifts through bare branches, soft as smoke, soft as their loose-packed feathers, engineered to move through air with-out making a sound. They are mating, their murmurous calls flung out in lassos of sound that seem to circle our house as we lie awake, eaves-dropping on this avian love song. The owls can hear a mouse moving beneath a foot of snow, and their eyes close from the top down, like humans'. But they are not like us at all. It is our luck to lie here, overhearing the way the male calls out in his low voice and the female answers, *I'm here, I'm here, I'm here.* One March two owlets hatched in an old hawk's nest high in an oak on the back hill. That summer the owner of Blue Moon Commu-nity Farm, our CSA just a few miles away, told us she was losing her chick-ens to great horned owls, which I've heard described as "tigers of the sky."

H is for Shagbark Hickory

Known for their messy, layered bark, shagbark hickories look like ruffians crashing the autumnal feast, their bright yellow leaves a trumpet blast of color. Tom's favorite tree, they are known for their exceptionally hard wood, used to make tool handles, skis (like my forty-year-old pair), and in another era, wagon wheels. Native Americans ground and mashed their sweet nuts to create hickory milk, used in making cakes. Every year we plan to gather the harvest, but are beaten to it by the resident gray squirrels.

I is for Island Lake

A shallow spring-fed lake, up to a dozen feet deep in places, Island Lake sits like a chip of blue opal in a bowl of farm fields. Surrounded by cattail wetlands, it's mostly DNR land, a wild haven (outside hunting season) for cranes, ducks, geese, swans, coots, mergansers, foxes, coyotes, muskrats, deer, kingfishers, cedar waxwings, and the tree swallows that swoop over the water, kissing its surface. On spring nights the lake is alive with spring peepers and chorus frogs, succeeded by bullfrogs as the water warms up. The lake is a dreamy place to float in a canoe on a June afternoon, amid yellow water lilies dotting the water like small suns. I think again, as I always do when on the lake, of how immersion in virgin water as one's first act of allegiance might shape a life. The island, bristling with trees, floats in the center, a green omphalos, a place of refuge, another world. I have still never set foot upon it.

J is for Jack-in-the-Pulpit

Like a little man, the jack (or spadix) stands inside the purple-and-green-striped hoodlike pulpit (or spathe) in the damp shade of the oaks on the north side of the house. The plant's common name, Indian turnip, suggests edibility, though all parts are poisonous. A circle of tiny flowers hides inside the pulpit, cinched like a jeweled belt around the base of the jack. Either all male or all female, the plant can switch genders depending on the food supply, with females being hardier. Because it was one of the first wildflowers I learned, kneeling beside my mother in the woods, it seems magical, the green jack standing there, slightly phallic in his green bower, saying a spring prayer. A pair of trilliums nod nearby, their petals immaculate, pure as white linen.

K is for Killdeer

As long as we have lived here, killdeer have nested at the edge of the bit of meadow that's too steep to plow, their distinctive *kill-jer* alarm slicing the air in plaintive strokes of sound. Their call carries me back to the earliest fields of my life, in Pennsylvania, where I fell in love with them for their broken-wing trick of luring intruders away from their nest, which is the merest indentation, a slight scrape scratched in gravel. I loved matching up the brown-and-white-masked member of the plover family with the painted illustration in the *Golden Guide to Birds*. I love what their call evokes of vulnerability, empathy, and the desire to protect, love the connections they summon between *now* and *then*, *here* and *there*, and *home, home, home*.

L is for Little Brown Bat

They swoop rapidly over the hill in the evening, moving by echolocation so accurate I can feel the slight breeze of their body as they pass inches from my face, squeaking in voices too high-pitched for me to hear. Bats eat half their body weight in insects every night. About two inches long, dressed in brown plush that they keep scrupulously clean, bats like water, which may account for their presence here, near the lake. As a child living in a colonial house with bats in the roof, I feared them. But the bats here fill me with a sense of wonder at how harmoniously they live, with groups of up to a hundred females in nursery colonies, each with one pup. In the winter they hibernate in barns, hollow trees, and caves, clustered together in one warm, breathing patchwork of fur and folded membranous wings. Threatened by white-nose syndrome, which has reached Wisconsin, the entire bat population is at risk. I can't imagine a summer night without these small paparazzi.

M is for Monarda

In midsummer monarda's mop-top flowers explode over the prairie like lavender fireworks, creating a nectar haven for bees, butterflies, moths, and hummingbirds. Also known as bee balm, horse mint, Oswego tea, and bergamot, it fills the air with a minty, sage-like fragrance. It smells like the Earl Grey tea I fell in love with years before I ever saw the charming, disheveled-looking flowers, which remind me of girls in frilly dresses. Like Proust biting into his madeleine, a whiff of monarda carries me back to every soothing cup of Earl Grey. Stopping amid a stand of it on our prairie, wrapped in an invisible cloud of scent, I feel certain—at least for the moment—that all will be well. As perhaps it may, for indigenous people had dozens of uses for this starburst flower, using it for tea and to ease digestive upsets and respiratory troubles. Although monarda is native to the eastern United States, I never encountered it there. So I was surprised to learn that after the colonists threw English tea overboard during the Boston Tea Party, they subsisted on brewed monarda. Imagine—comfort and revolution in a single cup.

N is for Nuthatch

Dapper and meticulous in their gray suits and black caps, nuthatches spend half their lives upside down. Half yogi, half climber, they astonish me as they spiral their way around tree trunks, finding food other birds miss. My *Birds of Wisconsin Field Guide* tells me their name comes from a hoary Middle English nickname, *nuthak*, for the way they wedge seeds into crevices and then hack them open. I watch them stuff seeds under the roof then fly away, reminded that I must create my own field guide for home ground, my observations telling me where—and who—I am now.

O is for Oak Savanna

Before I moved to the Upper Midwest, the word *savanna* summoned Africa, not these open-canopied, widely spaced oaks, a partially restored understory of native grasses and wildflowers dancing beneath them. Only a tiny fraction of Wisconsin's savanna remains, the rest having been destroyed by human incursion. Controlled by fire, savanna must be burned to maintain its balance. Savanna is open yet protected, and parklike in appearance. It exerts a primal pull on our imagination, which always makes me wonder if it is our original landscape, somehow encoded in the genes from the unknown place in Africa where we all began, the gaps in the trees calling us home. At the bottom of the back hill is the Grandmother tree, linchpin of this place. Her thick roots grip the ground like bony gray fingers. I love sitting with my back up against her rough bark, held in tree time, the great trunk's slow music calming my anxious heart. Up above, oriole nests hang like knitted wool bags, the birds streaking back and forth in bursts of black and orange flame. In the Celtic tree alphabet the word for oak is *duir*, which means "door," as well as solidity and protection. The World Tree must be an oak.

P is for Phoebe

Grayish-green, her plumage elegant but muted, a phoebe spends her days in the oak beside the liquid propane tank. Visible from my study window, she darts back and forth from a branch, catching insects midair, a maneuver called "hawking." She does this for hours, my companion as I sit at the desk, engaged in my own, often futile flight after words. I love watching the phoebe alight; she fluffs and spreads her tail open, as if pleased with her catch. Yesterday, during an unseasonable snowstorm, the phoebe flew up and down in front of my window as if she wanted something. She landed on the spiky dried seed heads of purple coneflowers, only to flutter up again in a way that made me feel helpless. Later I heard the radio alert that songbirds were starving in the storm. Oh, little bird with the name I would have given my daughter if I'd had one, please be safe as your song stitches the air with purpose—*phoe-be, phoe-be, phoe-be.*

Q is for Queen Anne's Lace and Queen of the Prairie

Two queens inhabit our property, one a migrant, one native. Queen Anne's lace, or wild carrot, arrived with the colonists. The most common plant in

America, it is considered a weed. But it was a plant of my childhood, familiar from my first bouquets. My mother told me the legend behind it,
explaining that Queen Anne challenged her ladies to make lace as beautiful
as her favorite flower. No one knows who won the contest, but the single
reddish-purple floret in the middle of the plant's flat white crocheted-lace
top remains, the place where Queen Anne pricked her finger. In late summer the flower heads of Queen Anne's lace curl up into baskets like bird's
nests, filled with seeds. I have read that these baskets open and close,
depending on the moisture in the air. Someday I would like to sit in the
meadow all day so I could watch this happen. It would be like watching
them breathe.

The other royalty here, queen of the prairie—also known by the charming name meadowsweet—is the native, its fluffy, lilac-scented plumes of
flowers rising like pink fire or clumps of cotton candy. Fragile looking, it is
in fact rugged and tenacious. Native people used it as a medicine for heart
troubles, as well as a love potion or aphrodisiac, an interesting combination of applications. Spreading by rhizomes, it can be aggressive. Although
queen of the prairie is beautiful, its diaphanous flowers do not possess
much in the way of nectar, so it is not useful for pollinators. But we have
just a few queen of the prairie plants and so treasure them for their loveliness alone. When I walk up the driveway at sunset, their flowers float
above the prairie, ephemeral as clouds, their pale pink smoke lit up by the
deeper magenta of the setting sun. Filmy and insubstantial as they are, they
seem to embody, if ever so briefly, the shapes of dreams the prairie has
about itself.

R is for Red Fox

Foxes have always lived here, with a large den on our neighbor's land
and an auxiliary den where the scrap of meadow bordering our land abuts
farmer John's corn and soybean fields. At first we saw them rarely. One
midsummer day, a vixen crossed my path like a flash of fire, a dead rabbit
in her mouth, her slotted yellow eyes blazing. Another time, a fox popped
up in the tall grass of the meadow as I sat on the back hill. We stared into
one another's eyes for a long moment, me like a woman under a spell in a
fairy tale. The foxes were elusive but always about, one pair streaking up
the hill like russet comets as we skied home across the fields, the precise,
flower-like prints of their feet pressed into nearly straight lines. Then one

year eleven kits were born. They rolled and tumbled before the main den like orange puffballs, and we watched, delighted, as the parents took them out, one by one, to learn how to hunt. Perhaps there were too many for the food supply, for ever since they dispersed at the end of that summer, we've only seen their prints out in the fields, leading to another den down by Island Lake. I miss their catlike ways, their amber eyes, and the sight of them running like creatures from another world.

S is for Sandhill Cranes

If the land here could speak, it would do so in the language of cranes, whose call seems the secret language of this place, their familiar *kar-r-r-o-o-o* filling the air as they mutter back and forth to one another in the cattail marshes around the lake. Primal and almost unearthly, their ululation seems to convey a message about what the earth remembers and what persists, eternal and unchanged. Although some describe their call as grating, I find it both lovely and haunting, a piece of the larger story of wind and water and the mystery of migration echoing in every note. Melancholy and comforting, it is my favorite sound in the world, the audible embodiment of *here*. Like Buddhist monks, the cranes move with unparalleled elegance, each step cadenced. With their gray feathers, sometimes stained muddy brown, their scarlet caps, and their bright red eyes, they are a commanding presence who look, in outline, as if they have just flowed from a monk's sumi brush. Their courtship dance, with its bows, jumps, and leaps, remains the most spectacular ballet I've ever witnessed. One evening last summer Tom and I counted over a hundred cranes gleaning grain in a freshly cut field of winter wheat. We looked at them, then at one another, blessed to have seen such a gathering.

T is for Wild Turkeys

We call the hen turkey who nests near our land every year Clara, and like to imagine she's the same bird, though she's probably not. I love the way she strides up the back trail like a dowager, her step picky, her eyes everywhere, her bluish bald head dipping up and down. Although she is a big bird, she can take off like a whirligig, flying straight up if need be. Though she is not as striking as her male counterpart, whose fantail spreads to impress his harem, her feathers are beautiful. I have a vase full of the stiff, brown-and-white-striped, quill-like primary wing feathers I have picked up over the years, and another of the soft, bronze-and-brown tail feathers.

When her poults are old enough, Clara brings them through the yard, the troop of tiny gray feather dusters on stick-like legs toddling behind her. One year as they were learning to fly, they discovered our Hatteras rope hammock and spent an hour fluttering up and down on it. Later the same summer, as sleek adolescents, they jumped up on the stone bench with carved squirrel legs and preened beneath the shade of the oaks, the embodiment of "a green thought in a green shade." I had never seen anything so peaceful.

U is for Ursa Major and Ursa Minor

Big Bear, Little Bear. How is it you have been there my whole life, walking me slowly home across the northern sky, no matter where I move beneath it? Where would I be without you? How would I ever find my way without the North Star always there, at the tip of Little Bear's tail?

V is for Meadow Vole

The first vole I ever saw was one fleeing the flames as we did a controlled burn of the prairie. My heart ached for the little creature, whose nest must have been in flames. The experience set in motion a sense of conflict I've felt ever since, when we burn, over what survives and what is destroyed in the name of preservation. Tiniest denizens of this hill, mouselike, with soft brown fur, voles maintain a complex system of tunnels and trails among meadows, field, and prairies. Visible in winter as raised, tubular runways through the snow, their trails map a secret world, like the one populated by the Borrowers in books I loved as a child. Their tiny skittering tracks seem a foreign language, one describing a life where they must eat their body weight's worth of vegetarian fodder each day, watch out for hawks, owls, foxes, coyotes, snakes, and the humans who set fires to their grassy worlds so the blackened earth may be spiked with green again.

W is for White-Tailed Deer and Wood Duck

I've mentioned this before, but the moment we saw a deer outlined against the fading light, as we went down the driveway after purchasing our house, is embedded within me, an amulet I turn over from time to time. The deer's presence confirmed an important emotional truth about the place for me. I love it that Tom recognized this, naming Deer Run after the Wild Run Farm of my childhood. Their tails flickering like white handkerchiefs, the deer are elusive as tawny smoke, there and not-there all at once. We often see them in the distance, browsing in the tall grass beside the lake. Just on the other side of the barbed-wire fence separating our land from our farmer-neighbor's lies a deer trail, pressed deep into the grass by heart-shaped hooves, a record of comings and goings I know nothing about. Every now and then we startle a deer on the back trail, always with the indrawn breath that says *Deer, deer, deer!* I know the herd in Wisconsin is too big, that deer lack predators, and that chronic wasting disease is a problem. But deer are my totem animal, my soul creature, my secret self; I cannot be objective about them. In my next life I want to be born with a constellation of white flowers on my back. I want to lie curled in a hollow of sweet prairie grass, scentless and trusting, waiting for my mother to return and claim me.

The other day I looked up and saw a handsome male wood duck sitting on our roof. With his iridescent green head and crest, red eyes, and pink-and-white beak, he looked painted, too beautiful to be real. Wood ducks have always nested on this hill. For many years, they chose a hole in a wild cherry tree visible from the house, until it came down in a wind storm. The following spring, they flew around the spot where the tree had been, their shrill calls filled with grief and confusion as they looked for their former home. Luckily, they found another nest cavity on the back hill, and their young continue their remarkable journey, leaping from the tree not long after birth and following the mother on the long quarter-mile walk down to the lake.

X is for Sphinx Moth

I jumped the first time one of these black-and-white kamikazes with wings buzzed me at dusk, hovering and sipping nectar from a flower, just like a hummingbird. Up and down, back and forth it went, one of the few creatures (along with hummingbirds and bats) that can perform such aerial maneuvers. Bold as a bomber, it zoomed in, unfurling its long proboscis to sip at first one flower, then another. Think of having a tongue like that— the thinnest strip of fruit leather dipped in honey, rolled up like the string of a yo-yo when not in use.

Y is for Yellow Compass Plant

The tallest plant on the prairie, sometimes rising twelve feet high, the compass plant also grows deepest, driving its taproot as far as fifteen feet down.

Its leaves align north and south, and its bright yellow, sunflower-like rayed petals follow the sun, turning like slow wheels. Hence its common name, though it is also called rosinweed and turpentine plant. I love watching the flowers move, marking time like a floral book of hours, and am comforted by their regularity. But I have not summoned the courage to roll the plant's sticky sap into the gum-like ball chewed by Indians and pioneer children. Still, I wonder what it tastes like. Rosin, turpentine, or an intangible mix of sunlight, summer, and time?

Z is for . . .

the zigzag, zaps, and zings of summer lightning, the zed-shaped folds of the aurora opening its luminescent green curtains on a winter night when it's twenty degrees below zero, and the z-z-z-z-z-ing as we sleep—cat on the bed, collies on the floor beside us—the zodiac swirling around us like the wheel of life that is here, now, the only one we are given.

Midsummer Milkweeds

On the table before me this July morning I have a small vase of common milkweed, which blooms now all over the prairie. It seems a shame to pick it because it wilts almost instantly and is, like most things in the wild, best observed in its natural habitat. But I've been noticing its flowers all month as they form in clusters of airy, pinkish-mauve balls, and I wanted to consider them up close, as it is only recently that I happened to notice milkweed has an astonishing scent. When I was walking down our dirt driveway to get the mail, passing the acre or so of restored prairie, where milkweeds bloom in profusion, a wave of sweetness washed over me that I could not at first identify. I wasn't anywhere near the house with its roses and lilacs. Was it one of the invasive Japanese honeysuckles we're always routing out? Sniffing, I followed the scent to where it was strongest, only to discover the delicate blend was coming from the common milkweed, *Asclepia syriaca*. Why hadn't I ever noticed this scent? Turning some olfactory key in memory, it took me back to a moment in childhood I could not pinpoint, though sweat beaded my lip in Wisconsin with the same salty sweetness as it had in Pennsylvania some sixty summers earlier.

Like any northern child in the eastern three-quarters of this country, I grew up with milkweeds, delighting in their downy fluff, come late summer and early fall. Breaking off branches of dried pods, my brother and sister and I ran, releasing sparkling tufts behind us like trails of stars in daylight, their trajectories determined by the wind. You can mark the year's turning by how much down floats through the air, each flat brown seed clinging fast, a tiny gossamer parachute that could land anywhere (and does, if milkweed's proclivity for popping up in my flower beds is any indication). One star and then another. All of a sudden the air is full of them, like the sky on August nights during meteor showers.

In the autumn I helped my mother gather the dried and empty pods that rattled like ghosts, sere and gray, in the fields around our farm. Ever creative, she spray-painted them gold for holiday arrangements, filling my father's woodshop with great bunches of their branches, the shells open like shining containers. Years later I wrote terrible poetry about this, trying to force a metaphor between the milkweeds and my mother's tired body, her ovaries carved out in what now seems a barbaric and primitive attempt to beat back her perhaps hormonally influenced cancer. It took more years before I saw that the milkweeds were milkweeds and my mother herself, and it was better that way. But their stories overlapped in my imagination, illuminating one another in the way I remember her arrangements brightened dark corners of the house, catching the light like gilt icons in ancient cathedrals. If you stared at them long enough, you could begin to see a pattern, like the pictures in clouds, or colored Currier and Ives lithograph prints of natural scenes, where animals hide among bark and branches. In my mind they are still everywhere, dressed in gold paint and shining, even though she isn't anymore.

The clusters of milkweed that stand before me, wilting even more as I write, are so far away from being pods that it is hard to imagine that is what they would have become, left in the field, turning into the green velvet fruit that bursts open come late summer. Cream-colored, pink-tinged, each flower is star-shaped, five downward-facing petals arranged around a five-pointed crown. The *Wildflowers of Wisconsin Field Guide* tells me that milkweed has a unique pollination system. Sacs of pollen snag on insects' legs. Without even knowing it, insects insert the sacs into the slits of other blossoms, this sex-by-accident causing pollination. Lifting the clusters of pink stars gently, I ponder how many in this small bouquet are pollinated and how many are not. Their scent—a mix of tuberose, honeysuckle, and lilac—lingers on my fingertips like faint perfume. I wonder why someone has not thought of marketing it as the attar of fields and prairies, in the same way someone distilled lavender and other fruit and floral notes in a perfume called Innisfree I brought back from Ireland.

Perhaps something as potent yet intangible as the scent of milkweed is not meant to be preserved but to be appreciated on the fly, so much a part of us that it is noticed only after many passings, like my walks up and down this dirt driveway. Authentic knowledge is always local and immediate.

Dipping my nose in the starry cluster, I think about how true this is. Yesterday I saw the first monarch butterfly flitting among the parts of the prairie where the milkweeds are most dense, its black and amber wings glowing like panels from my grandmother's amber slag-glass lamp. Was it just hatched or was it laying eggs, and is there any way to tell the difference? I stared at it, shocked by all I do not know about what happens around me every day. I know monarchs lay their eggs only on milkweed. Their caterpillars ingest the toxic milky sap with no ill effects, becoming unappealing to birds and other insects in the process.

I've looked for oriole nests, their weave held together with material from the plants' stems, hanging high in the back-hill oaks like lumpy gray stockings. I've heard that the Ho-Chunk people who roamed this hill before me filled their bedding with milkweed down—imagine sleeping on a pile of thistledown stars! But beyond that? Sniffing the pink stars, I think about how long it takes to accrue true local knowledge. I could spend the rest of my life on these four acres, layering my knowledge of them over other landscapes I have known well, bits of each one shining through, and still not know them fully. There is some odd part of me that wants to keep it that way. Yesterday, for example, watching that monarch, I could—and should—have gone and looked up something that might have helped me determine for certain whether it had just hatched or was laying its eggs. I thought of my bookcase filled with field guides and also of a book of poems about monarchs by a nature writer I admire, a woman with whom I once took a workshop.

But I didn't go look any of it up, wanting to stay with the purity of direct experience. I remembered a doll mattress that I'd once imagined stuffing with milkweed stars when I was a child and how the fun of that project lay in the imagining and in the sense of possibility that imagining engendered. I thought of how, even when she was dying, my mother delighted in making something new, painting the empty shells, going so far as to touch up spots the spray had missed with a slender brush she swept along the edges of the shells. She was not thinking, as I do, about how they were like boats for the dead on a river of darkness, but of beauty and transformation, an ordinary weed made extraordinary when painted with a layer of shimmering gold, one thing become another.

These flowers, left to dry on the stalk, would have become something else, too. But the life in their pale green nubbly pods, plump with damp silk, has been cut short, made into words instead. I plunge my face into the blossoms one more time, savoring their indefinable fragrance, then carry the stalk to the compost heap, mulch for next year's garden. We have enough milkweed plants to qualify as a monarch way station, identified as such by a blue sign Tom posted down by the road. Thirty years ago, new to Wisconsin, I used to drive through coppery clouds of monarchs on my way to work. It hasn't been that way for a long time now. So I'm almost glad milkweeds are taking over in places on our land, given the crisis the monarchs are in, their population decimated by herbicides that have reduced their food supply. And if I am lucky, a milkweed will again volunteer among my perennials, its taproot almost ineradicable, deep and stubborn and wild.

A Jar of Wisconsin Honey

It was the end of summer, the evening before the first day of school, and I was just getting ready to put henna in my hair when the phone rang. It was our farmer-neighbor, John.

"You folks home this evening?" he asked in the gruff and peremptory way I have learned is not rudeness, but just his style, perhaps leavened by shyness.

"Yes," I said, hesitant, thinking of my henna project and all the other tasks waiting to be done.

"Well," he said. "Do you like honey?"

Do we like honey? Who doesn't like honey? "Yes, we love it," I replied, wondering what he was up to, this rumpled-looking man in his faded overalls and squashed straw hat, who, though in his late seventies, is out in the fields every morning before I am even awake.

"We emptied the hives last week and I've got a jar for you if you'd like it. I can bring it right over."

"Of course, of course," I said, already beginning to strip out of the stained pink cover-up I wear for messy tasks and putting my clothes back on.

I sometimes wonder what John thinks, seeing the hill he used to own as he farms the flat fields that surround it. Does he miss how open it was before he sold off a quartet of four-acre lots? Moving back and forth on his tractor, does he yearn for this place that was his for so long? The most private lot, with only one neighbor up the hill, our property abuts his fields on two sides, with an acre or so of prairie sloping down from oak savanna, a buffer between us and the road. When we first moved here, we'd hear John's cows moving about in the hayfield to the back of our house. He got rid of them years ago because they were no longer profitable. When they were gone, I missed the sound of them cropping grass or huffing soft breaths at night. John lets us run our collies in his fields in fall and winter, and we take his tractor path down to the wilder terrain around Island Lake and the DNR land beyond that. As a result we've gotten to know him. He and Tom sometimes stand talking in that age-old, arms-across-the-chest stance of men who, while conversing about ordinary concerns like the weather, brush up against larger mysteries of life with as much ease as our collies run through the tall grass, their fur damp and hay-scented afterward.

Although we've lived on this hill for twenty years, and John has always been friendly, his warmth has been edged with the reserve I have come to associate with the Midwest. Neither as direct and outspoken as people in my native Northeast, nor as open and spontaneous as the Californians who shaped me as I came of age, people in the Midwest seem to take a long time to get to know you, as if measuring you up. It's only this summer that John's taken to giving us feedbags stuffed with more sweet corn than we can eat, or that his wife has called to offer tomatoes to add to our already overflowing bins. I knew the gift of honey was an important moment. It meant he liked us.

A few minutes later, John roared up in a battered blue pickup with his Australian shepherd, a constant and taciturn companion, sitting beside him. John handed me a quart-sized Kerr canning jar of pale golden honey. Though honeybees will travel up to two miles gathering nectar, he said he thought most of it came from flowers on this hill.

"I reckon it's a mix of clover and dandelion," he said. And then, gesturing to the graceful plumes of goldenrod in luxuriant bloom all over, "It's got none of that goldenrod; that's cooking honey. If it seems like you've seen more bees this summer, they're mine; they're all over this hill." John and Tom entered into a complicated conversation about the extraction and refraction of honey, about which Tom later confessed he'd only understood around a third, as is often the case with John, who tends to presuppose a familiarity with things beyond us.

I held the honey up to the light, turning it, admiring its color. It seemed to almost glow. Wild food, made from the nectar of flowers, it was summer distilled into an elixir. No wonder honey summons such indescribable delight. I tipped the jar upside-down like a summer snow globe, watching paler golden bubbles float up like pearls. I was glad that I'd left the mint I'd considered evicting from the side of the house when I saw how its flowers attracted bees of all varieties. Though I'd almost abandoned my perennials in this summer of killer mosquitoes, I was relieved that many of the flowers that bees love had been hardy enough to survive my inattention: the tousled red or purple heads of bergamot-scented monarda; the beautiful blue-violet spires of Agastache, or anise hyssop; and the native yellow digitalis, or foxglove, where, from my study window, I'd observed bees crawling inside the tubular flowers. To think that I had contributed even in some small way to the jar of liquid gold was thrilling.

I'd noticed John's beehives, south-facing and tucked inside a former pigsty, neat as stacked laboratory drawers, when I drove past his farm and wondered if they were active. But I hadn't considered the logistics, that the bees from those hives were gathering nectar and pollen in my garden. What I was holding in my hands was the quintessence of this particular place and no other—the sweet embodiment of the taste of here. Even the honey from Blue Moon Community Farm, a mere five-mile bike ride away to the north, would not taste the same. That summer we had enlarged our garden, reveling in a culinary intimacy I had not experienced since I was a child on my parents' farm in Pennsylvania—where my mother put up army-sized amounts of food each summer. But the honey felt different, gleaned from a wild, magical, humming world that even so tart an observer as Jonathan Swift once described as "sweetness and light." It's one thing to eat a frittata made with eggs from down the road, stuffed full of potatoes, onions, peppers, and tomatoes just picked in your own garden. It's quite another to dip your teaspoon into the small golden pond of an open jar of honey, the taste of vanished hours alive again, bright days dissolving on your tongue.

Conversations with John can sometimes go and on, soaring along with a purpose we don't quite see, like a hawk scouting fields. But he had something he needed to do that evening and left after chatting. Tom and I went back to our various projects, and the jar of honey got placed on the round oak table in the sunroom. It was not forgotten, just there as life swirled on around it. But each time I passed, I looked at it, marveling at how the sun lit it from within, lambent as an amber mica lamp. Now and then I dipped a spoon in for a taste. It was simultaneously delicate and rich, which seems right for a marriage of clover and dandelion. Something about it reminded me of a bottle of mead a nearby raspberry farmer had given us when we got married.

Standing in a circle of rose petals, we'd taken sips of the mead from small crystal glasses as part of our ceremony. Tom later absconded with the bottle, which he's shown clutching in many of the wedding photographs, a big grin on his face. I loved feeling part of a tradition hundreds of years old. Mead, which is made from honey, was thought to be an aphrodisiac, and the word *honeymoon* may even have come from the passion it was said to elicit. I remember being surprised at how the mead tasted, not cloying at all but sweet, dry, and warming, almost like sherry, a perfect and sensual mingling. I wanted it to last forever, and now Tom has the empty bottle stashed away somewhere, with other saved things that serve no purpose but remembered joy.

If Tom and I had had honeybees of our own, we might have told them about our wedding, as the practice of telling the bees is an old one among beekeepers. In her delightful history of the honeybee, *Sweetness and Light*, Hattie Ellis notes that honeybees were once considered part of the family, so much so that all important events, such as marriages or deaths, had to be reported to them or they might fly away. A practice recorded in England and Ireland since the seventeenth and eighteenth centuries, the custom included, according to Ellis, "tapping the hive with a key, whispering the news to the insects, and leaving an appropriate gift—a piece of wedding cake or funeral biscuits dipped in wine—at the hive's entrance." The custom survives to this day, as I discovered while traveling in Ireland several years ago. During a stay at a bed-and-breakfast on the rugged Beara Peninsula in the southwest, Tom and I commented on how delicious the honey was. Our hostess told us it was from her own hives, then explained how the bees knew of all important happenings in the family. "It's bad luck not to tell them," she said. "We don't want them leaving now, do we?" As she spoke, I thought of all I might tell bees if I had them—that my mother had died when I was young, that my first marriage had imploded, that I'd birthed two books instead of children, that I was traveling Ireland with Tom, second husband and the love of my life.

⌣

A week later the jar of honey was still on the table in the sunroom. Tom likes to eat breakfast out there, and knowing how much he likes honey, preferring it to jam on his toast, I'd warned him off.

"Don't eat all the honey," I said, reminding him that I wanted some too, though I am more moderate in my consumption. Because the honey had been in full view, it became an impromptu late-summer centerpiece, the embodiment of plenty and a reminder that even in this era of environmental degradation and destruction some things continue, despite their ever more fragile balance. A tangible symbol of what richness we may soon miss, it's made me think a lot about this substance—what the ancients must have had in mind when they spoke of the nectar of the gods—as well as about these beautiful, hardworking, and endangered makers. It's taken me back to my first taste of honey, when my mother sprinkled crushed aspirin in a teaspoonful dipped from her faceted crystal honey pot and spooned it between my fevered lips. This was in the 1950s, before we knew aspirin was dangerous for children, but my mother was on the right track with the honey, as my grandmother was when she gave us honey and lemon for sore throats, for honey has been used medicinally for thousands of years.

When I had the flu in college, a Vermont boyfriend dosed me with a potent mix of honey, blackberry brandy, and bourbon. He piled me beneath a red-and-black-striped Hudson's Bay blanket in his dorm room to drunkenly sweat it out. While the snow blew hard against the window, I read Sylvia Plath's startling bee poems in the just-released *Ariel*. In my honey-and-alcohol-infused state, they thrilled me with their sharp, stinging language, even as they frightened me with their ferocity and hallucinatory power. It wasn't until years later that I learned Plath had planned to end the book with "Wintering," a poem that concludes on a note of hope: "The bees are wintering. They taste the spring." It was her husband, Ted Hughes, who selected the icier piece, "Words," where "from the bottom of the pool, fixed stars / Govern a life."

Some years later, during my homemade granola and yogurt phase in California, I made honey my exclusive sweetener, consuming it with so many gallons of Earl Grey tea that the two flavors became linked, and I had to give them up for a while, overcome by the intensity of the combination. As a runner, I sometimes dosed myself with a spoonful of honey after reading in *The Cook's Companion* that its simple sugars are absorbed easily into the body, providing an almost "instant 'lift' with no strain on the digestive system." On my lunch breaks from the small university bookstore where I worked during those years, I sat on a bench in the Rancho Santa Ana Botanic Gardens, entranced as wild bees darted in and out of the famous Bee Tree, glittering like tiny tigers in the brilliant desert light.

It was in California too, that I once got out of the car in the middle of the Central Valley, climbed a fence, and walked down a green alley alive with flickering white blossoms and the sound of bees, busy pollinating the almond groves around me. Though I had a number of hours of driving ahead, I lay down and listened, thinking of Yeats's "bee-loud glade." I could have stayed a lifetime in that dappled light, so still that bees now and again landed on me for a moment before taking off again, in search of something sweeter.

∽

When I moved to rural Wisconsin after many years in town, I thought I might keep bees. If Sylvia Plath could do it, so could I. I was so enthralled with the idea that I took a workshop, "Backyard Beekeeping Basics," taught by Sarah Shatz and Claire Strader at Madison's iconic Willy Street Co-op. There I learned about honeybee history and was surprised to discover that bees are not native to North America but originated in Asia, slowly moving into Europe, where they have been valued for millennia. Beekeeping is thought to have originated with the Egyptians. Bees were worshipped in many cultures, including that of the Greeks, who called their priestesses *Melissae* or "bees." Bees were brought to North America by colonists, to whom they were valuable for both honey and wax. How were they carried, I wonder, on those long ocean voyages, so far away from flowers? But bees were so successful in the colonies that escapees moved west ahead of settlers, coming to be known as "white man's fly" by Native Americans.

We learned in the workshop that honeybees live in an intricate social hierarchy made up of castes. There are the queens, one per hive, whose primary job is to lay eggs and produce a pheromone-like substance, with which they communicate with other bees and keep the hive working. The male drones, which make up about 5 percent of the hive, exist only for the purposes of reproduction. If drones are still alive at the end of the summer they are driven off to die—a horrible fate. Finally, there are the admirable female worker bees, some 90 to 95 percent of the hive's population, who do all the labor. They clean the hive, secrete wax and royal jelly (the queen's only food), protect and cool the hive, care for the queen, and forage, filling their pantaloon-like pollen sacs with the magical dust from which honey is made.

The workshop also taught me how complicated beekeeping really is, with its removeable-frame hives (invented in the mid-nineteenth century to extract honey without killing the bees, replacing traditional conical straw skeps), which must be constantly monitored and maintained. I took detailed notes about starter packages of bees (which at the time all came from California in two-pound boxes), frames and frame spacers, queen excluders, bottom boards, propolis, smokers, bee brushes, and capping scratchers, until my head was spinning. Overwhelmed with information before we even got to the process of extraction—a sweet, sticky, and time-consuming process accomplished frame by honey-packed frame in a metal centrifuge—I was at the same time moved by how much work goes into caring for these beautiful and industrious insects. I felt awed and humbled by their nonhuman intelligence and their ability to work together for the collective good of the hive.

I left the workshop still yearning to have my own bees. But like so many things one daydreams about—raising goats, say, or having my own chickens, like my mother's bustling flock of Rhode Island Reds—I set the idea aside for the time being. It seemed easier to imagine than enact, given that I had a demanding job as a professor and writer, a husband, a step-daughter, extended family, numerous pets, a house, and a garden all making claims on my time and energy. While backyard beekeeping is a popular hobby, it's one that comes with a lot of responsibility, each bee a tiny soul deserving attention and protection. I also felt daunted by the threat of the bee mite (though there are organic methods to combat this infestation) and colony collapse disorder, not to mention the tragedy of a hive that fails to winter over. If I get upset over accidentally washing a spider down the drain, how would I handle the loss of an entire hive or multiple hives?

On the other hand, if I raised bees, I'd be contributing in some small way to the preservation of these hard-working and necessary creatures that play such a crucial role in our ecosystem, pollinating over a third of our fruits and vegetables. The USDA estimates that "one in three mouthfuls of food we eat directly or indirectly benefits from honeybee pollination," including "apples, oranges, strawberries, tomatoes, blueberries, and carrots." Colony die-off also threatens crops like cotton, coffee, soybeans, almonds, and alfalfa. Every beehive truly makes a difference. I thought of John's bees skimming in an invisible tracery of flight over and around our hill, their small furry bodies shuttling faithfully back and forth between the hive and the flowers, doing what they know to do. I felt saddened by what they are up against, given herbicides (which John himself uses more and more of every year on his corn and soybeans), habitat loss, parasites, and loss of biodiversity. As a resident on this hill, I ought to do my part, however small it might be.

So much of life is about having to make choices. I keep the idea of having my own hives humming in the back of my mind, as a possibility for retirement. I read books about beekeeping and bees, maintain a thick file of articles on the subject, plant flowers that I know bees love, and hope that these sweet creatures will still be here when I have time to attend to them in the way they deserve. I've joined the Bee Conservancy, and I give gifts of beeswax candles. *Someday*, I think, imagining myself as an apprentice beekeeper, clad in white garb like a contemporary acolyte in the cult of the ancient bee goddess, but with more urgent purpose. *Someday.* Then I dip a spoon into John's honey, fortifying myself for the day ahead, swallowing it down the way I take fish oil or vitamin C, but with so much more pleasure, the taste of summer alive in my mouth as fall makes its slow arrival.

Autumn Equinox,
with Asters

Then all at once, summer collapsed into fall.
—attributed to Oscar Wilde

It's the first day of fall, and the asters fill half our small prairie, the smudges of purple an intimation of the season arriving, their dark fire burning through the goldenrods' fading yellow flame. New England asters, New York asters, Michaelmas daisies, and aromatic asters whose flowers tolerate frost, sometimes lasting into November. All of them native to North America, no matter how you name them. And all of them shining, their delicate amethyst rays fringing sunshine-yellow hearts, more this year than I can ever remember, the succession of flowers on the prairie a psalm I am still learning, the seeds Tom planted just this week perhaps years away from bloom.

When I die, I want to come back and lie on the ground like those seeds, waiting, looking up through fronds of big bluestem and Indian grass at the sun and rain. And at the stars, for which these flowers the color of purple grapes are named, the word *aster* having come down to us through Greek, but so familiar we think of it as our own. As did my ex-husband's grandmother, who loved them because her name, Astrid, means "star" in Danish. Astrid, who told me stories of riding her bicycle for miles in southern Denmark, seeking out the best berries, so intent that evening came on before she was ready, the sky salted with stars, the sounds of small animals rustling around her in the grass. When she looked up at night, a girl on an island she'd later leave forever, did she see herself reflected? Do asters grow in Denmark, or did she learn to love them here? When she emigrated to northern Minnesota, were the stars above the ones she knew from home, their familiar patterns pricked out in the bitter winter dark?

I was the one who found Astrid the morning after she fell, lying for hours on her cold bathroom floor, no stars to light the darkness that seemed like it would never end. "I thought it was an angel come to take me," she said. "Then I saw that waterfall of hair come down and I knew it was you." I haven't had long hair in over forty years. And Astrid's been gone even longer, having passed after I moved away from California, still ill myself, with nothing I could do but burn a purple candle for her spirit. It was autumn then too, asters blooming in my Oregon yard, their color burning through the misty light like amethyst crystals in geodes.

I remember how small Astrid was in my arms, my hair falling around us both like a shawl in which I wished I could enfold her, gently, the way I folded laundry last night on her ironing board. Its 1940s metal legs creak, and it's forever hard to open, but it's so much a part of my life I had to ask my grown stepdaughter to give it back, recalling Astrid's meticulous stitches and perfect, pressed-open seams, her Rowenta iron hissing on its stand. The ironing pad still smells of real starch and hot cotton, history condensed there, immaculate with loss.

I don't know why I'm thinking these things this morning, trying to name what I love, walking early on the prairie among the asters' sharp autumn scent that does not make me sad but beholden, the last faint stars vanishing into lavender sky above, the workday pressing in. But I do know this. We are all small animals. We are all purple stars, light fallen from sky to ground and blooming, rooted against great odds. Astrid had these flowers shaped like stars. And I do too, their lion faces lifted to the light, even as the days grow shorter around this little square of prairie that is forever mortal, forever threatened by invasive weeds, though asters will always belong here. This morning the only prayer I know is these asters themselves, standing here before me. Their yellow hearts. Their purple solace. I bend my face to theirs.

Goldengrove Unleaving

This earth we are riding keeps trying to tell us something with its continuous scripture of leaves.

—William Stafford, *Scripture of Leaves*

It's late October and while I've had my head down, too busy with the work of the world, autumn has swept through, a hussy trailing her brilliant skirts. I caught the beginning of the season, that pause like a held breath when we linger on the threshold of true fall, the days bright and sunny, the nights clear and crisp, every hillside shining as the trees begin their slow undressing, revealing a little more each day. Then, when I wasn't looking, autumn had its way with us, its bronze and copper and gold splashed across the hillsides like light spilled from a Renaissance paint box. Now it's almost gone. When I gaze out from the top of the hill where I live, over the surrounding farmland, the trees are stripped nearly to the bone, have become the charcoal scribbles they are in the winter, as if drawn with a pencil and then smudged a little, as I can recall my mother doing in her sketchbook when I was a child.

Here on the top of the hill, where frost comes last, many of the oak leaves are still in place. Backlit by morning sun, they are magnificent and glow as if from within, russet as the fur of the foxes that have their den here, dark amber as buckwheat honey, burnt orange as the rakish eyebrows on my tricolored collies' faces. They are brilliant. But my inner compass points north, and no matter how far I travel, no matter what other landscapes I live in, nothing will ever burn as bright for me as a New England autumn, the scarlet leaves of sugar maples more brilliant than anything else the nation can offer. "This is nothing," I tell Tom every year, my soul imprinted with colors that send me running to the thesaurus, looking for words to describe how brilliant things can be when they are dying. He understands, having lived in New England himself for a few years. "I haven't seen anything like it since," he said once, adding that the only thing he could imagine comparing it to at the time was a brightly colored bowl filled with Trix, the cereal he'd eaten in childhood.

The oaks here offer me much comfort. But as always in autumn, part of my heart yearns for another landscape, comparing the one I now inhabit to memories of others. I remember making leaf houses with my brother and sister at Wild Run Farm, arranging lines of leaves in a three-dimensional blueprint of rooms we could walk through, fascinated even as children by the architecture of domestic spaces. The enormous sugar maple dominated our backyard, each scarlet leaf more beautiful than the next, each one bigger than my hands. We ironed leaves between sheets of wax paper, wanting to preserve their beauty, making them into placemats for the kitchen table or hanging them in the windows, where they glowed, temporary stained glass that over time dried up and lost its color. I raked leaves with my parents when I was still small enough that wielding a full size rake was difficult. Once the leaves were mounded into piles, their scent crushed open around us, my father buried us, raking them over us until we felt invisible, hidden deep inside our rustling caves. And of course there was the scent of leaf smoke, blue against deeper blue in the autumn twilight, reducing the fragile pyres of oak and birch and maple to feathers of white ash, where, if you looked carefully, you could see the skeletal outline of a leaf tremble for a moment, like a ghost of itself, before it broke apart into dust.

Years later I sat at a window in Vermont with my college roommate, Connie, watching as sunset illuminated the mountains that surrounded us in every direction. We had both just left home, and the autumn colors, our sitting there together drinking them in, and the sense of time passing moved me so much I felt as if I was the first one who had ever experienced it. I felt the need to make some statement about the season. I wrote out a line about the trees with an italic pen—"All we have are these trees, with their ever-changing leaves"—and hung it on the door to our room, shy but hoping to attract attention, labeling it with my initials. I was thrilled when an upperclassman, on his way to visit his girlfriend down the hall, noticed it and commented favorably, saying, "Ah, it seems we have a poet in our midst."

I still didn't feel as cool as Hannah, a Quaker girl from New Hampshire, in the room next door, who seemed to possess an elemental connection to the season. Each day she dragged enormous plastic bags full of leaves mixed with water into our common bathroom and left them in the tub, marinating the brew into some sort of natural dye with which to color the hanks of wool she knitted into mittens during class. I wanted to be as composed and self-possessed as she seemed, but had to content myself with reading Keats's "To Autumn" over and over until I'd memorized it, or reciting Hopkins's "Margaret, are you grieving / Over Goldengrove unleaving?" in rounds with Connie. We both wanted to be poets and loved Hopkins's invented words. "Wanwood," "leafmeal," "ghost guéssed," we'd chant to one another as we walked to the dining hall in the indigo dusk, dreaming of writing something that descriptive, that musical, that over the top. Striding along with Connie, I fancied that no one had ever felt the season as intensely as we did, no autumn ever as brilliant as those of late adolescence, when the world seems somehow to be ending and beginning at the same time.

After college, when I moved to California, I missed northeastern autumns with a physical ache. The great, shaggy bowl-shape of the coastal oak trees and their inland cousins, the live oaks, was familiar, but they were also disconcerting and evergreen, holding on to their small, shiny, holly-like leaves all year. I scoffed at them at first, although I grew to love them for their gritty ability to endure the harsh Mediterranean climate. I ached for the palette of changing colors I'd grown up with, not quite sure how to orient myself or prepare for winter without them.

The first few years in California, autumn was so painful for me that David took me on an annual October pilgrimage to the mile-high hamlet of Oak Glen, located in Yucaipa, in the San Bernardino Mountains. Despite its name, Oak Glen was famous for its apple orchards and scenery that looked a little like New England, if you ignored the fact that the surrounding mountains were seven or eight thousand feet high. The apple trees erupted in bursts of sudden gold, the "flame / of each one igniting like a match / struck upon memory or dream," as I wrote in a poem from that time. The apples were good, though I looked in vain for names I knew from the Northeast—pippin, russet, and my favorite, Northern Spy. I was touched by the tenderness of David's gesture. But fall in Oak Glen wasn't what I ached for.

When David and I later made our home alongside the Marys River in western Oregon, he counted eighty oaks on the property, most of them around the house. Surveying the grassy sward, spread like mossy velvet beneath the moss-draped trees—which I later realized was oak savanna—visitors often remarked that our place looked like a park. It was beautiful, and the leaves were brighter than in California, although they tended toward yellow, a more subdued array than New England's cochineal, marigold, and vermilion. Raking them was an arduous task; our hands blistered before we were through. One year we fell behind and failed to finish raking before the autumn rain began. Unable to burn our enormous smoldering piles in the insistent silver drizzle, we committed an unforgivable and ecologically irresponsible act, raking great swaths of them into the river and letting it wash them away. Where did it take them, I wondered, remembering the girl in college brewing her mysterious leafy dye, imagining their colors washing down the Marys River into the Willamette, then the Columbia, and then into the cold, green Pacific.

Years after that, when we were living in a charming but rundown rental house in a leafy neighborhood next to Lake Mendota in Madison, raking became manageable again, though country life had left me unprepared for the peculiar process of hauling the leaves to the edge of the street, where they lay in glowing drifts, waiting to be vacuumed up by city vehicles and taken who knew where. When David and I split up, I remained in the house. Cleaning leaves out of the gutters with a garden trowel by myself or raking them to the curb alone after divorcing was at first an exquisitely painful process. But it was one that also gave me strength. The familiar heft of the rake in my hand was soothing, and each cleared segment of the yard felt like a new room I could step into, one of my own where, while things might look the same, everything had changed.

Walking in the neighborhood, I sometimes encountered the delicate black imprint of a leaf, its skeleton atomized on the street, like a temporary fossil that would, like my sorrow over the end of my marriage, take several years to wash away. Gazing down at the imprints, I remembered discovering these afterimages for the first time the winter my mother died. Even as a grieving child, I'd felt riven by the spirit-prints of leaves etched on the sidewalks, wondering if she too had left her shape behind somewhere. Rediscovering them in my adult life, I possessed perspective. *If you lived through your mother dying, you can survive this*, I told myself. When my friend Holly sent me a poem that described the process of being "comforted and shaken by change," I adopted the line as my motto, grateful that I could, at least in part, hitch myself to the eternal wheel of the seasons.

Oak savanna wraps the hill where I live now like a leafy stole. Even though it's overgrown in places, it retains the character of that particular ecosystem, which combines the spaciousness of grasslands with the sense of protection afforded by the red and white oaks. I sometimes still feel exposed in the spare topography of the Upper Midwest. But here on the hill I am shielded, protected by the oaks, even after the winter winds shake down their last leaves, crumpled by then into papery fists that scud across the crust of snow like miniature coracles. Here too raking the leaves is a monumental task. Tom and I kept up well at first, raking pile after pile, then burning them, batch by fragrant batch, in the rusty burn barrel or on a patch of weathered grass. Then one year, when I'd broken my back and wasn't able to help, Tom got behind and resorted to raking the leaves into huge piles at the edge of the woods. In just a couple seasons, those piles became the best compost we've ever had, rich, black, filled with nutrients. We've been making leaf compost ever since. I learned too that raking them over my flowerbeds offered protection to the plants and overwintering insects. We stopped raking the entire lawn, realizing it was better to let leaves lie.

By the time I go out to rake each fall, late in the season, most of the leaves are down. The motion, like sweeping or dancing, but with more muscle, calms me with its regularity, like breathing, like waves rising and falling. I love the *skrish, skrish, skrish* of the rake's tines as they scrape through the cool, still-green grass and the inimitable scent that rises, somehow conveying life and death in one inhalation. I delight in finding woolly bears, caterpillars of the Isabella moth, their bands of orange and black an accurate predictor of the winter ahead, at least according to *The Old Farmer's Almanac*. I am always careful to move these late hatchlings to a safe place under the leaves, where they will hibernate, one of the few caterpillars in the world to do so, their furry coats a necessity. Canada geese call, another part of the fall ritual, reminding me of how my father, who loved them, would pause in his raking and watch them, saying "You know they mate for life"—his thoughts, I knew instinctively, always of my mother. Schools of blackbirds twist and turn in the sky, moving in perfect unison like schools of fish, skeining and unskeining. Now and then they land, settling into trees like lengths of black lace tossed here and there, the air itself vibrating, alive with the twitter of their many voices.

I rake and rake, growing warm enough that I need to tie my faded purple Squaw Valley sweatshirt around my waist. The fallen leaves crackle and scritch, brittle, folded in on themselves like so many fortune cookies. Those left on the trees blaze, the color of my mother's copper cooking pans from France. Remembering what I was taught by my scientist father, I think about how it is only now, when chlorophyll cuts out and trees grow a separation layer at the base of each leaf, that we see the yellows, oranges, and reds, decay-resistant carotenoids and anthocyanins. Like a hidden story, the colors have always been there, present but obscured by summer, which lingers longest in the green veins of the occasional leaf the way the soul must linger in the body.

When I am finished raking I lie down in the shifting, whispering pile, sometimes with Tom, sometimes alone. I inhale the scent I forget every year until it assails me again, now, in this season when twilight is one shade deeper than blue, when the leaves crackle, a husk mattress beneath me, when everything rustles then falls still. A single black field cricket chirps near the stone wall, its bright note faint and elegiac, and I find myself hoping it gets into the house so it can survive the winter and gift us with the luck crickets are said to bring. I lie back in my raft of leaves, wondering if "leaf-bed," might pass Hopkins's muster, and stare up at the few leaves shining above me. I feel completely at home for a moment, all my years of wandering having brought me to this. Perhaps, like the leaves with their layers of color, we are all more brilliant inside than we imagine. Perhaps each of us burns within, our soul glowing and burnished as old gold shining just beneath the green.

Wild Swans

The tundra swans arrived the day before Thanksgiving, descending like a band of luminous angels to tiny Island Lake, its cattail marshes rattling with the first chill of winter in Wisconsin. Navigating by the stars and their memory of earth's moonlit landscape, they came, traveling from their summer breeding grounds in shallow pools, lakes, and rivers in the Arctic toward their winter residence in Chesapeake Bay and the marshes of Virginia and North Carolina. White as alabaster, warmed by swansdown the color of snow that has not yet fallen, the great birds swept in, accompanied by their pearl-and-silver-plumaged young, who were making the journey for the first time. Resonant with the mystery of the world's great migrations, they arrived, and because they seemed to appear out of nowhere, it was hard not to see them as the messengers that angels are said to be—saints, perhaps, or the spirits of ancestors—descending through layers of black toward their own faint reflections, the lake's surface glinting, dark as tarnished mirror. It was the time of year when the veils between worlds are said to be thinnest, when one walks about feeling spiritually porous. What could we learn from this unexpected visitation?

Not that we saw them arrive, mind you. A quarter mile away, nestled under the quilts in the north-facing bedroom of our house on the hill, our daytime selves suspended in a starry net of dreams, we did not witness the splash and din of their arrival. We did not (at least at first) hear their rich bugling cry—*whoo-hoo, whoo-hoo, whoo-hoo*—that is neither honk nor coo but something wilder and stranger. We did not see them set their wings, stretched as wide as six feet, for landing, gliding in over the black water. We did not even know they were present, settled in as if they had always been there, until the next morning when, out in the fields with the dogs,

Tom saw them, drifting like dreams on the dark blue water at the farthest side of the lake. "What are those big white birds?" he told me he wondered, unable to believe his eyes, at first mistaking them for the snow geese that also visit these waters, before it occurred to him that they might be swans.

A trudge back up the hill for binoculars confirmed his intuition. They were swans, real as the shape of my own fingers, adjusting the binoculars that I might see the birds more clearly after Tom pulled me, half awake, down the hill, under the barbed-wire fence, and across the fields stippled with fallen cornstalks, broken cobs glowing here and there like dull brass in an otherwise bare landscape. "There are swans on the lake," he said, dragging me along. "Hurry! There are swans!"

And there they were, the distinctive black beak and the small yellow spot at the base of the upper mandible, like a decorative bead of yellow jasper or a tear made from sunlight, identifying them as native tundra swans, not the mute swans I'd glimpsed now and then at a park or zoo while growing up in the Northeast. Necks held straight up, the swans drifted and preened and fed on wild celery and arrowhead tubers, perhaps recalling the manna grass and marine eelgrass of summer. Tundra swans, which used to be called whistling swans for the sounds their wings make in flight, often travel in groups of several hundred. According to my worn Audubon guide, they present a spectacular sight "when they make mass landings in places like the Niagara River. Unfortunately, they are sometimes swept over the falls to their death." Our group was small, about two dozen, and given the number of smoky gray young, seemed to be composed of several family groups traveling together. Like adolescents not quite ready to leave home, cygnets remain with the parent flock for at least a year, learning the route and where to feed and rest.

Drifting like a flotilla of small boats—did the sight of swans inspire the first sails?—the great white birds seemed a miracle we'd stumbled on by accident. It had been a difficult season. My sister's husband had been diagnosed with cancer. My writing mentor and dearest friend was experiencing severe pain and the ravages of age. I was feeling more worn down than usual by my work teaching young writers and not thankful enough for a life that is, in many ways, blessed and abundant. Life is always harder than we think it should be. But it is ours, isn't it? And here were these magnificent birds, sailing along on our lake, going about their business and filling me with an awe that knocked me sideways and took me outside my small human concerns. Bound by cycles of seasonal change and patterns of birth and renewal, the sight of the swans comforted me on some essential level, offering what I can only describe as the solace of wild things. If they could manage to do something this enormous, guided by star patterns and earth's magnetic fields, I could navigate my life, couldn't I?

Gazing at the swans, I thought about something Rachel Carson said in her acceptance speech for the John Burroughs Medal: "If we have ever regarded our interest in natural history as an escape from the realities of our modern world, let us now reverse that attitude. For the mysteries of living things . . . are among the great realities." Migration is surely one of them. Looking at the swans put my own life in perspective, allowing me to see it as the speck it is, compared to this greater shimmering whole I was privileged to witness.

As we watched the flock, a cob and pen set forth, moving from one floating sedge island to another, their three cygnets strung between them like a garland. They paddled and drifted, then paddled and drifted again, seeming to move effortlessly through the still landscape, their reflections following them through the water. I thought about what it must be like to live this way, stopping partway through a journey of over 3,600 miles to rest for a day or two until the wind changes and something—instinct, perhaps, that thread of innate, blue *knowing*, or simply the urge of a winged creature to be in the air again—pulls them aloft, sometimes to heights of six to eight thousand feet, and onward. I imagined them spiraling back up into the darkness in a whirlwind of feathers, like some heavenly host, a feather or two dropping behind them like white leaves. I could see how, as I'd read, they might spook a driver whose path they happened to cross.

Studying the swans as they drifted on the lake like music made visible, I understood why they have engaged my imagination. Swans often appear in stories having to do with transformation, as if something about their beauty and elegance suggests a hidden life we all contain. I remembered how, as a child who never felt like she fit in anywhere, I identified with "The Ugly Duckling," a story that seemed to offer the hope that, though shy and awkward, I too might possess some secret interior beauty, not unlike the Inner Light my Quaker-educated mother spoke about. At night I read from my mother's many books of fairy tales, entranced by images of swan maidens and swanskins and the seven brothers who were turned into swans, saved only by their industrious sister who wove them flax shirts that made them boys again. When I was seven or eight, I fell in love with Tchaikovsky's

Swan Lake, which I discovered while working my way through my parents' leatherette-bound edition of the *Standard Treasury of the World's Great Music*. I'd drop the diamond needle on my father's RCA Victrola, listening past the initial hiss and scratch for the music that summoned me to be a swan maiden, dancing on an icy lake. When I fell ill at my grandmother's big house in Philadelphia, I loved how she tucked me up in her own bed, the swan lamp on the bedside table left on all night, as if it were flying beside me, keeping watch.

Oddly, given the place they occupied in my private mythology, I could hardly remember having seen a swan in the wild. Once, just months before my mother died, we kids were taken to a lake somewhere in southern Westchester County, where we ate ice cream and watched mute swans sailing across the sunlit water, their necks tall and proud as the figureheads that boatbuilders carved for good luck. My father took us there again that winter to go ice-skating, and I skimmed over the frozen surface, numb with loss, wondering if the swans we'd watched were trapped somewhere under the ice. Later, when he remarried too quickly, I remembered reading the "The Children of Lir" in my mother's book of Irish fairy tales. In that story a wicked stepmother turns her children into swans and sends them away for nine hundred years. Would something like that happen to me, I wondered, or would I just have to keep washing the kitchen floor ten times until I got it right?

It was only as an adult, when I traveled in England and Ireland, that I saw swans as it seemed to me they were meant to be seen. I spent an hour one September afternoon sitting beside the lake near Ann Boleyn's childhood home, Hever Castle, near Edenbridge in Kent, watching swans skim across the water. They seemed infinitely sad and stately when juxtaposed against her unhappy story. In Ireland I saw a pair of swans on a river in Kildare, not long after praying at Saint Brigid's Well for healing. They seemed to mean something numinous, though I didn't know then how prominent a role swans play in Celtic legends. According to James MacKillop in Oxford's *Dictionary of Celtic Mythology*, they are often depicted as "the epitome of purity, beauty, and potential good luck," as well as symbols of "communication between the Otherworld and the world of mortals."

But as Tom and I watched the swans on our lake, I was absorbed only by the immediacy of their presence, not what they might represent in my imagination. All I could do was stand with my back against one of the oaks that fringe the water, drinking in the sight, thinking again of what my father had told me—that not only geese but swans mate for life. If one bird dies, he'd said, the survivor often will not mate again. Following my mother's too-early death, he'd remarried not just once but twice, each time with disastrous results. Late in his own life he admitted that in each case he'd been trying to replace her, telling me my mother was the love of his life. If only he had behaved more like the swans he admired. It might have saved everyone in our family a lot of pain.

Tom took photographs, including one of the largest swans (a cob?) standing high on its black-stockinged feet, neck curved, chest out like a schoolyard bully, flapping its enormous wings. Looking on, I thought of how fierce swans are said to be, attacking intruders and defending their mossy mounded nests. Later that afternoon, as our collies loped along-side the Yahara River a few miles away, we looked up and saw a small flock of a dozen swans, flying in the direction of Island Lake. Were they our swans, or part of another group? We could not know, of course, though we liked to think they were the ones we'd seen that morning, headed back to their temporary home.

Recalling Yeats's swans that "suddenly mount / and scatter wheeling in great broken rings / upon their clamorous wings" in "The Wild Swans of Coole," I listened for the whistle of their wings over the water but could not hear it. There was nothing but the sound of the river running beside me and the sight of the swans themselves, burnished by the light, merging with the clouds they so resembled. The day after Thanksgiving the wind shifted and the swans were gone, vanished as mysteriously as they had come. Without them scattered across its surface, like cotton ball clouds fallen from a child's painting or the white water lilies that bloom there in summer, the lake looked empty, forsaken, waiting.

❧

The next time we walk outside at night I will ask Tom, who knows the stars better than I do, to point out Cygnus, the stellar swan, its wings out-stretched above us, sailing down the Milky Way, the River of Heaven. Some say Cygnus represents Orpheus, who was changed into a swan at his death and placed near his magic harp—the constellation Lyra—in the sky. But as we look up, our faces faintly illumined as he traces the celestial bird's outline, I'll think of the tundra swans. I'll think of how they sojourned for a brief while beside us, delighting us with their purity, elegance, and mystery. A part of me will want to know what the swans' appearance meant, pressing it for some sort of message. But in the end, seeing them will have been enough, and I will be thankful for that. One should not, after all, question the holy too closely, though it is good and right and proper to recognize it as what it is. Still, I'll wonder where the swans are now, hoping they are in a marsh or coastal lowland, and that we'll see them again on their way back to the Arctic in the spring, this small body of water in Wisconsin encoded in their memory now, the way they are in ours. I'll think of them all winter, they who the Greeks made a symbol of their Muses, they whose name comes from the meaning of the word *song*.

Elegy in December

In the midst of winter, I found there was, within me, an
invincible summer.

—Albert Camus, "Return to Tipasa," *Personal Writings*

The first day of December and I wake to snow, little bits of it flicking down, so light it's blown every which way, swirling in from all directions. Then it gets heavier and more deliberate, each of the thousands of leaves we haven't had time to rake dusted with it, like the confectioner's sugar my mother used to sift through a doily over a pan of brownies, delighting us with the lacy pattern. *It's just a flurry*, I tell myself as I make tea, worrying about my long commute to work over Wisconsin country roads. I am never ready for winter, never ready for this time of year when my mother leaves again, getting into my father's little red Austin 850 before Thanksgiving for the long drive from New York State to the Cleveland Clinic, where she will begin a clinical trial in immunotherapy, a primitive precursor to chemo that will not save her. "Did it ever occur to you that maybe she hoped it would work too?" my father said once, when I asked in anger how he could have taken her so far away from us when she was dying.

But now I wonder most how she must have felt leaving us. "I'll be home for Thanksgiving," she said as she hugged us kids to her, ran her hands down the length of my braids she'd woven that morning. And when she wasn't, they promised Christmas, the napkins I was embroidering for her present—an "M" for "Mommy" stitched on each one in blue floss—stabbed with fear and hope. She died a little after midnight on December 16, 1962. Which is why I can't ever enter this month without feeling as if I walk down chill halls, alone with my brother and sister, haunted by the way she looked back at us as she got into the car with my father, our family so soon to be broken by her death. Every death since echoes hers, every move, loss sculpted into my being, ice that will never melt.

December, December, and the snow comes down. Two friends have lost their fathers in one week, and driving to work, my mind skittering like a trapped bird over what to do in class, I'm suddenly in tears over Beethoven's First Symphony in C major on National Public Radio, remembering how much my own father loved it. He'd sit in the wing chair by the fireplace in the colonial house where I grew up, a wall of books behind him, listening to Beethoven and conducting. My generous, colorful, improvident father, with his books and his pipe smoke, his shiny black hair and beautiful storytelling voice. Everyone adored my father, a man my stepbrother once told me he thought was the kindest person he'd ever met. A man who seemed larger than life, always the center of every party. No one saw his sadness—the impoverished Depression-era childhood, his family so poor they shivered in a tent; the blood and gunpowder of Omaha Beach; his inability to save my golden mother and how he never really recovered from her loss. My beloved, unreliable father, inadequately mourned because his death summoned hers. My father, dust on Hermit's Peak, the New Mexico mountain where he asked that we scatter his ashes. "We all have wounds that shape us," I tell my students. "It's the lives we make despite those wounds and the stories we tell about them that matter." And I quote again Isak Dinesen's beautiful words: "All suffering is bearable if it is seen as part of a story." "You must believe this," I tell my students. "You must tell your stories."

December, December, and the snow comes down, a little more lightly now, as if it can't make up its mind, as if even seasons struggle to be born. At home I go to the coat closet, pull out my father's old Harris Tweed jacket and drape it around my shoulders. It smells of my house now, but I press my face into its weave, imagining his pipe smoke and Old Spice, slip my hands into the pockets as if there will be some message there for me, though I know they are empty. The jacket was the only thing I wanted after he died, the one thing that was quintessentially *him*, with its scratchy brown wool ("woven in the Outer Hebrides of Scotland!" he used to exclaim with pride), its leather elbow patches and worn buttons—what I think of when I see him in my mind.

"I talk to you all the time in my mind," my friend and former mother-in-law and second mother, Helen, said to me some summers back, when I hugged her goodbye after a visit, my eyes filled with tears, knowing I would not see her alive again. "It's such an amazing journey I'm on," she said about aging toward her own death. "I'm learning something new every day." May we each live with as much grace as she did, even at the end, and with as much courage as my mother, whom my father once described as "the bravest person I ever knew," a woman who picked out a special gift for each of her children from the Sears catalogue even as she lay on her deathbed. My father, who must have known something of courage himself—the boy without enough food in the Depression, the twenty-four-year-old army lieutenant leading his men up that beach in France, the bereaved father taking his kids to a bookstore every weekend after my mother died and buying us each a book, as if words on a page could anchor us to the world.

Sometimes they did. Even now, when I look at the titles of childhood books from that time, they speak of more than their own story; my emotional history is preserved there too, invisible between their pages. *The Cricket on the Hearth. Swiss Family Robinson. Miss Bianca. Nobody's Girl.* Each one with a book plate inside the front cover, featuring a girl by a tree, her long hair blowing in the wind, and the words "A present from Daddy" in his precise biochemist's hand. Turning the pages, I am gifted again, remembering when I held each book for the first time, lost in wonder, no scent sweeter than a new book. My father taught me this.

December, December, and the snow comes down. Season of darkness. Season of loss that becomes presence in absence, which is a gift too because it reminds us that we love. And love is all, isn't it, the thing that matters? As Thornton Wilder says, "There is a land of the living and a land of the dead, and the bridge is love, the only survival, the only meaning." I've carried those words in my head for years, pierced and comforted by their wisdom. Only love gets to live forever, immaculate and transcendent, so brilliant a light we seek to embody it in human form and call it holy. And who wouldn't want to give it shape? Poems, essays, stories—these are the purest divinities I know, though I loved the plain Quaker meeting houses and spare New England churches of my girlhood, loved the sound of my father's voice, reading to us from the King James Bible at Christmas, loved the idea of the divine as a light within us each. "The Creative," my friend Holly called it—with a capital C, as befits the sacred. If we tell our stories about our loved one, does it mean those lights burn forever? Is our end just another beginning?

December, December, and the snow, everything concentrated into a slow gathering-in. Is it any wonder we light candles in this season, set them in wide-silled windows to guide the traveler home? But how hard it is to see a beginning in a human end. "Grief has its own timeline," I write my friend Joanne in Portland. Joanne, who must rush back into teaching, still raw from her father's death in Vermont. Joanne, who writes that she is living in a dream-time, a liminal place between worlds, where the boundaries are blurred. "Stay there as long as you need to, darling," I write back to her. "That is holy country." And then I pray for her, and for my friend Susan, who has lost her father too. I kneel at my makeshift muse's altar and pray, both their fathers' spirits in the wind, like the hawk Susan once described her father watching with such pleasure.

"We'll weather the blast and land at last on Canaan's happy shore," my father used to say, only half joking, quoting an old hymn when something got me down as girl. Is that shore where all our fathers are now? "He's pure spirit," Tom said to me when my father died. "He's soaring. He's everywhere." Many years before, I'd said almost the same thing to my father. He was visiting me in California. We were walking in the drenched, winter green of the Rancho Santa Ana Botanic Gardens in Claremont, the San Gabriel Mountains like jagged, gray paper cutouts at our backs, when he turned to me and said, his voice breaking, "I really loved your mother, you know." As if there were ever any doubt. He was wearing the Harris Tweed jacket, and when I put my arm around him I felt its weave, scratchy and familiar as childhood, against my cheek. "I know," I told him. "But don't you see," I continued, gesturing to the shimmering gardens, "she's everywhere. She's here." In that moment she was. And still is, though it is not the same as seeing her, watching her push back her blond curls, hearing the voice I cannot now remember ring out from somewhere down the path, its nasal Philadelphia accent forever the sound of home.

December and December, and the snow comes down. "I believe in the benevolent and beneficent power of the Creative," I tell my students. "I don't think it gives us things to write about that we aren't prepared to handle, even if they seem frightening and sad." But life does, doesn't it, over and over? Two days before Thanksgiving my favorite student this semester, a woman close to my own age, who has returned to school to become a social worker after losing a job in corporate America, comes to my office and breaks down. She tells me she has been diagnosed with an aggressive form of breast cancer, the lump there almost overnight. We keep in touch by email over the holiday weekend, and I marvel at her courage as she deals with oncologists and surgeons, the installation of a port for chemo. I am struck by the synchronicity of this event, remembering my mother, wondering what I am meant to learn from this beyond the mysteries of compassion. I don't tell my student, of course; this is her story, not mine. My job is to listen and support, to tell her she has an A in the class so far and that's what I intend to give her. "Skip the last paper," I tell her. She argues at first, and then agrees. "You saw the writer in me," she says in an email. Reading it at work, I weep at my desk.

December, December. The snow comes down, and I ponder the difficult and radiant lives of women, my student's courage a shining example, like that of my college friend Marilyn, whose surgery for uterine cancer is scheduled to take place a few days before Christmas. In the middle of our lives, fate has brought us to the same part of the country, where we are renewing our friendship so many decades after we were scared freshmen, meeting in line in the dining hall at college in Vermont. I marvel that I have known her since we were eighteen, her masses of golden, pre-Raphaelite hair no less beautiful for being threaded with gray. When we walked in the white oak woods together last month, after going for apples, the light illuminated her hair so it floated around her in a halo I wanted to touch, each strand shining. "You're a lifeline for me," she writes, "even when we are not together." "Let her be okay," I pray at my muse's altar, imagining how Marilyn would laugh if she saw me. How she might say, "I'm a secular Jew from Long Island, for heaven's sake. But okay, I'll take your prayers." Marilyn, with whom I stayed up night after night in the college library, writing papers, smoking Winstons, crying over the boys we imagined had broken our hearts, laughing at the absurdity of it all. No one but us remembers the details of those days, the Green Mountains holding us in their piney embrace, everything urgent and aching, but all the time in the world to figure out our lives.

December, December. The snow comes down, and the year runs out. But there is no end to the story of family and friends, to all those candles in all those windows. Even when our own lives end something goes on shining, doesn't it? A breath. A trace. A murmur under everything. A leaf like a cup filled with perfect crystals of snow, which I see everywhere when I step outside with the dogs, my father's Harris Tweed jacket wrapped around me, large and warm as life.

Valentine

> Where Thou art—that—is Home—
>
> —Emily Dickinson, *The Complete Poems*

It's the middle of winter, but tonight I am in summer's warm arms, a Boston lettuce for our salad torn in half before me. You're at the stove, stirring Indonesian sweet potato peanut soup. I'm at the sink, staring down into pale green whorls. "The heart's the best part," my mother says, a thousand Junes ago. Then a breath and I'm back, the moment sliding by, a window raised inside me, the hearts of the world lined up like school children waiting for the bus.

Hearts of palm, artichoke hearts, the heart of the country, hearts of darkness, heart songs, heart throbs, pour your heart out, wear your heart on your sleeve, set your heart free like the old Judy Collins song said, lose heart, take heart, Have-a-heart traps, the death of the heart, the heart is a lonely hunter, Joan of Arc's heart that was too pure to burn, the hoofprints pressed like hearts deer leave behind in snow, the heart-shaped rock my friend found on top of a mountain a month after her husband died.

In fifth grade I wrote a fifty-page handwritten report called "A Short History of the Human Heart," as if, with my colored pencils and tracing paper, I knew everything there was to say on the subject. Aren't we all experts? And aren't we all beginners when it comes to the heart, its four chambers never big enough to contain us, though we haven't room for more? It takes so much work to get to the heart of the matter, the red fruit at the core of each conversation, little bonfires leaping between us when we kiss or hug or even just shake hands.

When I was a girl and had to recite poems by heart at school, I memorized them with my body while the fist in my chest punched at my ribs. It's still the same today, my heart in my throat as if it could speak; the feeling is always red. I know Tom's face by heart too, and that of the daughter I never had. But I've nearly forgotten my mother's, dead and gone forever when I was a child. My engagement ring has two gold hands holding a gold heart, just like hers, though Tom did not know that when he chose it. I wear the tip pointed toward my own heart, according to tradition; it is a sign I am taken.

My father once helped me make a clay heart for a science fair project. Larger than life-size, it hung on a metal stand, wired with lights that mimicked a pulse. I didn't win a prize, not even honorable mention. I don't know what happened to that heart I'd spent a whole weekend molding and painting. When my father died, there was no autopsy, so we never knew for certain if it was his head or his heart. But when I stood in the room where he'd fallen, when I lay my body down over the place where they'd found him, to touch what he'd touched last, I knew. It was his heart, the only muscle that we say can be broken.

In the 1960s there was a salad called hearts of lettuce, iceberg wedges topped with Thousand Island dressing. No one eats it now. Iceberg lettuce has gone out of fashion. I still don't know why the heart is the best part, though my mother never lied about anything. Or why we say *lub-dub, lub-dub* to describe the sound the heart makes, the small ocean of the body rising and falling, rocking us each on the water, the way it did when I memorized poems: as if to say *I rise, I fall, I rise again. I rise, I fall, I'm gone.*

Envoi

My Pink Lake and
Other Digressions

Call the world if you Please, "the vale of Soul-making."
—John Keats, *Letters*

Ah, the sweet relief of digression. I slip into it with a sense of recognition and release, as if entering the pond where I first learned to swim or putting on my frayed purple velour bathrobe at the end of the longest work week in the world. This is how my mind always works best, sliding sideways from one subject to another, moving associatively, a butterfly flitting from one flower to the next, dipping and sipping deep, an invisible trail of scent stretched behind me. One minute I hear Tom's voice in the kitchen, cajoling our collie, who is grieving, like me, for his sister dog, Annabelle, buried on the back hill two days ago. "Eat something, Togo," Tom says. "Please eat." And the next minute I hear my father's voice, fifty years ago, offering the family dog half a buttered bagel and saying "That's my boy, that's my boy."

My father and his red wool work shirt. The kitchen with his watercolor paintings of Revolutionary War soldiers, old copper pans from France shining on the wall beside the brick oven, and the battered round table where my sister and I drank all those ironstone china cups of tea after school, gossiping about the day. Her eyes were so much like our mother's—dead when we were such little girls—I sometimes told her so. But when I did she'd turn snotty, scathing, critical, saying, "You're so *sensitive*." As if sensitivity were a crime. And meanwhile, Day Lily Creek babbled along outside through the lower meadow, its surface catching the light, reflecting it in rippling panels like moiré silk on the ceiling.

I follow the long, looping lassos of thought that is not thought exactly but something looser, something liquid that rises and falls, like waves or currents of air. "Everything is connected to everything else," my mentor, friend, and creative mother, Holly Prado Northup, said once, explaining what she thought I was trying to do in the wild, breath-driven rushes of words I read from my journal each week in her writing workshop, so shy I could hardly speak. "Have you seen the film Jeanne Moreau directed called *Lumière*?" she asked. "Moreau does visually what you're trying to do with words. You've got to go see *Lumière*." I never did see the movie, but felt pleased, as if I'd been seen, which I had. Around the same time I read Virginia Woolf's diary, thrilled by what she wrote about proceeding at a "rapid, haphazard gallop, . . . sweeping up accidentally stray matters which I should exclude if I hesitated, but which are the diamonds in the dust heap." I was looking for diamonds too.

Holly, with her blond hair backlit by sun streaming through the window from her round, walled garden with the little fairy-tale gate, talking about what she called "a sense of possibility" in poetry. How many Tuesday mornings did I spend in her workshop? How many long drives from Claremont into L.A. did I make, the San Gabriel Mountains so sharp against the blue that I'd cut my hand if I touched them? Where would I be if I had not had those mountains? Where would I be if I had not met Holly? As lost, I think, as the tiny sugar ant that skitters across my page as I write this seems to be, though perhaps it knows exactly where it is going.

Holly validated something in me by believing, by intimating that there was and is another way of understanding the world than what I'd learned in school. I'd forced myself to be analytical there, though it felt like being locked in a cage, my mind a wild mustang that had never known a bridle, the bit cold and sharp in my soft mouth. And meanwhile, on the other side of the fence lay a landscape filled with all the surprises that happen if one looses the strictures linear reasoning places on the mind, shucking them off like a too-tight dress, peeling the green husk of life back from the pearl kernels of sweet corn underneath.

Even in my grief, even in my sadness over losing Annabelle, our beautiful female collie, all wind-rush and fur-silk and jingling tags I think I hear down the hall at night, my mind moves in its reliable motions, and this is comforting. Out and out and out, my mind swims into the surf, riding the waves back in, the way I did one afternoon at San Onofre Beach, my body aligned so well with the music of the earth I could have died then, water spangled on my skin, my bikini top off because the beach was so empty.

Waves and mountains—they are my favorite forms of prayer—the scent of salt air and California bay laurel steeped in sunny canyons just two of my many homes.

Digressions, tangents, intuitive through lines, spines. Life never follows a narrative arc. When I was a teacher, I drove my students crazy, making them laugh, making them say, "Oh, no. Here we go again. Danger, danger, Will Robinson! We're going *off* topic!" One minute I'd be talking about James Baldwin's magnificent and heartbreaking story "Sonny's Blues." Then I'd say, "Okay, chickadees. Let's look at how many times windows occur in the story." And I was off, hopscotching from Baldwin's windows, to the hundreds of windows Andrew Wyeth painted (looking in and looking out), to the intrinsic nature and purpose of windows, to "Let's get out pen and paper and write for five minutes about what we see from the window we look out of most often, and then five more on what characters in the story see."

And then it was time to hear some of their words, halting and shy, and then back to the story again, diving into its beautiful and terrible complications of race and art. There was one passage I always read aloud, voice shaking at the loveliness of Baldwin's words, remembering how one of my own professors wept once while reading to a class, her pearl earrings trembling. Then I had the students read it too, word by word, the circle I'd required them to sit in infused by sudden magic, a ring of light held together by the sound of their voices:

> Then Creole stepped forward to remind them that what they were playing was the blues. . . . And the music tightened and deepened, apprehension began to beat the air. Creole began to tell us what the blues were all about. They were not about anything very new. He and his boys up there were keeping it new, at the risk of ruin, destruction, madness, and death, in order to find new ways to make us listen. For, while the tale of how we suffer, and how we are delighted, and how we may triumph is never new, it always must be heard. There isn't any other tale to tell, it's the only light we've got in all this darkness.

"I thought we were talking about windows," one husky boy said as we left class that afternoon. "But we were really talking about race, weren't we?" I remember him still, a young man who had perhaps traveled farther than any student I ever had, from his conservative upbringing in northern Wisconsin to my English class. There he found himself in a small discussion group with two feisty African American girls from Milwaukee. By the end of the year they were housemates. "College opened my eyes," he said once, during a conference over a paper. "What if I hadn't come here? What if I hadn't changed?"

I wanted to weep at what can happen, at what the human heart can open and hold. There are miracles everywhere. Even at a land-grant school in what at first seemed to me the middle of nowhere, but was of course a place like any other, beloved to my students because it was theirs. I cared about them with an affection so fierce it hurt, learned more from them than they ever did from me. I was there through circumstances of love and work, but determined to do my best by them. The Midwest was never a place I'd planned to end up. My yearning for somewhere else is a permanent lump in my throat, an irritation, an itch I can't scratch, a question I won't ever be able to answer.

But I've made a home here on the north side of the drumlin, haven't I—learning the flowers, trees, animals, the mineral scent of snow in winter, the scent of sweet earth turned over in spring? Last night I sat on the deck with Tom, eating artichokes and arborio rice in the soft May air, the oaks just opening their tiny fists of green leaves, mayapple parasols shining beneath them, and Island Lake shimmering in the distance, its waters a mirror lit pink by the setting sun. So many evenings I've sat out there with the collies, who both rushed out, excited, barking like wild things the instant I opened the door. Now there is just Togo, who lies quiet at my feet, head on his paws, looking out toward the hill where Annabelle is buried beneath the mulberry tree.

It's almost my birthday. Tom asks if I remember the year when he inquired what I wanted and I replied, "All I want is the pink lake." And he gave it to me, in the photo that hangs in our bathroom, and in so many other ways, the two of us sitting on this deck more evenings than I can remember, dogs at our feet, Annabelle's ears always perked, alert triangles of black velvet I loved to stroke. The pink lake was all I needed, then and now. Pink lake and a pink sky. In summer I will sit here sipping rosé, remembering the vat my father made when I was a child, and the essay he wrote about it called "Pink Wine." I wept, reading it after his death, thinking of how all he ever wanted to do was write. I keep it on a bookshelf in my study, tucked inside the pages of his unpublished novel.

And even as I answer Tom, I remember more. My mind slides to my first kitchen at Wild Run Farm. My mother says, "I'm in the pink," explains what it means, and then waltzes around on the old-fashioned, rose-patterned linoleum, singing, "Brown paper packages tied up with string, these are few of my favorite things." She holds in her arms Tina, a puppy with orange eyebrows like those on the dog I just buried. The puppy will be dead in a few weeks, hit by a car as we walk down the road together to Perkiomen Creek. My mother will die of cancer two years later. Our beautiful collie is dead now, her suffering over, heaven for dogs an endless green field where they can run and run. "Dog years," another of my teachers, Mark Doty, calls them in a book remembering Arden and Beau. These have been ours, the animals who companion us for a measure of our time on the planet.

The next morning my throat constricts at the sight of Togo, lying near Annabelle's favorite spot beside the front door. A half wall by the door makes the area denlike; it was always, indisputably hers. The last month of Annabelle's life the dogs often lay there together, Togo watching her, gazing into her eyes when she woke, the two of them communing about something we were not privileged to know. There's a mark on the wall where she'd brush it with her fur, turning in her dog-circle before lying down. I will never wash it away. How to go on without her?

And yet, somehow, we all do go on, don't we, the ever-present question of what to make for dinner and where to go next sometimes one and the same. Life keeps opening up before me, like all those blue-gray highways I have traveled, moving from one place to another in this big country. The names of states pile up inside me, like the drawer in my grandfather's mahogany secretary desk, crammed with a life's worth of photos I've never had time to arrange. Every instant is a sandalwood-scented mala bead I run through my fingers to remember. Virginia Woolf called them "moments of being." How to string them together, how to hold joy and sadness cradled in my palm at the same time? I wrote a line about this once, published it in a book of poems. But when I look I cannot find it. Does this mean I am meant to learn it all again?

"I meant to write about death," Woolf wrote in her diary, "only life came breaking in as usual."

And all those moves, what do they mean? I always intended to stay in one place, didn't I? A friend who was born here laughs and says my sensibility is bicoastal, not midwestern at all. I wonder how a sensibility can be shaped by a place and what that means. Is there a way to map it, and if so, what would it look like? Would it be like nineteenth-century ribbon maps, unfolding in long, interconnected scenes, or the spiral-bound TripTiks I used to get from AAA before driving cross-country? I loved how the agent would print the TripTik maps out, highlighting the trail of my journey with a florescent orange Magic Marker.

I think I understand the mystery of place for a moment as I lie on the ground beside our dog's grave, letting earth hold me as it holds her. Always, no matter where I have lived, I have known to do this, the bones of the earth forever there beneath mine. The scent of the herb called Sweet Annie floats all around me, rising from the dried boughs I piled upon her grave. I've grown Sweet Annie for years, but learned just the other day that its proper name is *Artemisia annua*. It is a beautiful name, from one of my favorite Greek goddesses, patroness of animals. But I like common names best for the folklore they reveal. Sweet Annie is perfect for Annabelle, and I am glad I never got around to making all the fragrant wreaths I planned on as gifts at Christmas, glad the boughs are here, spilling their green seeds into her black fur.

Sitting up, I notice that the cat's grave beside our dog's fresh one has, in just two years, been covered by violets. I remember a pet cemetery I saw once on an estate in Wales, each beloved creature honored, and then a line from a poem I wrote my sister years ago. "At home, violets open their blue lamps," I said. And then: "In the spring rain, even the cut branch blooms." I was talking about boughs pruned from the apricot tree in my California yard, which bloomed even after they were cut. The sight of those pale pink stars was so startling I felt something stir inside me, like the first faint inklings of the child I would later lose. I was shocked that the severed limb persisted in blooming, nature profligate and elemental. It hurt to look, though I did. I made jam from the tree's fruit that year as I did every summer, stirring up great vats of the sweet gold on the Western-Holly stove, ladling it into Kerr canning jars. That apartment over a carriage house was like the inside of a rolltop desk. It was the first home of my adulthood, and I lived there for ten years. I loved it so much I paid rent on it when David and I spent a year in Texas for one of his jobs. I wanted to be sure it was there to come back to.

The real wonder is that we can (and do) go on living, even when we lose what we love most, even as I pick my way with care around the slippery, tar pit edges of clinical depression, afraid I'll be pulled in again, tugged under into the black slick of it, forgetting the way home to joy, that under-valued commodity we forget so easily because happiness takes care of itself.

Woolf again, in *To the Lighthouse*: "What is the meaning of life? . . . The great revelation perhaps never did come. Instead, there were little daily miracles, illuminations, matches struck unexpectedly in the dark; here was one."

Tonight my miracle is a window cranked open on the May evening, cool air moving over me in waves as I lie down beside my man, wearing a summer nightgown for the first time this season, its worn cotton batiste delicious against line-dried sheets that smell of wind and sun and new beginnings. All night the window stays open on the garden that smells of rain and possibility, that thing Holly taught me to look for in poems. All night as I lie awake, so sad about Annabelle I cannot sleep, still listening for the sound of her breathing, I pick the stars out as they hang in the still mostly bare branches of the oaks like lanterns guiding the way. Years ago my father read a story to me with this line: "When you love someone who lives on a star it is lovely to look at the sky at night." Is our dog a star now, like my father and mother?

I count my stars. I "count my blessings instead of sheep," the way Bing Crosby advises Rosemary Clooney to do in *White Christmas*. The bed is a boat that carries me through darkness, everyone I love aboard ("It's the ark of us," I said to Tom), even if I can't see them on earth anymore. Our beloved dog lies down in the den of my heart, her brother curled on the green braided rug beside our bed. The window is open on frog-song and Canada goose–murmur, crane-call and coyote-yip, their voices stitching the air together in an invisible quilt of sound I pull over my shoulders, everything connected to everything else—as it always has been, as it will still be, come tomorrow, come morning.

Author's Note

This book began when Tom and I moved to the patch of prairie and oak savanna in the Wisconsin farm country described in these pages. Although far from wilderness, the wildness that persists here, and the land that supports that wildness, even in the face of the Anthropocene, have been my teachers and guides. I am grateful to the spirit of this place for all it has given and the many ways it sustains us. We are blessed to live on Indigenous Ho-Chunk land.

Almost ten years in the making, this book was written around the edges of full-time teaching and pursued more single-mindedly when I retired. I never anticipated putting the finishing touches on this book in the midst of the Covid-19 pandemic. That experience taught me many things, most notably how fortunate I am to live in a beautiful place. It has also underscored the importance of homeplaces, without which we are nothing, and how vital it is to protect and restore them. While *The Green Hour* is a celebratory rather than explicitly environmental book, our work with the land here is a constant reminder of the responsibility we bear as the stewards of this place. As Robin Kimmerer has said in *Braiding Sweetgrass*, "Even a wounded world holds us, giving us moments of wonder and joy." Like her, we have chosen "joy over despair." The project is ongoing.

Acknowledgments

Some of the essays in *The Green Hour: A Natural History of Home* have appeared in the following journals and anthologies, sometimes in different versions or with different titles. I am grateful to the editors at each publication.

1966: A Journal of Creative Nonfiction: "Planting Pansies"
Arts & Letters: A Journal of Contemporary Culture: "My Mother's Dress"
Brevity: "Valentine"
Briarcliff Review: "Midsummer Milkweeds"
Calyx: A Journal of Art and Literature by Women: "Autumn Equinox, with Asters"
Catamaran: "California Girl"
Chautauqua: "Wild Swans"
Chattahoochee Review: "Beyond Wild Run Farm: A Travel Guide to an Eastern Pennsylvania Childhood"
Cimarron Review: "My Pink Lake and Other Digressions"
Feminist Studies: "At the Bottom of the Ocean: Psych Ward, 1986"
Flyway: A Journal of the Environment: "A Jar of Wisconsin Honey"
Kenyon Review: "An Alphabet of Here: A Prairie Sampler"
Parabola: "Coyote Crossings"
Quarter after Eight: "A Strand in Her Intricate Weave"
Reed Magazine: "The Landscapes inside Us"
South Dakota Review: "Strange Angels: Encounters with Sandhill Cranes"
Sou'Wester: "Goldengrove Unleaving"
Under the Sun: "My Thoreau Summer" and "*Genius Loci*: Gazing into the Green"
Upstreet: "In the Presence of Water"

Water-Stone Review: "Flower Moon: A Wisconsin Books of Hours"
Wild Apples: A Journal of Nature, Art, and Inquiry: "Window Tree"
Zone Three: "Elegy in December"

"At the Bottom of the Ocean: Psych Ward, 1986" was listed as a "Notable" essay in *Best American Essays 2014.*

"Wild Swans" and "California Girl" were listed as "Notable" essays in *Best American Essays 2015.*

"Coyote Crossings" also appeared in *Nothing to Declare: A Guide to the Flash Sequence* (White Pine Press, 2016).

"The Persistence of Rivers" won the 2016 Jeanne Leiby Prose Chapbook Contest sponsored by *The Florida Review* and was published by Burrow Press in 2017. Gratitude to Susa Fallows and Lisa Roney of the *Florida Review,* to contest judge Vanessa Blakeslee, and Ryan Rivas of Burrow Press.

"Wild Swans" also appeared in *If Birds Are Near,* edited by Susan Rogers (Comstock/Cornell University Press, 2020).

"My Pink Lake and Other Digressions" also appeared in *Best American Essays 2020.* I am grateful to André Aciman and Robert Atwan for selecting it.

Special thanks to Martha Highers at *Under the Sun* for her support of my work and help making "*Genius Loci*: Gazing into the Green" the essay it needed to be.

Thank you to Dennis Lloyd, director of the University of Wisconsin Press, for championing this book from the beginning. Your moving responses, careful and insightful reading, and thoughtful feedback helped shape the collection and make it a better book. Thanks to acquisitions assistant Jackie Teoh. You are a gem—smart, funny, kind, and the best hand-holder I ever met. Warm thanks to Adam Mehring for your editing acumen, kindness, and patience and to Meg Wallace for copyediting. Gratitude to Jennifer Conn for the sensitive art direction and special thanks to Casey LaVela for finding the perfect title. Thanks to Kaitlin Svabek for your help bringing this book into the world. Thanks to Neil West for an interior book design that presents my words exactly as I imagined.

Thanks to artist Helen Klebesadel for the gorgeous painting on the cover of the book, which speaks to the green heart of these essays, and to Trudy Gershinov of TG Designs for the inspired and beautiful jacket design.

The first inklings this might be this book emerged at the Orion Writers Conference at Sterling College in 2009. I am grateful to the conference for a fellowship that made it possible for me to attend.

Thanks to Charles Goodrich and Oregon State University's Spring Creek Project for Ideas, Nature, and the Written Word for a collaborative writing residency at the cabin at Shotpouch Creek in the Oregon Coast Range in 2011. It provided sacred time for work on this book.

I am grateful to the University of Wisconsin–Whitewater for a course release in 2011 and a faculty sabbatical in 2013, which provided time and space to work on this book.

At the University of Wisconsin–Whitewater I am grateful to my students in Creative Nonfiction, Nature Writing, and Gender, Ethnicity, and the Environment for allowing me to try ideas out and inspiring me with their brave, beautiful, and necessary work. Gratitude to all my colleagues, especially in the writing program, for their inspiration and support, and to the College of Letters and Sciences for creating an environment that nurtures creative work.

Thanks to Mark Doty for his long-ago suggestion (when I was his student at Vermont College of Fine Arts) that my mother is the "tutelary spirit" in my work. You were right, Mark.

Thanks to Nancy Benzschawel for finding the little house we named Deer Run.

Thanks to my Madison writing group, the Lake Effect Poets, for allowing me to occasionally inflict prose on them.

Thanks to science writer Scott Spoolman and geologist John Luczaj for the last-minute consultation about our glacial erratic. You guys rock!

Thanks to Briana Frank of Tree Health Management, ecologist Micah Kloppenburg, and the folks at Prairie Nursery, who have all taught us and helped us find our way with the land.

Thanks for Grace Miele Owen for our summer at South Pond in Marlboro, Vermont.

Thanks to my brilliant stepdaughter, Katie Umhoefer, for her consultation on book design.

Thanks to poet Wyn Cooper for his sensitive reading and edits. Gratitude and bows to Alice Peck for her exquisite attention to these pages and for accompanying them (and me) not just as an editor but as a companion soul.

My parents, Hank and Mary Townsend, understood the importance of wild places. This book is informed by their memory and spirit.

Thanks to my late stepbrother, Peter Wittreich, for your love, enthusiasm, legacy, and support of Annabelle at a critical moment.

Thanks and love to my brother and sister, Steve and Jennifer Townsend, for the well of memories we share, from the days at Wild Run Farm and beyond. "Beyond Wild Run Farm" is for you.

Thanks to Robert Alexander for the years of friendship, encouragement, and support of my writing.

Thanks to Martha York, wise guide on the psyche's journey.

Thanks to Beth Lueck for your empathy, laughter, and encouragement; Jackie Melvin for your faith and golden understanding of the soul; Carter McKenzie for your poet's heart. Thanks to Marilyn Gardner for being proud of me and telling me so.

Thanks to Peg Volkmann for her gentle support, encouragement, and enthusiasm.

Thanks to the memory of Holly Prado Northup, mentor, creative sister, beloved friend. Her spirit illuminates everything I write.

Thanks to my writing partner, Judith Sornberger, and to Catherine Jagoe, Sara Taber, and Marilyn Annucci, who were the muses and midwives of this book. It would be less without your careful readings, suggestions for revision, inspiration, and encouragement. Judith was also my sister-adventurer at Shotpouch. Thanks, Jude, for your ability to see potential in the rawest scrap of writing, for your laughter, and for your company on the winding road of the word.

Togo and Annabelle—the brother and sister pair of tricolored collies who appear in these pages—both died while this book was being written. Their presence was a blessing that made our lives and the experience of this place richer.

Tom Umhoefer not only shares the adventure of life at Deer Run but read and reread these pages, cooked countless dinners, encouraged, consoled, and put up with a partner whose thoughts were all too often elsewhere. Thank you, Tom, for endless cups of tea and for believing in me every day, even when I did not believe in myself. You are my home, my everything. So may it always be.

Notes

Genius Loci

5 "And how shall they comfort each other": Adrienne Rich, "In the Wake of Home," in *The Fact of Doorframe: Poems Selected and New, 1950–1984* (New York: Norton, 1984), 324.

8 Hildegard of Bingen called *viriditas*: Matthew Fox, *Illuminations of Hildegard of Bingen* (Santa Fe, NM: Bear & Company, 1985), 30.

8 Robin Wall Kimmerer's "grammar of animacy": Robin Wall Kimmerer, "The Grammar of Animacy," in *Braiding Sweetgrass* (Minneapolis: Milkweed Editions, 2013), 48–59.

11 "Where do we find ourselves?": Ralph Waldo Emerson, "Experience," in *Emerson's Essays* (New York: Dutton, 1971), 228.

11 "songlines and placelines of our lives": Sharon Blackie, "The Danger of Writing Books," November 10, 2019, https://sharonblackie.net/the-danger-of-writing-books.

11 nostalgia was the clinical description for homesickness: Paul Gruchow, "Home Is a Place in Time," in *Grass Roots: The Universe of Home* (Minneapolis: Milkweed Editions, 1999), 7. Many people have written about the history of nostalgia. I first encountered it defined as an illness in Gruchow's work. Most recently, Canadian critic David Berry has written a cultural history, *On Nostalgia* (Toronto: Coach House Books, 2020).

11 "the instrument of my own discovering": Kathryn Aalto, "Nan Shepherd," in *Writing Wild: Women Poets, Ramblers, and Mavericks Who Shaped How We See the Natural World* (Portland: Timber Press, 2020), 72.

12 We know trees breathe: Andy Coghlan, "Trees May Have a 'Heartbeat' That Is So Slow We Never Noticed It," *New Scientist*, April 20, 2018, www.newscientist.com/article/2167003-trees-may-have-a-heartbeat-that-is-so-slow-we-never-noticed-it/.

13 "It's a journey with my soul that I am taking": Kate Wolf, "Unfinished Life," *Gold in California: A Retrospective of Recordings, 1975–1985* (Los Angeles: Rhino Records, 1977), audio CD, track 8.

13   "a *refugia*, a place of safety": Kathleen Dean Moore, "Ethics and Extinc-
      tion," in *Great Tide Rising: Towards Clarity and Moral Courage in a Time of
      Planetary Change* (Berkley: Counterpoint, 2016), 139–40.

14   "ceremonial time": Paula Gunn Allen, "The Ceremonial Motion of Indian
      Time: Long Ago, So Far," in *The Sacred Hoop: Recovering the Feminine in
      American Indian Tradition* (Boston: Beacon, 1992), 147–54.

A Strand in Her Intricate Weave

18   "I am the dryad of the wood": Arthur Ketchum, "The Spirit of the Birch,"
      in *Silver Pennies: A Collection of Modern Poems for Boys and Girls*, edited by
      Blanche Jennifer Thompson (New York: Macmillan, 1954), 79.

20   "I am the dryad, slim and white": Ibid., 80.

Beyond Wild Run Farm

22   "two watch coats, four pairs of stockings, and four bottles of cider": Bor-
      ough of Pennsburg, Montgomery County, Pennsylvania, www.pennsburg
      .us/borough-history.

Planting Pansies

33   "There's pansies, that's for thoughts": William Shakespeare, *Hamlet*, in *The
      Complete Pelican Shakespeare*, act IV, scene 4, line 175 (London: Penguin,
      1969), 963.

33   But there are other names for pansies too: Laura C. Martin, *Garden Flower
      Folklore* (Chester, CT: Globe Pequot, 1987), 11.

33   heartsease—which is Elizabethan in origin: Diana Wells, *100 Flowers
      and How They Got Their Names* (Chapel Hill, NC: Algonquin, 1997),
      217–18.

34   But it was also used to heal wounds: Botanical Online, "Properties of Pan-
      sies," botanical-online.com/en/medicinal-plants/pansy-properties.

34   The heart-shaped leaves were also used to cure broken hearts: Martin, *Gar-
      den Flower Folklore*, 11.

34   where even a bit of the juice "on sleeping eyelids laid": William Shake-
      speare, *A Midsummer Night's Dream*, in *The Complete Pelican Shakespeare*,
      act II, scene 1, lines 171–72 (London: Penguin, 1969).

35   "a miniature impression of a cat's face": Wells, *100 Flowers*, 217–18.

36   Flavigny candies are made from a single anise seed: "Anise of Flavigny,"
      en.wikipedia.org/wiki/Anise_of_Flavigny.

My Mother's Dress

42   "Sweet Mary," she writes: Elizabeth Conway Doak, unpublished memoir,
      author's collection.

My Thoreau Summer

47 "I went to the woods to live deliberately": Henry David Thoreau, *Walden* (New York: Viking, 1985), 394.

52 "Bright star, would I were stedfast as thou art": John Keats, "Bright Star," in *English Romantic Writers*, by David Perkins (New York: Harcourt, 1967), 1205.

52 "a bowl, / with all its cracked stars shining": Anne Sexton, "To John, Who Begs Me Not to Enquire Further," in *Selected Poems of Anne Sexton* (Boston: Houghton Mifflin, 1988), 26.

California Girl

69 "a California girl, in aesthetics and attitude": Roseanne Cash, *Composed: A Memoir* (New York: Penguin, 2010), 89.

70 The Golden State has been described as existing "west of the West": Leonard Michaels, David Reid, and Raquel Scheer, eds., *West of the West: Imagining California* (New York: Harper, 1991), epigraph.

74 "The space is vast": Tony Duquette, *Our Lady of the Queen of Angels: A Celebrational Environment* (Los Angeles: Anthony and Elizabeth Duquette Foundation, 1981), n.p.

The Landscapes inside Us

92 "Going to the mountains is going home": John Muir, *Our National Parks* (Eugene: Doublebit Press, 2020), 1.

95 "People ought to saunter in the mountains—not hike!": Quoted in Albert Palmer, *The Mountain Trail and Its Message* (Boston: Pilgrim Press, 1911), 26–27. This booklet records Palmer's experiences hiking with John Muir, founder of the Sierra Club.

96 "I only went out for a walk": John Muir, *John of the Mountains: The Unpublished Journals of John Muir* (1938), edited by Linnie Marsh Wolfe (Madison: University of Wisconsin Press, 1979), 439.

Coyote Crossings

101 Coyote is both creator and destroyer: Ami Ronnberg and Kathleen Martin, eds., *The Book of Symbols: Reflections on Archetypal Images* (Cologne: Taschen, 2010), 276.

101 The Navajo call Coyote "God's Dog": Hope Ryden, *God's Dog: A Celebration of the North American Coyote* (Lincoln, NE: Author's Guild Backinprint.com Editions, 2005), xii, xiii.

The Persistence of Rivers

106 Rachel Carson so aptly describes as "the sense of wonder": Rachel Carson, *The Sense of Wonder* (New York: Harper & Row, 1965), 45.

108   which means "place where the cranberries grow" in Lenape: Sandy Hingston, "20 Local Native American Place Names and What They Mean," *Philadelphia Magazine*, October 12, 2015, www.phillymag.com/news/2015/10/12/philadelphia-native-american-place-names/.

108   "Whatever landscape a child is exposed to early on": Barry Lopez, "Replacing Memory," in *About This Life: Journey on the Threshold of Memory* (New York: Knopf, 1998), 206.

114   "I bring you some water lost in your memory": Patrice de La Tour du Pin, *Le Second Jeu*, quoted in Gaston Bachelard, *The Poetics of Reveries: Childhood, Language, and the Cosmos* (Boston: Beacon, 1971), 96.

122   "a stream is an expression of its watershed": Gretel Ehrlich, "Stream," in *Home Ground: Language for an American Landscape*, edited by Barry Lopez (San Antonio: Trinity University Press, 2006), 344.

125   "standard of comfort by which you measure whatever else is real in the world": Susan Hand Shetterly, *Settled in the Wild: Notes from the Edge of Town* (Chapel Hill, NC: Algonquin, 2010), 89.

128   the Kalapuya name for Marys Peak . . . means "Place of Spirit Power": "Marys Peak: Island in the Sky," Oregon State University Environmental Arts and Humanities Program blog, April 3, 2017. http://blogs.oregonstate.edu/eahgrad/2017/04/03/marys-peak-island-sky/.

129   "where we are interacts reciprocally with who we are": Reg Saner, "Over the Rainbow, My Kind of Place," in *Landscape with Figures: The Nonfiction of Place*, edited by Robert Root (Lincoln: University of Nebraska Press, 2007), 6.

133   "the line of beauty" that Thoreau says dwells "in the curve": Henry David Thoreau, "The Service," *Henry David Thoreau Online*, www.thoreau-online.org/the-service-page2.html.

133   "We don't tend to ask where a lake comes from": John Daniel, "Beginnings," in *The Far Corner: Northwest Views on Land, Life, and Literature* (Berkeley: Counterpoint, 2009), 49.

136   "story is our only boat for sailing the river of time": Ursula Le Guin, "Another Story or The Fisherman on the Inland Sea," in *The Found and the Lost: The Collected Novellas of Ursula Le Guin* (New York: Gallery/Saga, 2016), 197.

Four and Twenty

140   some sort of "natural telepathy" or "group soul" we call a murmuration: *Audubon Magazine*, March–April 2009, www.audubon.org/magazine/march-april-2009/how-flock-birds-can-fly-and-move-together; Royal Society for the Protection of Birds, "Starling Murmurations," www.rspb.org.uk/birds-and-wildlife/wildlife-guides/bird-a-z/starling/starling-murmurations/.

140   Biologists speculate that "each bird tracks the movements of just seven neighbors": Royal Society for the Protection of Birds, "Why Birds Flock

Together," https://www.rspb.org.uk/birds-and-wildlife/natures-home-mag azine/birds-and-wildlife-articles/features/why-birds-flock-together/.

In the Presence of Water

144   Mendelowitz's massive *History of American Art*, characterized Inness as an "Independent": Daniel Mendelowitz, *A History of American Art* (New York: Holt, Rhinehart, and Winston, 1970), 309.

145   "The aim of art," Inness wrote, "is not to instruct": Ibid., 311.

145   "vanished . . . into something better": Mary Oliver, "Sleeping in the Forest," in *Twelve Moons* (Boston: Little, Brown and Company, 1979), 3.

148   "Water is always trying to tell us something": John Jerome, *Blue Rooms: Ripples, Rivers, Pools, and Other Waters* (New York: Henry Holt and Company, 1997), 9.

High Wind Warning

149   "Western wind, when will thou blow": John Frederick Nims, "Western Wind," in *Western Wind: An Introduction to Poetry* (New York: Random House, 1983), 6.

151   "Who has seen the wind / neither you nor I": Christina Rossetti, "Who Has Seen the Wind?" www.poetryfoundation.org/poems/43197/who-has-seen-the -wind.

Window Tree

153   "White coral bells upon a slender stalk": Norman Lubhoff and Win Stracke, eds., "White Coral Bells" (trad.), *Songs of Man* (New York: Prentice-Hall, 1965), 189.

155   "I have seen you taken and tossed": Robert Frost, "Tree at My Window," in *The Poetry of Robert Frost* (New York: Holt, Rinehart and Winston, 1974), 251–52.

155   "The story of my life is the story of trees I've loved": Deena Metzger, in book description for *Writing for Your Life a Guide and Companion to the Inner Worlds*, http://deenametzger.net/published-works-3/writing-for-your-life/.

156   trees were seen as "sacred powers, mediators between the worlds": Caitlin Matthews, *The Celtic Spirit: Daily Meditations for the Turning Year* (New York: HarperSanFrancisco, 1999), 257.

157   Thoreau "traveled a great deal in Concord": Thoreau, *Walden*, 326.

157   "trees truly are mediators between worlds": Matthews, *Celtic Spirit*, 257.

157   as William Faulkner says, "it's not even past": William Faulkner, *Requiem for a Nun* (New York: Random House, 1951), 92.

Strange Angels

159   Sandhill cranes are large birds: Eek! Environmental Education for Kids, "Sandhill Crane," www.eekwi.org/animals/birds/sandhill-crane; Canisius

Ambassadors for Conservation, "Sandhill Crane," www.conservenature
.org/learn_about_wildlife/prairie/sandhill_crane.htm; Wikipedia, "Sandhill
Crane," en.wikipedia.org/wiki/Sandhill crane; All About Birds, "Sandhill
Crane: Life History," allaboutbirds.org/guide/sandhill_crane/lifehistory;
National Geographic, "Sandhill Crane," www.nationalgeographic.com/ani
mals/birds/s/sandhill-crane/.

161 there will soon be jumbled and untidy platform nests: Audubon, "Sandhill
Crane," www.audubon.org/field-guide/bird/sandhill-crane.

162 Emerson's "concentrated eternity": Ralph Waldo Emerson, quoted in John
P. Miller, "Transcendental Education," in *Educating for Wisdom and Compassion* (Thousand Oaks, CA: Crown, 2006), 89.

163 Gallagher's poem "Each Bird Walking": Tess Gallagher, "Each Bird Walking," in *Willingly* (Port Townsend, WA: Graywolf Press, 1984).

165 dancing is a "normal part of motor development for cranes": International
Crane Foundation, www.savingcranes.org/species-field-guide/sandhill-crane/.

165 "What is that knocking?": D. H. Lawrence, "Song of a Man Who Has
Come Through," featured poem in *The Reader*, January 12, 2016, thereader
online.wordpress.com/2016/01/12/featured-poem-song-of-a-man-who-has
-come-through-by-d-h-lawrence/.

Flower Moon

169 Quartz and feldspar stripes ripple through the darker gneiss: Science writer
Scott Spoolman and University of Wisconsin–Green Bay geologist John
Luczaj provided information that gave an approximate identity and age for
our glacial erratic. Email correspondence with author, October 13, 2020.

169 feldspar can align our chakras: Personal conversation with Doris Deits, pro-
prietor of the Peaceful Heart metaphysical bookstore, Oregon, Wisconsin,
November 2020.

170 "Think of yourself as a windowpane": John Makransky, *Awakening through
Love: Unveiling Your Deepest Goodness* (Somerville, MA: Wisdom, 2007), 165.

173 "Often I am permitted to return to a meadow": Robert Duncan, "Often I
Am Permitted to Return to a Meadow," www.poetryfoundation.org/poems/
46317/often-i-am-permitted-to-return-to-a-meadow.

An Alphabet of Here

178 The word means "littlest ridge," from the Irish Gaelic *droimnín*: "Drumlin,"
https://en.wikipedia.org/wiki/Drumlin.

178 they usually occur in groups called swarms: Scott Spoolman, *Wisconsin State
Parks: Extraordinary Stories of Geology and Natural History* (Madison: Wisconsin Historical Society Press, 2018), 153–54.

179 Native Americans ground and mashed their sweet nuts to create hickory
milk: Max Witynski, "Nuts for Hickory," *Wisconsin Academy of Sciences,*

Arts, and Letters Magazine, Spring 2018, www.wisconsinacademy.org/maga
zine/spring-2018/wisconsin-table/nuts-hickory.

180 The plant's common name, Indian turnip, suggests edibility: "Jack in the Pulpit," www.prairienursery.com/jack-in-the-pulpit-arisaema-triphyllum.html.

181 their name comes from a hoary English nickname, nuthack: Stan Tekiela,
Birds of Wisconsin Field Guide (Cambridge, MN: Adventure Publications,
2020), 215.

182 the word for oak is *duir*, which means "door": Liz Murray and Colin Mur
ray, *The Celtic Tree Oracle* (New York: Saint Martin's, 1988), 36.

185 the embodiment of "a green thought in a green shade": Andrew Marvell,
"The Garden," www.poetryfoundation.org/poems/44682/the-garden-56d22
3dec2ced.

Midsummer Milkweeds

189 milkweed has a unique pollination system: Stan Tekiela, *Wildflowers of Wisconsin Field Guide* (Cambridge, MN: Adventure Publications, 2009), 111.

A Jar of Wisconsin Honey

194 Swift once described as "sweetness and light": Hattie Ellis, *Sweetness and
Light: The Mysterious History of the Honeybee* (New York: Harmony, 2004),
epigraph. A bee novice, I deeply admired honeybees but knew almost nothing about them. Sarah Shatz and Claire Strader's class Backyard Beekeeping
Basics, offered through the Willy Street Co-op in Madison, Wisconsin, in
2014, was an excellent introduction and is the source of much of the information about bees in this essay. Wolfgang Thaler and Herbert Habersack's
NOVA film, *Tales from the Hive*, provides an up-close view of the hive (www
.pbs.org/wgbh/nova/bees). Another organization worth knowing about is
the Bee Conservancy (https://thebeeconservancy.org).

195 Mead, which is made from honey, was thought to be an aphrodisiac: Ellis,
Sweetness and Light, 93.

195 Ellis notes that honeybees were once considered part of the family: Ibid.,
136.

196 "The bees are wintering. They taste the spring": Sylvia Plath, *Ariel* (New
York: Harper and Row, 1965), 67, 85.

196 providing an almost "instant 'lift' with no strain on the digestive system":
Doris McFerran Townsend, *The Cook's Companion* (New York: Rutledge/
Crown, 1978), 332–33.

197 thinking of Yeats's "bee-loud glade": William Butler Yeats, "The Lake Isle of
Innisfree," in *Collected Poems* (New York: Macmillan, 1974), 39.

198 The USDA estimates that "one in three mouthfuls of food we eat": USDA,
"Bee Benefits to Agriculture," *AgResearch Magazine*, March 2004, https://
agresearchmag.ars.usda.gov/2004/mar/form/.

198 Colony die-off also threatens crops: Since this essay was written, the bees' plight has worsened. In addition to the damage wrought by mites and colony collapse, growing evidence implicates pesticides, particularly those incorporated into plants' structures.

Goldengrove Unleaving

204 reciting Hopkins's "Margaret, are you grieving / Over Goldengrove unleaving?": The title of this essay comes from Gerard Manley Hopkins's poem "Spring and Fall," www.poetryfoundation.org/poems/44400/spring-and-fall.

205 "comforted and shaken by change": Poem by Holly Prado in author's possession.

Wild Swans

209 they present a spectacular sight "when they make mass landings": John Bull and John Farrand Jr., *The Audubon Field Guide to Birds* (New York: Alfred A. Knopf, 1977), 464.

210 "If we have ever regarded our interest in natural history as an escape": Rachel Carson and Linda J. Lear, *Lost Woods: The Discovered Writing of Rachel Carson* (Boston: Beacon, 1998), 96.

211 "the epitome of purity, beauty, and potential good luck": James MacKillop, *A Dictionary of Celtic Mythology* (New York: Oxford University Press, 2000), 394.

212 Yeats's swans that "suddenly mount / and scatter wheeling in great broken rings": W. B. Yeats, "The Wild Swans at Coole," in *The Collected Poems* (New York: Macmillan, 1974), 129.

Elegy in December

215 "All suffering is bearable if it is seen as part of a story": Brent Mohn, "A Talk with Isak Dinesen," *The New York Times Book Review*, November 3, 1956, 49.

216 "There is a land of the living and a land of the dead, and the bridge is love": Thornton Wilder, *The Bridge of San Luis Rey* (New York: Harper, 1955), 148.

My Pink Lake and Other Digressions

224 proceeding at a "rapid, haphazard gallop, . . . sweeping up accidentally stray matters": Virginia Woolf, *The Diary of Virginia Woolf*, Volume 1, *1915–1919*, edited by Anne Olivier Bell (New York: Harcourt Brace Jovanovich, 1978), 233.

225 "Then Creole stepped forward to remind them that what they were playing was the blues": James Baldwin, "Sonny's Blues," in *Jazz Fiction*, edited by Sascha Feinstein and David Rife (Bloomington: Indiana University Press, 2009), 17–48.

227 Woolf called them "moments of being": Virginia Woolf, "A Sketch of the Past," in *Moments of Being: Unpublished Autobiographical Writing* (New York: Harcourt Brace Jovanovich, 1976), 73.

227 "I meant to write about death": Virginia Woolf, *The Diary of Virginia Woolf*, Volume 2, *1920–1924*, edited by Anne Olivier Bell (New York: Harcourt Brace Jovanovich, 1978), 167.

229 "What is the meaning of life?": Virginia Woolf, *To the Lighthouse* (New York: Harcourt Brace, 1955), 240.

229 "When you love someone who lives on a star it is lovely to look at the sky at night": Antoine de Saint-Exupéry, *The Little Prince*, translated by Richard Howard (New York: Harcourt, 1971), 76. I recently discovered that I've spent most of my life remembering this line incorrectly. In the book, the line reads, "If you love a flower that lives on a star, then it's good, at night, to look up at the sky."

ALISON TOWNSEND is the author of two books of poetry, *The Blue Dress* and *Persephone in America*, which won the Crab Orchard Open Poetry Competition. Her poetry and nonfiction appear in numerous journals, including *The Southern Review*, *The Kenyon Review*, *Parabola*, and *Under the Sun*, and have been recognized in *Best American Poetry*, *The Pushcart Prize*, and *Best American Essays 2020*. Her many awards include the 2020 Rattle Poetry Prize. She is professor emerita of English at the University of Wisconsin–Whitewater, where she taught creative nonfiction. She and her climate-activist husband live on four acres of prairie and oak savanna in the farm country outside Madison, Wisconsin.